EXPLORING SOCIOLOGY

Readings for Introductory Sociology

First Edition

Edited by Mark Plume

Virginia Commonwealth University

Bassim Hamadeh, CEO and Publisher
Jennifer Codner, Senior Field Acquisitions Editor
Michelle Piehl, Senior Project Editor
Christian Berk, Production Editor
Emely Villavicencio, Senior Graphic Designer
Trey Soto, Licensing Coordinator
Natalie Piccotti, Director of Marketing
Kassie Graves, Vice President of Editorial
Jamie Giganti, Director of Academic Publishing

Copyright © 2021 by Mark Plume. All rights reserved. No part of this publication may be reprinted, reproduced, transmitted, or utilized in any form or by any electronic, mechanical, or other means, now known or hereafter invented, including photocopying, microfilming, and recording, or in any information retrieval system without the written permission of Cognella, Inc. For inquiries regarding permissions, translations, foreign rights, audio rights, and any other forms of reproduction, please contact the Cognella Licensing Department at rights@cognella.com.

Trademark Notice: Product or corporate names may be trademarks or registered trademarks and are used only for identification and explanation without intent to infringe.

Cover image copyright © 2015 iStockphoto LP/Maxiphoto.

Printed in the United States of America.

CONTENTS

SECTION 1: **THE WISDOM OF SOCIOLOGY:** *WHO* **YOU ARE,** *WHERE* **YOU ARE, AND** *WHEN* **YOU ARE DETERMINES, TO A LARGE EXTENT, WHAT YOU THINK AND HOW YOU ACT** 1

CHAPTER 1 Introducing Sociology 3

How to Think Sociologically 4
Steven M. Buechler

SECTION 2: **DOING SOCIOLOGY: REVEALING OUR SOCIAL WORLD THROUGH RESEARCH** 23

CHAPTER 2 Social Research Methods 27

A field study on watching eyes and hand hygiene compliance in a public restroom 29
Stefan Pfattheicher, Christoph Strauch,
Svenja Diefenbacher, and Robert Schnuerch

SECTION 3: **CULTURE: DIFFERENT WAYS OF SEEING AND BEING** 47

CHAPTER 3 Culture 49

Body Ritual among the Nacirema 50
Horace Miner

SECTION 4:	CREATING ROUND PEGS FOR ROUND HOLES: SHAPING HUMANS AND THE INFLUENCE OF GROUPS	59
CHAPTER 4	Socialization	61
	Final Note on a Case of Extreme Isolation Kingsley Davis	62
CHAPTER 5	Groups	71
	Why We Conform Rafael Narvaez	73
SECTION 5:	STAYING WITHIN THE LINES: DEVIANCE AND SOCIAL CONTROL	83
CHAPTER 6	Deviance and Social Control	85
	Eating Your Friends Is the Hardest: The Survivors of the F-227 James M. Henslin	86
SECTION 6:	TYPES OF INEQUALITY: SOCIAL CLASS, RACE, AND GENDER	97
CHAPTER 7	Social Class	99
	How Inequality Wrecks Everything We Care About Chuck Collins	100
CHAPTER 8	Race	107
	White Privilege: Unpacking the Invisible Knapsack Peggy McIntosh	109
CHAPTER 9	Gender	115
	Gender Inequality in Culture Industries Denise D. Bielby	117

SECTION 7:	SOCIAL INSTITUTIONS: THE INVISIBLE HANDS OF SOCIAL STRUCTURE	131
CHAPTER 10	The Bonds that Bind: Marriages and Families	133
	The Way We Wish We Were: Defining the Family Crisis Stephanie Coontz	135
CHAPTER 11	Pathway to the American Dream?: Education	151
	Educational Attainment and Economic Inequality: What Schools Cannot Do John F. Covaleskie	153
CHAPTER 12	Faith, the Individual and Society: Religion	165
	Religion Is Socially Learned Phil Zuckerman	167
CHAPTER 13	Work, Money and You: The Economy	183
	Rise of the Hipster Capitalist Elizabeth Nolan Brown	184
CHAPTER 14	Power, Politics and Authority: Government	193
	All Politics Is Identity Politics Ann Friedman	194
	References	203

THE WISDOM OF SOCIOLOGY

WHO YOU ARE, *WHERE* YOU ARE, AND *WHEN* YOU ARE DETERMINES, TO A LARGE EXTENT, WHAT YOU THINK AND HOW YOU ACT

The wisdom of sociology is that it reveals to students the hidden social forces that are common to all people, and as a result, we are all more alike than different. Sociology highlights the influence of social forces on all people regardless of culture, ethnicity, gender, tradition, or faith, which reflects what I believe to be the central revelation of sociology—*our lives are shaped in large part by external forces.*

The value of sociology is composed of three important elements. First, acquiring an understanding of the sociological perspective and developing a sociological imagination are essential elements of being an educated person. Understanding that by living among others in a human society necessarily leads to an individual being influenced by social forces is fundamental to understanding the sociological perspective and development of one's sociological imagination. Seeing ourselves as influenced by social forces and social elements that are external to us helps us see that others are also subject to those influences. Second, by understanding that we are all subject to external and coercive social forces allows us to be more civil, more humane to our fellow humans. I believe that a person who understands and can employ the sociological perspective, an educated person, has an enhanced potential for civility, sympathy, and empathy. I also believe that the vast majority of people desire these qualities in themselves and those they encounter. Finally, I believe that sociology is a scientific discipline that has contributed—and will continue to contribute—to the larger body of human knowledge through the use of rigorous scientific investigation. These contributions, which are the result of a variety of research methods, have enriched the lives of the peoples of many cultures by highlighting the plight of marginalized people, changing public discourse, public policy, laws, and social attitudes. However, the consumption, digestion, and utilization of these data rely entirely on a population of educated people. My fondest hope is that through the instruction of sociology, I will contribute to that population and students who take sociology will join that population.

CHAPTER 1

INTRODUCING SOCIOLOGY

The following article by Steven M. Buechler gives you a fairly brief but concise overview of the sociological perspective. The author does a good job of giving you a broad-stroke description of sociology while also illustrating what elements of social thought are not truly a part of the sociological view. The article helps you understand how sociologists view the world and asks you to put things in motion by employing your sociological imagination. It further explores the eight sociological assumptions, which make up the foundation of the sociological perspective and help guide sociological inquiry (as we will see in section 2). This work also examines the critical nature of sociology, the penetrating analysis that sets sociology apart from all other social science disciplines.

Some Things to Keep in Mind

As you read the following article about how to think sociologically, here are some things you might want to think about.

1. What makes sociological thinking different from other ways of thinking?
2. What are the eight sociological assumptions?
3. As you read through each of the eight sociological assumptions, try to think of an example that illustrates that assumption.
4. What is sociology's double critique?

HOW TO THINK SOCIOLOGICALLY

Steven M. Buechler

People have always tried to make sense of the world around them. Myths, fables, and religion provided traditional ways of making sense. More recently, science has provided additional ways of understanding the world. Sociology is part of the rise of science as a means of making sense of the world.

As we know in our own time, there can be tension between religious and scientific views. Contemporary disputes over evolution, sexuality, marriage, and even the age of our planet often pit religious values against scientific interpretations. More broadly speaking, both at home and abroad, religious fundamentalisms rest uneasily alongside modern, secular worldviews. These familiar tensions have a history that takes us back to the origins of sociology itself.

Sociology and Modernity

The rise of sociology is part of a much larger story about the emergence of the modern world itself. Modernity emerged in European societies through a long process of social change that unfolded from the sixteenth to the nineteenth centuries. During this time, virtually everything about organized social life in Europe was fundamentally transformed. In our day, we speak of globalization as a force that is changing the world in the most basic ways. But current patterns of globalization can be traced back to the rise of modernity itself; in many respects, they are a continuation of the changes that ushered in the modern world.

Economically, modernity transformed most people from peasants to workers in a complex division of labor. Politically, modernity created distinct nation-states with clear boundaries. Technologically, modernity applied scientific knowledge to producing everything from consumer

Steven M. Buechler, "How to Think Sociologically," *Critical Sociology*, pp. 3-15, 281-290. Copyright © 2014 by Taylor & Francis Group. Reprinted with permission.

goods to lethal weapons. Demographically, modernity triggered population growth and massive migration from small, familiar, rural communities to large, urban, anonymous cities.

When social worlds change like this, some people benefit while others are harmed. In addition, most people find rapid change and its inevitable conflict to be unsettling, and they seek to understand what is happening. It was this moment that gave rise to sociology. Explaining modernity became sociology's task at the same time that modernity was making sociology possible in the first place.

The link between modernity and sociology was the Enlightenment. This intellectual revolution accompanied other revolutionary changes occurring throughout Europe. In the broadest terms, the Enlightenment challenged religious belief, dogma, and authority. It sought to replace them with scientific reason, logic, and knowledge.

Four basic themes pervaded Enlightenment thought (Zeitlin 1987). First, human reason was the best guide to knowledge, even if it meant that scientific skepticism displaced religious certainty. Second, reason must be paired with careful, scientific observation. Third, Enlightenment thought insisted that social arrangements be rationally justified; if not, they must be changed until they could be rationally defended. Finally, Enlightenment thought assumed that with the systematic application of reason, the perfectibility of people and the progress of society were all but inevitable.

Enlightenment thought contained some potentially fatal flaws. It was a Eurocentric worldview, created by privileged white men, that made universal pronouncements about all people in all times and places. While applauding Europe's progress, it ignored the colonial domination of the rest of the world that provided the labor, goods, and wealth that underwrote that progress. Generalizations about "humanity" meant "males," to the exclusion of women, and pronouncements on the "human race" meant white Europeans, to the exclusion of darker people, who were viewed as subhuman.

The Enlightenment was much more than a justification of imperialism, sexism, and racism, but it could become that as well. More than two centuries later, the jury is still out on whether Enlightenment biases can be overcome and its promises be fulfilled. Some postmodernists see little hope for this to happen. Others, myself included, think that the critical spirit of the Enlightenment can help uproot its biases. The project is already under way as feminists, people of color, and postcolonial writers find their way into contemporary sociological discourses (Lemert 2013).

In its own day, the Enlightenment provoked a "romantic conservative reaction" (Zeitlin 1987) that rejected the elevation of reason and science over faith and tradition. It defended traditional customs, institutions, and ways of life from the new standard of critical reason. The debate between Enlightenment progress and conservative reaction set the agenda for sociology as the social science of modernity. Progress or order? Change or stability? Reason or tradition? Science or religion? Individual or group? Innovation or authority? Such dichotomies framed the subject matter of the new science of sociology.

The classical era of sociology refers to European thinkers whose ideas brought this new discipline to maturity from the late eighteenth to the early twentieth centuries. The very different sociologies of Auguste Comte, Herbert Spencer, Ferdinand Tönnies, Karl Marx, Max Weber, Georg Simmel, Emile Durkheim, and others are variations on sociology's main theme: How do we understand modern society? Given these efforts, we might think of sociology as the ongoing effort of human beings to understand the worlds they are simultaneously inheriting from earlier generations and maintaining and transforming for future generations.

This approach has been described as the "sociological imagination." It arises when people realize that they can only know themselves by understanding their historical period and by examining others in the same situation as themselves. We think sociologically when we grasp how our historical moment differs from previous ones and how the situations of various groups of people differ from each other (Mills 1959).

The sociological imagination is guided by three related questions. The first concerns the social structure of society. How is it organized, what are its major institutions, and how are they linked together? The second concerns the historical location of society. How has it emerged from past social forms, what mechanisms promote change, and what futures are possible based on this historical path? The third concerns individual biography within society. What kinds of character traits are called forth by this society, and what kinds of people come to prevail? The sociological imagination is thus about grasping the relations between history and biography within society.

The sociological imagination sensitizes us to the difference between "personal troubles" and "public issues." A personal trouble is a difficulty in someone's life that is largely a result of individual circumstances. A public issue is a difficulty that is largely owing to social arrangements beyond the individual's control. The distinction is crucial because common sense often interprets events as personal troubles; we explain someone's difficulties as springing from individual shortcomings. The sociological imagination recognizes that such difficulties are rarely unique to one person; they rather happen to many people in similar situations. The underlying causes derive more from social structures and historical developments than the individual alone. If our goal is "diagnosis," the sociological imagination locates problems in a larger social context. If our goal is "treatment," it implies changing the structure of society rather than the behavior of individuals.

This applies to success as well. Common sense often attributes success to individual qualities. The sociological imagination asks what social and historical preconditions were necessary for an individual to become a success. Many successful people, in Jim Hightower's memorable phrase, "were born on third base but thought they hit a triple." The point is that whereas common sense sees the world in individual terms, sociological thinking sees it in structural terms. Only by seeing the connections between structure, history, and biography can we understand the world in a sociological way.

This discussion implies that professional sociologists and ordinary people see the world differently. This is often true, but the issue is more complicated. Modernity has also led ordinary people to develop a practical sociology in their everyday lives. Think about it this way. Sociology sees the world as a social construction that could follow various blueprints. Indeed, social worlds *are* constructed in very different ways in different times and places.

In our time, an awareness of the socially constructed nature of social worlds is no longer the privileged insight of scholars, but has become part of everyday understanding. Whether owing to rapid change, frequent travel, cultural diffusion, or media images, many people understand that we live in socially constructed worlds. Some people are distressed by this fact, and others rejoice in it, but few can escape it. Thus, an idea that was initially associated with professional sociology has become part of the everyday consciousness of ordinary people today.

The result is that many people without formal sociological training understand social processes quite well. Put differently, the objects of sociological analysis are people who are quite capable of becoming the subjects of the sociological knowledge created by that analysis. Although few people can explain how quantum mechanics governs the physical world, many can describe sociological processes that shape the social world.

Certain circumstances prompt people to think sociologically. Perhaps the key stimulant is when familiar ways of doing and thinking no longer work. It is when people are surprised, puzzled, challenged, or damaged that they are most likely to think sociologically (Lemert 2008). People then develop sociological competence as they try to make sense out of specific, individual circumstances by linking them to broader social patterns. In this way, sociological awareness begins to understand bigger things as a by-product of wrestling with the practical challenges of everyday life.

Circumstances do not inevitably provoke sociological consciousness. Some people redouble their faith or retreat into ritualism. So perhaps we can conclude this way. Societies confront people with problems. These problems have always had the potential to promote a sociological awareness. In our times, there is a greater awareness of the socially constructed nature of the world. This makes it even more likely that when people in this society are confronted with practical challenges, they will develop sociological competence as a practical life skill. In late modernity, everyone can become a practical sociologist.

Thinking Sociologically

The sociological perspective involves several themes. They overlap with one another, and some may be found in other social sciences as well as everyday consciousness. Taken together, they comprise a distinctive lens for viewing the social world. Here are some of those themes.

Society Is a Social Construction

People construct social order. Sociology does not see society as God-given, as biologically determined, or as following any predetermined plan beyond human intervention. At the same time, this does not mean that everyone plays an equal role in the process or that the final product looks like what people intended.

Social construction begins with intentions that motivate people to act in certain ways. When many people have similar goals and act in concert, larger social patterns or institutions are created. Goal-driven action is essential to the creation of institutions, and it remains equally important to their maintenance and transformation over time. Put succinctly, society is a human product (Berger and Luckmann 1966).

Basic human needs ensure some similarities in the goals that people pursue in all times and places. But these pursuits also unfold in specific historical circumstances and cultural contexts that have led to a dazzling variety of social worlds. This variety is itself the best evidence of the socially constructed nature of social worlds. If biology or genetics were the determining force behind social worlds, wouldn't they look a lot more similar than what we actually see around the globe?

Social constructionists thus insist that society arises from the goal-driven action of people. But they also recognize that the institutions created by such actions take on a life of their own. They appear to exist independently of the people who create and sustain them. They are experienced by people as a powerful external force that weighs down on them. When this external force becomes severe enough, people are likely to lose sight of the fact that society is a social product in the first place.

The value of the social constructionist premise is this dual recognition. On one hand, society is a subjective reality originating in the intentions of social actors. On the other hand, it becomes an objective reality that confronts subsequent generations as a social fact that inevitably shapes *their* intentional actions—and so it goes. Understood this way, the idea that society is a social construction is at the heart of the sociological perspective.

Society Is an Emergent Reality

Another premise of sociology is emergentism. This reveals sociology's distinctive level of analysis. For psychology, the level of analysis is the individual, even if it is acknowledged that individuals belong to groups. For sociology, the level of analysis is social ties rather than individual elements. Emergentism recognizes that certain realities only appear when individual elements are combined in particular ways. When they are, qualitatively new realities emerge through these combinations.

Take a simple example. Imagine a random pile of ten paper clips. Now imagine linking these paper clips together to form a chain. There are still ten paper clips, but a new emergent reality has appeared that is qualitatively different from the random pile because of how the elements are related to one another. Or consider human reproduction. Neither sperm nor egg is capable of producing human life on its own; in combination, qualitatively new life begins to emerge from a particular combination of elements.

Sociology specializes in the social level of analysis that emerges when elements are combined to create new, larger realities. Emergentism also implies that when we try to understand elements outside of their context, it is at best a simplification and at worst a distortion. The parts derive meaning from their relationship with other parts, and the sociological perspective is fundamentally attuned to such relationships.

Society Is a Historical Product

Thinking historically is a crucial part of the sociological imagination (Mills 1959). Classical sociologists thought historically because they lived in times of rapid social change and it was a major challenge to understand such change. Modern sociology tends to be more static, and modern people tend to be very present-oriented. Both professional and practical sociologists would benefit from a more historical perspective on the social world.

Seeing society as a historical product means recognizing that we cannot understand the present without understanding the past. Historical knowledge of past social conditions provides crucial comparisons. Without such benchmarks, it is impossible to understand what is genuinely new in the present day. Without a historical referent for comparison, sociology is clueless when it comes to understanding social change. Historical knowledge also provides the raw material for categories, comparisons, typologies, and analogies that are crucial to understanding both the present and possible future worlds.

The concept of emergentism applies here because the importance of seeing relationships between elements also works chronologically. If we look at society at only one point in time, we sever it from its past and its potential futures. Its very meaning arises from these relationships; to ignore them is to distort even the static understanding of society at one point in time. Consider the difference between a photograph and a film that presents a succession of images. We can learn something from the still photo, but its meaning often changes dramatically when we see it as one of a series of interrelated images.

Society Consists of Social Structures

Sociologists use the term *structure* to refer to the emergent products of individual elements. Structure implies that the social world has certain patterns or regularities that recur over time. Put differently, sociologists are keenly interested in social organization.

Structures are products of human purposes, but they acquire an objective reality and become a powerful influence on human action. Think about how physical structures like buildings shape action. We almost always enter buildings through doors; in rare cases we might do so through windows, but walking through walls is not an option. Social structures are less visible and more flexible than buildings, but they also channel people's actions, because they make some actions routine and expected, others possible but unlikely, and still others all but impossible.

Like buildings, social structures often have a vertical dimension. Social structures ensure that some people are better off than others and that some are not very well off at all. Some residential buildings have penthouses at the top, premium suites near the top, standard accommodations below them, and housekeeping staff in the basement. Social structures are also stratified, granting power, privilege, and opportunity to some while limiting or denying them to others. Sociologists are especially interested in the hierarchical dimension of social structures.

Sociologists traditionally thought of social structures as powerful forces weighing down upon the individual. In this image, structures constrain freedom of choice and behavior. But this is a one-sided view. Structures are constraining, but they are also enabling. These established patterns of social organization also make many actions possible in the first place or easier in the second place. Without preexisting social structures, we would have to do everything "from scratch," and the challenge of sheer survival might overwhelm us. The trick is thus to see social structures as simultaneously constraining and enabling social action (Giddens 1984).

Society Consists of Reflexive Actors

People in society are aware of themselves, of others, and of their relationships with others. As reflexive actors, we monitor our action and its effects on others. We continue, modify, or halt actions, depending on whether they are achieving their intended effects. According to one school of thought, we are literally actors, because social life is like a theatrical performance in which we try to convince others that we are a certain kind of person (Goffman 1959). To stage effective performances, we must constantly be our own critic, judging and refining our performances. Reflexivity thus means that when we act, we are conscious of our action, we monitor its course, and we make adjustments over time.

To stage such performances, we must undergo socialization. Along the way, we acquire a language that provides us with tools for reflexive thinking. We also acquire a self. Oddly enough, to have a self requires that we first have relationships with others. Through those relationships, we imaginatively see the world from their perspective, which includes seeing ourselves as we imagine we appear to them. It is this ability to see ourselves through the perspective of others—to see ourselves as an object—that defines the self. Reflexive action only becomes possible with a self.

Reflexivity makes ordinary people into practical sociologists. To be a competent person is to be a practical sociologist. We cannot help being sociologists every time we ponder a potential relationship, reconsider a hasty action, or adopt someone else's viewpoint. All such situations call upon and refine the reflexivity that is the hallmark of social action as well as a defining characteristic of the sociological perspective.

Society Is an Interaction of Agency and Structure

Social structures and reflexive actors are intimately connected. Unfortunately, much sociology emphasizes one side of this connection at the expense of the other. Agency-centered views stress the ability of people to make choices out of a range of alternatives in almost any situation. The emphasis on choice implies that people control their own destiny, at least within broad limits. Structure-centered views stress the extent to which people's choices are limited by social structures. The emphasis on structures implies that people's options—if not their lives—are essentially determined by larger social forces over which they have little control. Both approaches have merit, but the challenge is to see structure and agency in a more interconnected way.

Marx once said that people make their own history (acknowledging agency), but under circumstances they do not choose but rather inherit from the past (acknowledging structure). Here's an analogy from the game of pool. Each time you approach the table, you "inherit" a structure left by your opponent when they missed their last shot. Yet, for every layout of balls on the table, there is always a shot that you can attempt, and that action will alter the structure of the table for subsequent shots. In this analogy, structure (the position of balls on the table) both limits and creates opportunities for agency (taking a shot), which in turn alters the structure for the next round of shooting. If pool is not your game, chess is also a good analogy. The point is that agency and structure are two sides of the same coin; each conditions the possibilities of the other as we make our own history in circumstances we don't choose.

The close connection between structure and agency has led one theorist to reject the notion of structure altogether, because it implies something that exists apart from agency. Anthony Giddens (1984) talks about a *process* of structuration. In this view, actors use preexisting structures to accomplish their goals, but they also re-create them as a by-product of their actions. Consider a wedding ceremony. It is a preexisting cultural ritual people use to accomplish the goal of getting married. The by-product of all these individual marriages is the perpetuation of the cultural ritual itself. Generalize this to any situation in which we draw upon an established part of our social world to achieve a goal; in using this part we also sustain (and perhaps transform) it as a part of social structure.

Society Has Multiple Levels

Although society has multiple levels, sociologists often focus on one level at a time. Think about using Google Maps to locate a destination. You can zoom out to get the big picture at the expense of not seeing some important details. Alternatively, you can zoom in on some key details at the expense of not seeing the big picture. Combining these differing views will orient you to your destination, but we must remember it is ultimately all one interconnected landscape.

Sociologists nevertheless distinguish between macro and micro levels of society. When we look at the macro level, we typically include millions of people organized into large categories, groups, or institutions. The macro level is the "big picture" or "high altitude" perspective in which society's largest patterns are evident and individuals are invisible. When we look at the micro level, we might inspect no more than a dozen people interacting in a small group setting. Here, the role of particular individuals is very prominent, and larger social patterns fade into the background.

Some of the best sociology involves understanding not only structure-agency connections but also micro-macro links. Every macro-structure rests on micro-interaction, and every micro-interaction is shaped by macro-structures. The previous example of a wedding also illustrates this point. On the macro level, weddings are a cultural ritual that inducts people into the institution of marriage and the family. However, weddings, marriage, and the family would not exist on the macro level without countless, micro-level interactions. The macro-level institution depends on micro-level actions to sustain it. At the same time, anyone who has ever gotten married will tell you that macro-level, cultural expectations about weddings impose themselves on people as they plan for this supposedly personal event. Every micro-level wedding depends on a macro-level, cultural blueprint for its social significance. The micro and macro levels of society are one interdependent reality rather than two separate things.

Society Involves Unintended Consequences

One of the more profound insights of the sociological perspective concerns unintended and unanticipated consequences of action. Much human action is purposive or goal-directed. People act because they want to accomplish something. Despite this, they sometimes fail to achieve their goals. But whether people achieve their goals or not, their actions always create other consequences that they don't intend or even anticipate. Shakespeare made a profoundly sociological point when he had Juliet fake her own suicide to dramatize her love for Romeo. Unfortunately, the plan never reached Romeo. Juliet neither intended nor anticipated that Romeo would find her unconscious, believe that she was really dead, and take his own life in response. Nor did he intend (or even realize) that she would awaken, discover his real death, and really take her life in response. Talk about unintended consequences!

This principle acknowledges the complexity of the social world and the limits on our ability to control it. It says that despite our best efforts, the effects of social action cannot be confined to one intended path; they always spill over into unexpected areas. The principle is also a cautionary message for those seeking to solve social problems. Such efforts might succeed, but they often bring other consequences that are neither positive nor intended.

Efforts to control crime provide an example. Consider policies to "get tough" on crime through harsher treatment like capital punishment and mandatory sentencing. Because the human beings who serve as judges and juries are reflexive actors who take these facts into account, they are often less likely to convict suspects without overwhelming evidence because of the harshness of the sentence. Thus, the unintended consequence of an attempt to "get tough" on crime might be the opposite, because fewer suspects are convicted than before.

A related idea is the distinction between manifest and latent functions. A manifest function is an outcome that people intend. A latent function is an outcome that people are not aware of; it can complement, but it often contradicts, the manifest function. Crime and punishment provide yet another example. The manifest function of imprisonment is punishment or rehabilitation. The latent function is to bring criminals together where they can meet one another, exchange crime techniques, and become better criminals upon their return to society.

The concept of latent functions is crucial to sociological analysis. Sometimes we observe behavior or rituals that seem irrational, pointless, or self-defeating. This is the time to begin looking for latent functions. What we will often find is that such "irrational" behavior reinforces the identity and sustains the cohesion of the group that performs it. Thus, before we dismiss the tribal rain dance (because "rain gods" don't exist), we must explore its latent function. Even when people don't (manifestly) know what they are (latently) doing, their behavior can be crucial to group cohesion.

Recognizing unintended consequences and latent functions is not just for professional sociologists. Daily living requires managing risk, and ordinary people in everyday life recognize the tricky nature of goal-directed action. The folk wisdom that "the road to hell is paved with good intentions" acknowledges the potential disconnect between goals and outcomes. Such recognition, however, never completely prevents outcomes we neither intend nor expect. These principles give social life some of its most surprising twists, and sociology some of its most fascinating challenges.

No attempt to capture the sociological perspective in a small number of themes can be complete. Other sociologists would doubtless modify this list. But most would recognize these themes as central to thinking sociologically. As such, they provide a foundation for the more detailed investigations to follow.

Sociology's Double Critique

This final theme deserves special emphasis as the foundation of this book. Last but not least, thinking sociologically means looking at the social world in a critical way.

In everyday language, *critical* implies something negative. Being critical is often seen as being harsh, unfair, or judgmental. When we say someone is "critical," we often mean that their behavior is inappropriately mean-spirited. This is a perfectly reasonable use of everyday language, and the point it makes about how people should treat one another is also perfectly reasonable.

In sociological language, *critical* means something else. Doing sociology in a critical way means looking beyond appearances, understanding root causes, and asking who benefits. Being critical is what links knowledge to action and the potential of building a better society. Being critical in the sociological sense rests on the profoundly *positive* belief that we can use knowledge to understand the flaws of the social world and act to correct them.

The sociological perspective contains a double critique. First, mainstream sociology brings an inherently critical angle of vision to its subject. Second, some particular approaches in sociology carry this critique further by building on values that make sociological analysis especially critical of power and domination.

The critical dimension of mainstream sociology derives from the Enlightenment. Despite the flaws noted earlier, the Enlightenment advocated the use of reason, science, and evidence to critically examine religious truth, established doctrine, and political authority. Given its Enlightenment roots, sociology has always cast a critical eye on all types of claims, forms of knowledge, and exercises of power.

It is this quality that Peter Berger (1963) called the "debunking" tendency of sociological consciousness. Debunking means that the sociological perspective never takes the social world at face value and never assumes that it is what it appears to be. The sociological perspective rather looks at familiar phenomena in new ways to get beyond the immediately obvious, publicly approved, or officially sanctioned view. In this way, sociology sees through the facades of social structures to their unintended consequences and latent functions. Sociologically speaking, the problem might not be crime but laws, not revolution but government. Berger concludes that sociology is not compatible with totalitarianism, because the debunking quality of sociology will always be in tension with authoritarian claims to knowledge and power.

Although the world has changed since Berger wrote, the need for debunking is greater than ever. The political fundamentalisms of Cold War and rival superpowers have been replaced by other fundamentalisms that are logical targets for sociology's debunking insights. A world in which more and more people feel they know things with absolute certainty is a world that drastically needs the sociological perspective.

At the same time that some people embrace fundamentalist beliefs, others become suspicious and cynical about everything. This stance ("debunking on steroids") is too much of a good thing. For the ultra-cynical poser, all ideas, values, and beliefs are suspect, and none deserve support. Against this stance, sociology offers nuance and judgment. The sociological perspective recognizes that some ideas, values, and beliefs have more merit, logic, or evidence than others. Careful sociological thinkers make such distinctions. Indeed, the ultra-cynical mind-set itself needs debunking. Cynicism helps people avoid action or evade responsibility. A sociological perspective suggests that such inaction, or evasion, *is* action that tacitly supports dominant powers by refusing to challenge them in any way.

Mainstream sociology does not take the world for granted. Just when we think we have the answers, it poses another level of questions. For all these reasons, sociology in its most generic form has always included a critical angle of vision.

Although mainstream sociology is inherently critical, some versions of sociology take critique to another level by adopting certain values as the basis for their critique. In contrast to mainstream sociology, these approaches are devoted to a critical analysis of how social structures create relations of domination.

This fully critical sociology is best understood in contrast to mainstream sociology. Although mainstream sociology is critical because of its debunking tendency, it also adopts a scientific posture of detachment. Mainstream sociology seeks to be value-free, value-neutral, or objective. Put differently, mainstream sociology deliberately refrains from taking sides that would jeopardize its scientific neutrality. Mainstream sociology recognizes that *as citizens*, sociologists can be political actors. But it insists that in their role as scientific sociologists, they must maintain their objectivity.

Critical sociology differs from mainstream sociology on these issues. It emphasizes that in social science, humans are both the subjects and the objects of study. Notions of objectivity derived from the natural sciences don't necessarily translate into social science. But even if sociology could approximate objectivity, critical sociologists reject such a stance. It is not desirable, because the quest for objectivity diverts sociologists from asking the most important questions and from taking a more active role in the resolution of social problems.

Think of the contrast in this way. Mainstream sociology is primarily committed to one set of Enlightenment values having to do with science and objectivity. Critical sociology is primarily committed to another set of Enlightenment values having to do with freedom and equality. The latter values demand critical scrutiny of any social order that imposes unnecessary inequalities or restrictions on people's ability to organize their lives as they wish. These values require critical analysis of social arrangements that create conflicting interests between people and allow one group to benefit at the expense of another.

Critical sociologists deliberately focus on relations of domination, oppression, or exploitation, because these actions so obviously violate the values of freedom and equality. Critical sociologists are willing to advocate for groups who are victimized by such arrangements. Good critical sociologists realize they cannot speak for such groups. But they can explore how social arrangements make it difficult for some to speak for themselves, and they can underscore the importance of changing those arrangements.

Other issues distinguish mainstream from critical sociology. Mainstream sociology's commitment to science means it maintains a strict divide between scientific questions of what *is* and normative questions of what *ought* to be. Critical sociology wants to transcend this divide by linking critical analysis of how the world is organized now with normative arguments for how the world should be organized in the future. Behind such arguments are hopeful, or even utopian assumptions about alternative worlds that might be constructed. Critical sociology is simultaneously pessimistic about the current state of the world and optimistic about its possible futures. It examines our potential for living humanely, the social obstacles that block this potential, and the means to change from a problematic present to a preferable future.

The debate between mainstream and critical sociology is important and complex, and it will not be resolved by anything said here. But what can be said is that sociology is better because of the debate. Each side provides a corrective to the faults of the other. At the extreme, mainstream sociology becomes an inhumane, sterile approach that reduces human beings to objects of scientific curiosity; it needs a course correction through the humane values of critical sociology. At the extreme, critical sociology becomes an empty, ideological stance that denies the complexities of its own value commitments; it needs a course correction through the scientific caution of mainstream sociology.

Sociology's double critique thus derives from mainstream and critical sociology, respectively. My primary goal in this book is to illustrate critical sociology, but I also include the critical insights of mainstream sociology. I do so because these approaches sometimes speak to different issues, because neither seems adequate on its own, because they are often complementary, and because this best conveys the richness of our discipline itself. In the end, it is less important which side is "right" than that both sides coexist and continually provoke us to be reflexive about our role as sociologists and as actors in the world.

Sociology's double critique is also crucial to rethinking the flaws of the Enlightenment itself. Mainstream sociology's notion of debunking accepted truths grew out of the Enlightenment struggle against religion, but there is no reason it can't also foster critical examination of the Enlightenment itself. Critical sociology's challenge to domination also seems tailor-made to examining and overturning those forms of domination that the Enlightenment ignored, accepted, or promoted. Thus, for all its flaws, the Enlightenment provides tools for its own examination, critique, and transformation.

References

Berger, Peter. 1963. *Invitation to Sociology*. New York: Doubleday.
Berger, Peter, and Thomas Luckmann. 1966. *The Social Construction of Reality*. Garden City, NY: Anchor.
Giddens, Anthony. 1984. *The Constitution of Society*. Berkeley: University of California Press.
Goffman, Erving. 1959. *The Presentation of Self in Everyday Life*. Garden City, NY: Anchor.
Lemert, Charles. 2008. *Social Things*. 4th ed. Lanham, MD: Rowman & Littlefield.
———. 2013. *Social Theory: The Multicultural and Classic Readings*. 5th ed. Boulder, CO: Westview Press. Mills, C. Wright.
Mills, C. Wright. 1959. *The Sociological Imagination*. New York: Oxford University Press.
Zeitlin, Irving. 1987. *Ideology and the Development of Sociological Theory*. Englewood Cliffs, NJ: Prentice Hall.

Section 1 Discussion Questions

1. Describe what you thought sociology was before the first day of class. How much does that idea differ from what you know about sociology now? Using at least five examples, discuss how sociology is not common sense or common wisdom.
2. Discuss several ways sociologists differ from other social or behavioral scientists such as psychologists, economists, or historians in the way they examine human behavior.
3. Now, using your sociological imagination, examine and discuss the social and historical forces that have influenced your decision to attend college. Discuss this with the other students in your class. Do most of you have similar influences? Have many of you made the decision to attend college for the same reasons? You may find that most of you are in college for identical reasons, and you may even be able to see yourselves reflected in the trend of college attendance.
4. List and describe the ways using the sociological imagination can help individuals become more civil, humane, and compassionate.
5. In the past forty years, what has been the trend in college attendance in the United States? Is college attendance up, down, or flat? Discuss what you believe are the most significant social forces influencing this trend. Additionally, consider the diversity of college attendance. That is, have all ethnic, religious, gender, or social class groups seen the same trend in college attendance? If so, why? If not, why not?
6. Think of a problem that impacts you personally (e.g., the high cost of tuition, unemployment, or divorce) and explain how you would make sense of it differently if you viewed it as (a) only a personal problem or (b) influenced by a public issue. How do possible solutions to the problem differ depending on how you view it?
7. Sociology is a critical science because it places society under scrutiny so it can analyze, challenge, and turn over every leaf to get closer to a better understanding of how society really operates. Discuss how sociology challenges ideas about any or all of the following topics: racism, immigration, sexism, divorce, trans issues, and addiction.

Section 1 Exercises

1. This is a thought exercise for your sociological imagination. I want you to find a quiet, comfortable place where you can recline, relax, and won't be disturbed for about fifteen minutes. Go ahead, find a happy place.

Who you are:
Now, get really relaxed and read through this exercise. I want you to think about who you are ... by that I mean, how old are you? Are you male, female, or do you identify as a different gender? Are you middle class, lower class, or something else? Are you Black, White, Asian, Latinx, or some other ethnic identity? Are you able bodied or other abled? Did you grow up in a neighborhood with large houses and manicured lawns or in an apartment? Maybe you grew up in a mobile home. Did you and your family go on vacations? What kinds of vacations? International travel or staycations?

Where you are:
In this section, I want you to think about where you grew up or where you spent most of your life before coming to college. Was it urban or rural? Was it a big city, a mid-sized or small city? Was it a big town or small village? Was it in New England or the South, Southern California, or the Midwest?

When you are:
Well, this is pretty easy. Just think about the times you live in now. What are the social, political, economic, historical, and technological atmospheres like that you live in now?

The thought experiment:
Taking into consideration the three elements from above—who you are, where you are, and when you are—I want you to now imagine that it is 1950. It is 1950 where you are now; you are the same age you are now; and all those things about yourself are still true—you may be a nineteen-year-old Asian female who identifies as trans who grew up in rural Arkansas—and all those things are the same; the only difference is that you have traveled back in time to 1950.

Now, I want you to consider just one question: given who you are and where you grew up, would you be in college in 1950? Think about why you would or would not be in college in 1950. List and describe at least five reasons you would or would not be in college in 1950. Try to explain why this thought experiment is a wonderful way to illustrate the sociological perspective.

2. This exercise requires you to find several articles—in newspapers, magazines, blogs, or scientific journals—about a social pattern/trend that interests you. You should find at least five different articles. Read through all the articles, and summarize them using the sample table 1.1.

TABLE 1.1 Sample

Social Pattern/Trend	Social Forces					
	Demographic	Economic	Social Attitudes	Beliefs	Historical	Other

Describe the social pattern or trend you are examining in the first cell labeled "Social Pattern/Trend." Then, using the data from the articles you read, write brief descriptors in the cells under each of the column headings labeled "Demographic," "Economic," and so on. Once you have completed the table using the data from all [your] articles, step back and take a look at your completed table. Which column has the most entries? That is, what social forces seem to have the greatest influence on your chosen social pattern?

Finally, think about the connection between these social forces and the social trend you examined and the lives of individuals like yourself. Can you see how people's behaviors can be influenced by the times in which they live, their own demographic profiles, and social atmospheres that allow or don't allow certain behaviors? Examining and understanding these connections and their effects on yourself and others is the process of exercising your "sociological imagination." Just like working out certain muscles, the more you exercise your sociological imagination, the stronger it becomes!

3. For this exercise, you need to locate a research article (it must be from a peer-reviewed journal, a primary source, in any discipline that you want). It can be a print article or research that you find online. The most important element of the research is that it must be research that is counterintuitive. That is, it must be an article whose findings are contrary to popular or commonly held views on that topic.

Once you locate an article, you need to read and summarize the article. Your summary should include the major variables in the research, the methods used, the sample, findings, and conclusions that the author(s) have indicated. Also, include why you considered this to be counterintuitive. Indicate WHY this research was counterintuitive. That is, is this an example of research that dispelled a commonly held view on the topic, or were the findings contrary to what you thought, or both? Please feel free to include more in your summary than the elements I have included above.

4. These eight assumptions are essential to the sociological perspective. These assumptions are necessary to understand how sociologists view the social world (Buechler 2008). Try to think of examples for each one of the eight assumptions listed in the table below. Each one of the assumptions below was discussed in chapter 1 or in lectures on chapter 1.

For each of the eight assumptions in the table below, answer the question or complete the task that is presented using an example. Try to use examples from your own experiences if you can.

TABLE 1.2 The Fundamental Sociological Assumptions

Assumptions	Meaning	Question/Task
Number 1 Society is a social construction (see the discussion on Durkheim)	Society is a human creation. Society has a dual nature: while it is created by the actions of individuals, it becomes an objective reality that persists over time and influences the actions of the individual.	What is a social construction? How could you show using cross-cultural comparisons that society is a social construction? Give at least two examples from your own life circumstances of how you are affected by society as a social construction.
Number 2 Society is an emergent reality (see the discussion on dysfunctions and structural functionalism)	The reality of society is that it emerges from the interaction of individuals but is more than just the sum of the individuals. A social reality emerges that is greater than the sum of the parts.	Using the recent economic downturn as an example, show how the idea that society is an emergent reality can create new social realities.
Number 3 Society is a historical product (see the discussion about the sociological imagination)	In order to understand current social arrangements, we need to look at historical social organizations. This allows us to engage in comparative analysis and understand social change.	We have discussed the idea of change and the effect of historical period on biography extensively. Give two examples of how society has changed in your lifetime. Also, imagine you were born in 1915 in America. How could that historical reality have impacted your life? Give at least three examples of how that historical period in America could have impacted your life.

Number 4 Society consists of social structures (see the discussion about structural functionalism)	Society is made of social structures that constrain the individual but are also shaped by actors' actions.	We have discussed social structure in terms of social institutions. Give at least two examples of how institutions can constrain behavior and why they do.
Number 5 Society consists of reflexive actors (see the discussion on symbolic interaction)	We are aware of ourselves and others. We monitor and adjust our actions and beliefs based on the perceived social context and other elements of social interactions.	Give an example of how in a specific social situation you are aware of yourself and others and how that can influence how you act.
Number 6 Society is an interaction of agency and structure (see the discussion on the interactionist perspective)	Our interactions are shaped by social structures like the economy, and social structures are shaped by our interactions.	Give one example from your life of how you interact with a particular institution.
Number 7 Society has multiple levels (see the discussion about micro- and macrosociology)	Microsociological analysis focuses on the reality created through day-to-day interactions between individuals, and macrosociological analysis seeks to find the "big picture" by investigating large social structures, institutions, and large-scale patterns.	Give one example of microsociological analysis and one example of macrosociological analysis.
Number 8 Society involves unintended consequences (see the discussion about manifest and latent functions)	Sometimes, our actions have unintended consequences and affect ourselves or another person in a way we did not intend. Anytime a collective of humans is engaged in an endeavor, there is the manifest function of that endeavor and latent or unintended consequences of the interactions.	Give an example from your own life of how your actions had an unintended consequence and affected you or another person in a way you did not intend.

DOING SOCIOLOGY
REVEALING OUR SOCIAL WORLD THROUGH RESEARCH

Okay, sometimes people make mistakes in their observations of the social world, but why does that matter? Well, it matters on several levels. The casual observations and conclusions we make on a daily basis many times influence the way we treat others. What we know about others is based not only on faulty observations but faulty reasoning and beliefs. Often, this leads to treating others in ways that they may find insulting, condescending, or just plain rude. Frequently, the results of social research are used to influence the lives of certain groups through public policy, so we, as social researchers, cannot engage in faulty investigations, which lead to flawed conclusions—we just can't afford to get it wrong. Take a look at the example about Wolf Wolfensberger below.

In the social sciences, we conduct social research on the social world, and from that research, we draw conclusions that become published scientific findings. Many times, those findings are used to inform laws and social policies, influence therapeutic practices, or develop social theory. For example, the research of Wolf Wolfensberger (1972, 1991, 1998, 2005) helped transform the way the intellectually disabled are treated. Much of his analyses showed how society unconsciously distances itself from the disabled, treating them as different and therefore justifying services and facilities that segregate them. His research revealed that if those with intellectual disabilities were treated with the expectation that they could learn, grow, and contribute to society, there would be no need for "special schools." Ultimately, Wolfensberger's research influenced changes in social policy and practices concerning the treatment of the intellectually disabled. Much of his work has contributed to a more inclusive and mainstream treatment of the intellectually disabled, transforming and validating the lives of a generation of disabled citizens.

So, as responsible social scientists, we cannot afford to make poor observations and draw faulty conclusions because our conclusions inform laws, policies, and practices that have the potential to affect people's lives. If our work as social scientists may affect the lives of many people, we must take care to use a method of systematic investigation—the scientific method—that avoids the pitfalls of casual observation.

What Is Social Research?

> *If we knew what it was we were doing, it would not be called research, would it?*
> —Albert Einstein

When we discuss research in the social sciences, we are almost always talking about data that has been collected about some social process, phenomenon, or population. It could be the results of surveys about attitudes toward gun control laws or the effects of birth order on personal finances or how evicting people is a lucrative business in poorer communities in many American cities. Social research is evidence based. That is, social researchers collect primary or secondary data that is used to support a theoretical position, test a hypothesis, or build a better understanding of some social process, practice, or population.

Social research is the application of the scientific method to the investigation of the social world. Social research helps us understand the world beyond our immediate experience and provides us with an understanding of how the social world operates. Topics in social research might include poverty, race/ethnicity, social and gender inequality, social networks, interpersonal attraction, and the influence of peer pressure. Research on topics like these and others have the potential to provide vital information to government agencies, policy makers, nongovernmental organizations, and other interested groups.

Quite frequently, research is driven by personal interests. Some say that many social researchers are propelled into research by their own autobiographies, experiences in their own lives that create their research interests—sometimes referred to as "me-search." For me, this is true: my PhD dissertation was an examination of the well-being of adult children of alcoholics. I grew up in an alcoholic home and was fascinated by the topic, especially how children can emerge from such damaging home lives and still be well-adjusted, productive adults. While research on a topic may be influenced by personal interest, the collection, analysis, and interpretation of data must remain objective. A researcher has to let the data fall where it may and not influence the data to fall in the direction she *wishes* it to fall. Subjective biases and value judgments should never cloud the research process.

Investigators of the social world have a wide array of research designs and methods at their disposal. These include, but are not limited to, surveys, secondary data analysis, experiments, field experiments, participant observation, ethnographies, interviews, focus groups, and so on. However, each researcher has to decide which method(s) is best suited for their particular topic of investigation. Phone surveys are probably not the best method for asking adults about their participation in kinky sex, and hanging out in bars is not an effective way to survey what alcoholic beverages Americans prefer to drink. Neither of these would be very productive nor yield any useful or generalizable results. Ultimately, the methods researchers use to collect data have to be the best way for them to answer the questions they are asking.

CHAPTER 2

SOCIAL RESEARCH METHODS

Field Experiments

By definition, all experimental studies include the manipulation of one or more independent variables. Typically, with true experiments, this is achieved in a laboratory setting where investigators can control nearly every aspect of the experiment. This allows experimenters to be highly confident when making causal inferences—that their independent variable caused changes in their dependent variable—and reduces the possibility that extraneous variables have influenced their results. As we discussed, in sociology and many other social sciences, much of what is studied does not lend itself to laboratory conditions. Sometimes highly controlled laboratory conditions can alter participants' behaviors, limit the type of questions investigators can ask, or limit the generalizability of results. Moreover, many social scientists think that because laboratory experiments are so far removed from our actual daily lived experiences, their results tell us very little about how people act in real life settings.

Many researchers, therefore, have taken to the field to conduct their experiments. That is, they conduct their work in real-life settings like classrooms, factory floors, or on the streets—in the *field*. A **field experiment** uses elements of experimental design in natural settings rather than a laboratory. For example, Pfattheicher, Strauch, Diefenbacher and Schnuerch (2018), placed signs in a public bathroom that encouraged hand washing. The investigators used one set of signs that included a set of "watching eyes" above the text and another set of signs that used innocuous symbols with the text. Hand washing behavior was significantly increased when the "watching eyes" signs were used. Do you find this surprising? If so, why? If not, why?

Some Things to Keep in Mind

1. What type of research design does this work represent?
2. Why did the authors choose this particular design?
3. Was this an effective design?
4. What do the results suggest to you?
5. Can you think of alternative ways to explain the results?

A FIELD STUDY ON WATCHING EYES AND HAND HYGIENE COMPLIANCE IN A PUBLIC RESTROOM

Stefan Pfattheicher, Christoph Strauch, Svenja Diefenbacher, and Robert Schnuerch

1 | Introduction

All over the world, hand hygiene[1] is one of the most important means to prevent the transmission of pathogens and thereby reduce infections in professional contexts like the healthcare environment, as well as in home or community settings (e.g., Aiello & Larson, 2002; Bloomfield, Aiello, Cookson, O'Boyle, & Larson, 2007; Sax et al., 2007; World Health Organization, 2009). In developing countries, personal hand hygiene plays a crucial role in the prevention of life-threatening diseases such as diarrhea and is regarded as one of the most cost-effective preemptive measures (Bartram & Cairncross, 2010; Borghi, Guinness, Ouedraogo, & Curtis, 2002; World Health Organization, 2009). In wealthy countries, insufficient personal hand hygiene might be less life-threatening; nevertheless, it can contribute to elevated infection rates, particularly in pandemic situations (Aiello & Larson, 2002; Curtis & Cairncross, 2003). In this regard, hand hygiene can save more than a million people yearly from diarrheal diseases and can prevent viral infections like influenza (Curtis & Cairncross, 2003; Moyad & Robinson, 2008).

In addition to home and community settings, adequate hand hygiene is crucial and even legally regulated in several professional contexts such as the food processing industries and the healthcare sector (Allegranzi & Pittet, 2009; Kampf, Löffler, & Gastmeier, 2009; Medeiros, Cavalli, Salay, & Proença, 2011; Murphy, DiPietro, Kock, & Lee, 2011; World Health Organization, 2009). In hospitals, hand hygiene is particularly relevant with respect to patient safety, as it represents an

---

[1] In the present contribution, hand hygiene is used to summarize different hand hygiene procedures, namely washing hands with plain soap and water as well as hand disinfection using antimicrobial agents such as alcohol hand rubs (Diefenbacher, Siegel, & Keller, 2016; World Health Organization, 2009). In different settings, different hand hygiene procedures are required in order to perform optimal hand hygiene (e.g., at home vs. in hospitals).

Stefan Pfattheicher, et al., "A Field Study on Watching Eyes and Hand Hygiene Compliance in a Public Restroom," *Journal of Applied Social Psychology*, vol. 48, no. 4, pp. 188-194. Copyright © 2018 by John Wiley & Sons, Inc. Reprinted with permission.

effective way to prevent hospital-acquired infections among patients, a most vulnerable group of individuals, including infections with multi-drug resistant organisms such as MRSA (Allegranzi & Pittet, 2009; Backman, Zoutman, & Marck, 2008; Ducel, Fabry, & Nicolle, 2002; Kampf, Löffler, & Gastmeier, 2009; World Health Organization, 2009). Moreover, childcare centers and schools are receiving special attention given their double role as institutions that directly and indirectly interconnect a large number of people *and* as early-in-life providers of basic education on hand hygiene (Azor-Martínez et al., 2014; Meadows & Le Saux, 2004; Wang, Lapinski, Quilliam, Jaykus, & Fraser, 2017). Overall, hand hygiene is an effective strategy for preventing diseases and contributes to better health in a vast variety of contexts (Allegranzi & Pittet, 2009).

All of the above-mentioned hand hygiene-relevant settings differ in several regards: for example, in the frequency of situations in which hand hygiene is recommended; in the risk of negative outcomes when hand hygiene is not performed in those situations; or, in the scope and severity of the potential negative outcomes. A commonality of these different settings, however, is the lack of compliance with hand hygiene recommendations. In private settings, a typical situation recommended for hand hygiene is after toilet use (Bloomfield et al., 2007; Nicolle, 2007). Judah and colleagues (2010), for example, report that a quarter of adult commuters sampled in buses and trains in the United Kingdom had fecal bacteria on their hands. Other studies (e.g., Anderson et al., 2008; Cardinale Lagomarsino et al., 2017; Monk-Turner et al., 2005; Munger & Harris 1989; Nalbone, Lee, Suroviak, & Lannon, 2005) directly assessed hand hygiene after toilet use in public restrooms and found largely varying, but frequently suboptimal compliance rates between 30% and 90% for different populations (e.g., convenience samples of students or employees at their work place, male, female, or samples in different regions).[2] Studies on hand hygiene practices of food workers reported poor compliance with official hand hygiene recommendations during food production in 31% of catering businesses (Clayton & Griffith, 2004) and 27% in restaurants (Green et al., 2006). A smaller study reported a compliance rate as low as 7% during food production in restaurants (Strohbehn, Sneed, Paez, & Meyer, 2008).

The best studied hand hygiene context by far is the healthcare sector, specifically hospitals, where infections that patients might acquire during their stay are a major concern (Allegranzi & Pittet, 2009; Kampf, Löffler, & Gastmeier, 2009; World Health Organization, 2009). Nonetheless, compliance with hand hygiene recommendations is still alarmingly low. The mean compliance rate established by a systematic review of 96 original studies is reported as low as 40% (Erasmus et al., 2010).

As a consequence of the special importance of hand hygiene and low compliance in the same, it is crucial to identify methods that enhance hand hygiene compliance (Naikoba & Hayward, 2001). In particular, research should focus on easily applicable low-cost methods:

---

2 A huge portion of variation in reported compliance rates might be caused by (a) different operationalizations, that is, what specific behavior is considered in the study (e.g., washing with or without soap; disinfection yes or no), and (b) the facilities that are considered (i.e., commodes and/or urinals which can differ in perceived contamination of hands; Berry, Mitteer, & Fournier, 2015).

Small interventions could represent a low threshold for companies and institutions. If successful, such interventions could increase health, in the case of employers, save money due to fewer employee sick days, decrease infection-related absenteeism in schools, and increase patient safety in hospitals or other healthcare institutions. In sum, strategies toward increasing hand hygiene are urgently needed and should be in the focus of research. The present investigation takes one step in this direction; specifically, we tested whether a simple cue of being watched, that is, the presentation of stylized watching eyes, increases hand hygiene compliance after using a public restroom. In this way, we tested whether a low-cost method (i.e., the simple presentation of stylized watching eyes) can improve hand hygiene. This approach might not only serve applied value for companies, public institution, and people's health per se, but also contributes to our basic understanding about how hand hygiene can be improved. As outlined in detail to follow, we argue that (subtle) social presence offers this potential.

1.1 | Watching eyes and socially desirable behavior

There is long-standing, striking evidence that individuals modify their behavior when other individuals are present (Markus, 1978; Zajonc, Heingartner, & Herman, 1969). In particular, individuals act in a socially desirable way when being watched by others (Leary & Kowalski, 1990; Van Bommel, van Prooijen, Elffers, & van Lange, 2014). It appears that people not only modify their behavior when other individuals are present, but also when mere reminders of being observed (i.e., human watching eyes) are present in the environment (Haley & Fessler, 2005). In recent years, a growing number of researchers have shown that cues of being watched reduce socially undesirable behavior such as bicycle theft (Nettle, Nott, Bateson, & Noë, 2012) or littering (Ernest-Jones, Nettle, & Bateson, 2011). Similarly, cues of being watched increase socially desirable behavior such as cooperation (Bateson, Nettle, & Roberts, 2006) and donations to charity given relatively few other people were present (Ekström, 2012). Yet we want to point to several published null effects in the study of cues of being watched (Northover, Pedersen, Cohen, & Andrews, 2017). We discuss this issue in detail in the Discussion section.

In the present contribution, we argue that, due to its important role in the prevention of disease-spreading, hand hygiene reflects a socially desirable and expected behavior (Aunger et al., 2016). On this basis, we assume that individuals show stronger hand hygiene compliance when being watched. In fact, past research shows that an observer present in a public restroom increases the number of people who wash their hands after using the restroom (Munger & Harris, 1989). This finding could be replicated in other public restrooms (Cardinale Lagomarsino et al., 2017; Edwards et al., 2002; Nalbone et al., 2005) and for hand hygiene compliance in hospitals (Eckmanns, Bessert, Behnke, Gastmeier, & Rüden, 2006; Maury, Moussa, Lakermi, Barbut, & Offenstadt, 2006).

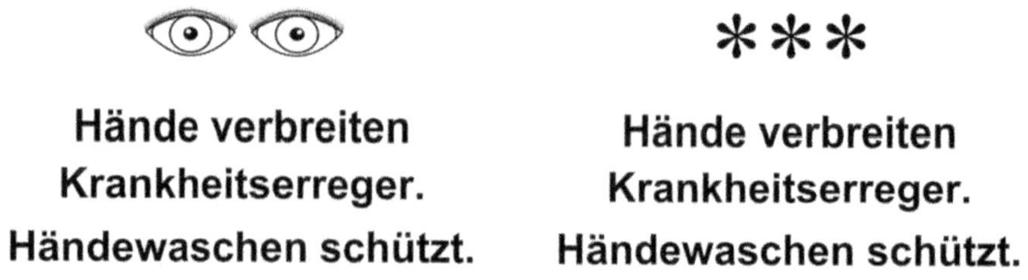

Hände verbreiten Krankheitserreger. Händewaschen schützt.

Hände verbreiten Krankheitserreger. Händewaschen schützt.

Fig. 1 The posters pinned in the restroom: Watching eyes (left) and the three stars (right) with the message about hand washing. The message (in German) says "Hands spread pathogens. Hand washing protects."

Recent studies have explored whether the presentation of watching eyes can be applied to increase hand hygiene behavior. Beyfus et al. (2016; see also King et al., 2016) demonstrate increased compliance with hand hygiene recommendations in a hospital when watching eyes are placed next to an alcohol foam dispenser compared to when no stimulus is presented. However, there were two notable disadvantages in that study: First, the image not only showed eyes but the eyes of a recognizable leader at the institution where the study took place. Second, the eyes pinned above the dispensers could be interpreted as angry. Therefore, the findings might not reflect the influence of a simple depiction of watching eyes. Instead, they could be driven by the participants' fear of being caught—by someone in leadership—violating the hand hygiene instruction and/or the apparent aggressiveness of the eyes. Interestingly, a similar study in the hospital context showed that angry watching eyes do not significantly increase hand hygiene behavior (Bolton, Rivas, Prachar, & Jones, 2015). Overall, research is needed to enhance knowledge on the possible effect of watching eyes on hand hygiene behavior. In the study reported below, we address this issue and examined whether (neutral) watching eyes increase hand hygiene compliance. The study took place in a women's public restroom.

2 | STUDY

2.1 | Methods

2.1.1 | Procedure and assessments

A field study was set up to assess the impact of watching eyes on hand-washing compliance after using a public restroom. The study took place at a central public restroom on a campus at a German university. The study was conducted in full accordance with the Ethical Guidelines of the German Association of Psychologists (DGPs) and the American Psychological Association (APA). No personal information was assessed; participants remained completely anonymous and were not identified in any regard during the study process. Moreover, by the time the data were acquired in June 2017, it was also not customary at Ulm University, nor at most other German universities, to seek ethics approval for simple, noninvasive field studies.

Hand hygiene compliance was defined as washing hands with soap. Data on whether individuals washed their hands with soap was collected with a soap dispenser provided by the company Ophardt Hygiene Technologies, Inc.[3] The dispenser set timestamps for each use. In addition, the times individuals entered and left the restroom were recorded by one hidden (female) observer situated about 15 meters away.[4] The recorded times of entering and leaving the restroom and the data from the soap dispenser were matched to determine who used the dispenser. Whether or not people used soap to wash their hands served as the binary dependent variable. In addition, we recorded (a) whether at least one other person was also present during the time individuals were in the restroom (control group = 83.3%, watching eyes = 78.8%, n.s.), and (b) the time, in minutes, that individuals spent in the restroom (control group $M = 3.46$, $SE = .09$; watching eyes $M = 3.22$, $SE = .08$, $t(352) = 1.93$, $p = .05$, Cohen's $d = 0.21$).[5]

2.1.2 | Watching eyes

Two posters were changed every 1–2 hr, reflecting two conditions (see Figure 1). In the control condition ($n = 144$), a poster carrying a message of advice on hand hygiene and a distractor (three stars) was displayed directly at the sink. The message read "Hände verbreiten Krankheitserreger. Richtig waschen schützt." (Hands spread pathogenic germs. Hand-washing protects). In the experimental condition ($n = 210$), the stars were replaced by a pictogram of neutral eyes looking straight ahead, taken from Keller and Pfattheicher (2011; see also Pfattheicher & Keller, 2015). The message of advice was therefore present in both conditions, but the presence of the watching eyes versus stars was varied. Both posters were the size of an ISO 216 paper sheet (210 mm × 297 mm). Posters were changed only when no individuals were in the restrooms and the procedure took only a few seconds. We used the pictogram of watching eyes because they were relatively neutral, that is, more parsimonious regarding the information that is salient in the situation. Accordingly, possible confounding factors that may come along with other (eye) manipulations (e.g., attractiveness, emotion) can be excluded. The applied eyes were tested previously in a study by Pfattheicher and Keller (2015). They found that these eyes reliably increase a sense of being watched.

---

3   We could have used a dispenser from another company as well. To be transparent, we mentioned that the dispenser is from Ophardt Hygiene Technologies, Inc.
4   The observer only entered the restroom to change the watching eye picture (experimental condition) and the three stars (control condition). The study took place in the main building of the university; there are typically other people also present outside the restroom walking by or sitting there. That said, the observer was probably not considered an "observer" but as a person just sitting there.
5   As reported in detail below, watching eyes increased hand hygiene compliance. Controlling for time spent and whether other people were present even strengthened the effect of watching eyes on hand hygiene behavior.

2.1.3 | Sample

Using G*Power (Faul, Erdfelder, Buchner, & Lang, 2009), a power analysis was conducted for a one-tailed z-test for a single binominal regression coefficient in a logistic regression. Power was set to .80 (Cohen, 1992) and a medium effect (odds ratio = 2.15; Rosenthal, 1996) was assumed which would correspond to an increase of hand hygiene compliance from 65% to 80% caused by watching eyes. We went for a medium effect to detect an effect that is of relevant size. This power analysis revealed a required sample size of $N = 220$ to detect a significant effect (alpha level of .05) given there actually is an effect. Data from 354 individuals between June 20 and 27, 2017, could be collected. Due to the fact that the experimenter was female while a regular change of posters in the restrooms was necessary, the study took place only in the women's restroom. Data of the study are available on the Open Science Framework (see https://osf.io/5dkf3). We used SPSS Statistics 24 (IBM Corp., Armonk/USA) to run the analyses. As we had a binary variable (hand hygiene yes/no), we ran logistic regression analyses. For testing interactions, we used the PROCESS macro provided by Hayes (2013).

3 | RESULTS

Overall, 76.6% of the individuals used the soap dispenser. Using logistic regression analysis, whether individuals used the soap dispenser (1 = yes, 0 = no) was regressed on the experimental condition (1 = watching eyes condition, 0 = control condition). This analysis revealed a significant effect of the experimental condition ($B = .67$, $SE = .27$, $p = .01$, odds ratio = 1.95, Nagelkerke $R^2 = .03$, $\chi^2 = 6.41$). Specifically, analysis suggests that individuals used the soap dispenser more often in the watching eyes condition (83.3%) compared to the control condition (71.9%).

To provide convergent evidence that *social presence* increased hand hygiene compliance (see also Edwards et al., 2002; Munger & Harris, 1989), we analyzed whether the presence of at least one other person during the time individuals were in the restroom (1 = yes, 0 = no) also increased hand hygiene compliance. This was the case ($B = .74$, $SE = .29$, $p = .01$, odds ratio = 2.10, Nagelkerke $R^2 = .03$, $\chi^2 = 6.14$). Specifically, when at least one person was present, individuals used the soap dispenser more often (79.4%) compared to when they were alone (64.7%). This finding is of high importance as it provides convergent and independent validity: either subtle social presence (i.e., watching eyes) or real social presence increased hand hygiene behavior. This speaks to the validity of the entire study. In addition, we tested whether the effect of the experimental condition (i.e., the presence of watching eyes) depended on the presence of other people in the restroom (see Ernest-Jones et al., 2011; Powell, Roberts, Nettle, & Fusani, 2012). No significant interaction was found ($p = .35$).

Next, we (exploratively) examined whether the effect of watching eyes depended on the time people spent in the restroom. To test this notion, whether individuals used the soap dispenser was regressed on the experimental condition (this time contrast coded to allow interpretation of main effects, +0.5 = watching eyes condition, −0.5 = control condition; cf. Hayes, 2013), the time spent in the restroom (centered to the mean), as well as their interaction (overall statistics of this model: Nagelkerke R^2 =.11, χ^2 = 25.60, p <.001). Analysis revealed a significant main effect of the experimental condition (i.e., the presence of watching eyes; B = .56, SE = .28, p = .05, Odds ratio = 1.75) and a significant main effect of the time spent in the restroom (B = .32, SE = .15, p = .04, Odds ratio = 1.38). The latter main effect indicates that the probability of hand washing increased the longer individuals stayed in the restroom. Most importantly, the two main effects were qualified by a significant interaction (B = −.83, SE = .31, p < .01, Odds ratio = .43). The pattern of the interaction is displayed in Figure 2.

Decomposing the interaction (Aiken & West, 1991; Hayes, 2013), watching eyes increased hand hygiene compliance only when individuals spent a relatively short period (1 SD below the mean; i.e., about 2 min) in the restroom (B = 1.52, SE = .41, p < .001, Odds ratio = 4.57). When individuals spent a relatively long period (1 SD above the mean, i.e., about 4.5 min) in the restroom, watching eyes did not significantly increase hand hygiene compliance (B = −.40, SE = .50, p = .42, Odds ratio = .67). That is to say, individuals already had a relatively high hand hygiene compliance when staying a relatively long time in the restroom. However, when staying a relatively short time in the restroom, hand hygiene compliance was lower and could be significantly increased by watching eyes. These interesting findings are further discussed below.

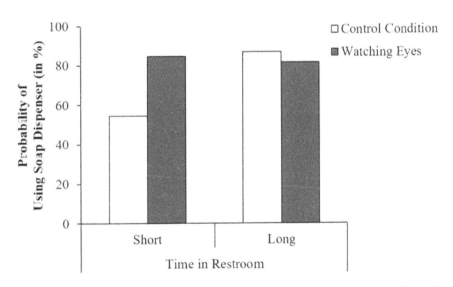

Fig. 2 Probability of using the soap dispenser as a function of the experimental condition and the time spent in the restroom.

4 | DISCUSSION

The present research deals with a question that is important for humans' health: How can we increase hand hygiene compliance? Building on (a) past research showing that watching eyes increase socially desirable and expected behavior (e.g., Ekström, 2012; Powell et al., 2012), and (b) the assumption that hand washing after using the toilet is socially desirable and expected (Aunger et al., 2016), we have assumed that the presentation of watching eyes has the potential to increase hand hygiene compliance. In line with this hypothesis, we show a significant increase of hand hygiene compliance when watching eyes were presented in a women's restroom, as compared with a neutral control condition.

The present work has several implications and contributes to the existing literature in a meaningful way. First, we extend previous research on watching eyes and hand hygiene behavior. Beyfus and colleagues (2016) as well as Bolton et al. (2015) tested the effect of *angry* watching eyes on individuals' hand hygiene; in addition, Beyfus and colleagues (2016) used the eyes of a recognizable leader at the institution where the study took place. In our study, we eliminated these interfering third variables by using simple, neutral-looking eyes and were able to demonstrate their positive effect on hand hygiene compliance. Thus, we can conclude that the *mere* presence of watching eyes has the potential to increase hand hygiene compliance.[6]

Second, amidst recent concerns about reproducibility in psychological science (Open Science Collaboration, 2015), replications should be of particular interest to the field (Brandt et al., 2014). Indeed, with the present study we conceptually replicate previous research showing that the (actual) presence of other people increases hand hygiene compliance (Eckmanns et al., 2006; Edwards et al., 2002; Maury et al., 2006; Munger & Harris, 1989). In combination with the finding that watching eyes affect hand-washing behavior, the present research provides convergent evidence that different forms of social presence can likely increase hand hygiene compliance.

Third, with the present study, we might also show *who* increases hand hygiene compliance when being watched. Taking into account the time individuals spent in the restroom, we document an effect of watching eyes only when individuals spend a relatively short period in the restroom. Remarkably, for these individuals, watching eyes had a big effect in terms of effect size (Rosenthal, 1996). In contrast, when individuals spent a relatively long period in the restroom, hand hygiene compliance was already high and could not be further increased by watching eyes. We speculate that staying for a longer period in the restroom is accompanied with defecation rather than urination only. In these instances, individuals might see a greater necessity to wash their hands with soap. Given this ceiling effect, watching eyes could not have an additional impact. We further

---

[6] By showing that watching eyes can increase hand hygiene behavior we do not claim that norms are irrelevant (they are indeed highly relevant); we merely argue that there are different routes to increasing hand hygiene behavior that do not exclude each other. One way is though norms (and safety climate and safety culture) and another is through simple nudges like watching eyes.

speculate that staying in the restroom for a shorter period of time is accompanied with urination only. In these instances, individuals might see less of a need to wash their hands with soap, leaving room for watching eyes to increase hand hygiene compliance.

4.1 | Limitations and outlook

Since the reported data are the result of a field experiment, limitations are particularly important to mention. First, we acknowledge that we cannot draw conclusions about *why* watching eyes have increased hand hygiene compliance in the present study. That is, we have not provided evidence for the psychological process in this field study. Recent research has accumulated evidence that individuals' avoidance (rather than approach) system underlies the effect of social influence in general and watching eyes in particular (Keller & Pfattheicher, 2011; Pfattheicher, 2015; Pfattheicher & Keller, 2015; Schnuerch & Pfattheicher, in press; Steinmetz & Pfattheicher, 2017). That is to say, individuals typically change behavior when being observed *not* to gain a positive reputation and to make a good impression in the eyes of others (i.e., approach) but typically to *avoid* the violation of social expectations, social punishment, and a bad reputation. On this basis, one can argue that the effect of watching eyes on hand hygiene compliance might be based on individuals' avoidance system, yet we have no empirical basis for this claim so far.

Second, in the present study, the advice to wash one's hands was present in both experimental conditions. Thus, we cannot conclude whether watching eyes per se increase hand hygiene compliance, or whether basic advice sets a precondition for watching eyes to operate. We assume that the message of advice smoothes the way for watching eyes to increase hand hygiene compliance. With information about the necessity of hand washing being activated, watching eyes might create the social expectation that hand washing should be done, leading to actual hand-washing behavior. Without information about the necessity of hand washing being activated, there is no information available that can be transformed into social expectations, affecting behavior. Future investigations could thus add a condition during which only watching eyes are present to assess the impact of the advice alone and to enable an estimation of possible interactions.

Also in light of recent meta-analyses and publications showing weak evidence of a main effect of watching eyes on prosocial behavior (e.g., Northover et al., 2017; Sparks & Barclay, 2013), it is relevant for future research to examine preconditions for watching eyes to affect human behavior (see also Northover et al., 2017; Pfattheicher & Keller, 2015). In the theoretical part of this contribution, we have argued that watching eyes increase socially desirable behavior. In this regard, we speculate that hand hygiene is strongly socially desirable; thus, as shown in the present contribution, watching eyes can increase this behavior. In contrast, transferring money to an anonymous stranger could be considered less socially desirable; the lower degree of social desirability might explain the found null effects with this dependent variable (Northover et al., 2017). Building on these considerations, a promising approach for future research would be to manipulate the degree of social desirability that is inherent in the investigated behavior and to test whether watching eyes increase prosocial behavior especially when it is socially desirable.

Third, we want to acknowledge that the study assessed data from females only and took place at a public restroom on a university campus. Thus, our conclusions apply to this specific group and this specific context. The question whether the effect found in the present study is also found in different places and populations can only be answered in future research. Given that hand hygiene behavior is likely socially desirable in different places and populations, we expect that watching eyes increase hand hygiene behavior in different contexts as well. In this regard, it seems particularly promising to test the effect of watching eyes in companies and public institutions. In fact, watching eyes reflect a low-cost method with the potential to increase hand hygiene compliance, which in turn might reduce germ transmission; as such, the application of watching eyes could increase health, save money for employers due to fewer sick days for employees, decrease infection-related absenteeism in schools, and increase patient safety in hospitals or other healthcare institutions. This, however, needs to be tested in future research.

To conclude, the present contribution shows the potential of watching eyes to increase hand hygiene compliance. As such, the present work opens a new avenue of research for studying hand hygiene compliance while emphasizing that individuals' behavior can be influenced by simple social nudges.

ORCID

Stefan Pfattheicher http://orcid.org/0000-0002-0161-1570

REFERENCES

Aiello, A. E., & Larson, E. L. (2002). What is the evidence for a causal link between hygiene and infections?. *The Lancet Infectious Diseases, 2*, 103–110.

Aiken, L. S., & West, S. G. (1991). *Multiple regression: Testing and interpreting interactions*. Newbury Park, CA: Sage.

Allegranzi, B., & Pittet, D. (2009). Role of hand hygiene in healthcareassociated infection prevention. *Journal of Hospital Infection, 73*, 305–315.

Anderson, J. L., Warren, C. A., Perez, E., Louis, R. I., Phillips, S., Wheeler, J., ... Misra, R. (2008). Gender and ethnic differences in hand hygiene practices among college students. *American Journal of Infection Control, 36*, 361–368.

Aunger, R., Greenland, K., Ploubidis, G., Schmidt, W., Oxford, J., & Curtis, V. (2016). The determinants of reported personal and household hygiene behaviour: A multi-country study. *PLoS One, 11*, e0159551.

Azor-Martínez, E., Gonzalez-Jimenez, Y., Seijas-Vazquez, M. L., Cobos-Carrascosa, E., Santisteban-Martínez, J., Martínez-Lopez, J. M., ... & Gimenez-Sanchez, F. (2014). The impact of common infections on school absenteeism during an academic year. *American Journal of Infection Control*, *42*, 632–637.

Backman, C., Zoutman, D. E., & Marck, P. B. (2008). An integrative review of the current evidence on the relationship between hand hygiene interventions and the incidence of health care–associated infections. *American Journal of Infection Control*, *36*, 333–348.

Bartram, J., & Cairncross, S. (2010). Hygiene, sanitation, and water: Forgotten foundations of health. *PLoS Medicine*, *7*, e1000367.

Bateson, M., Nettle, D., & Roberts, G. (2006). Cues of being watched enhance cooperation in a real-world setting. *Biology Letters*, *2*, 412–414.

Berry, T. D., Mitteer, D. R., & Fournier, A. K. (2015). Examining hand-washing rates and durations in public restrooms: A study of gender differences via personal, environmental, and behavioral determinants. *Environment and Behavior*, *47*, 923–944.

Beyfus, T. A., Dawson, N. L., Danner, C. H., Rawal, B., Gruber, P. E., & Petrou, S. P. (2016). The use of passive visual stimuli to enhance compliance with handwashing in a perioperative setting. *American Journal of Infection Control*, *44*(5), 496–499.

Bloomfield, S. F., Aiello, A. E., Cookson, B., O'Boyle, C., & Larson, E. L. (2007). The effectiveness of hand hygiene procedures in reducing the risks of infections in home and community settings including handwashing and alcohol-based hand sanitizers. *American Journal of Infection Control*, *35*, 27–64.

Bolton, P. G. M., Rivas, K., Prachar, V., & Jones, M. P. (2015). The observer effect: Can being watched enhance compliance with hand hygiene behaviour? A randomised trial. *Asia Pacific Journal of Health Management*, *10*, 14–16.

Borghi, J., Guinness, L., Ouedraogo, J., & Curtis, V. (2002). Is hygiene promotion cost-effective? A case study in Burkina Faso. *Tropical Medicine & International Health*, *7*, 960–969.

Brandt, M. J., IJzerman, H., Dijksterhuis, A., Farach, F. J., Geller, J., Giner-Sorolla, R., ... van't Veer, A. (2014). The replication recipe: What makes for a convincing replication? *Journal of Experimental Social Psychology*, *50*, 217–224.

Cardinale Lagomarsino, B., Gutman, M., Freira, L., Lanzalot, M. L., Lauletta, M., Malchik, L. E., ... Valencia, C. (2017). Peer pressure: Experimental evidence from restroom behavior. *Economic Inquiry*, *55*, 1579–1584.

Clayton, D. A., & Griffith, C. J. (2004). Observation of food safety practices in catering using notational analysis. *British Food Journal*, *106*, 211–227.

Cohen, J. (1992). A power primer. *Psychological Bulletin*, *112*, 155–159.

Curtis, V., & Cairncross, S. (2003). Effect of washing hands with soap on diarrhoea risk in the community: A systematic review. *The Lancet Infectious Diseases*, *3*, 275–281.

Diefenbacher, S., Siegel, A., & Keller, J. (2016). Verfahren zur Erfassung des Händehygieneverhaltens—Eine methodische Betrachtung aus verhaltenswissenschaftlicher

Perspektive [Methods for measuring hand hygiene behavior—A methodological examination from a behavioral scientific perspective]. *Hygiene & Medizin, 41,* D105–D119.

Ducel, G., Fabry, J., & Nicolle, L. (2002). *Prevention of hospital acquired infections: A practical guide.* Geneva: World Health Organisation.

Eckmanns, T., Bessert, J., Behnke, M., Gastmeier, P., & Rüden, H. (2006). Compliance with antiseptic hand rub use in intensive care units the Hawthorne effect. *Infection Control & Hospital Epidemiology, 27,* 931–934.

Edwards, D., Monk-Turner, E., Poorman, S., Rushing, M., Warren, S., & Willie, J. (2002). Predictors of hand-washing behavior. *Social Behavior and Personality: An International Journal, 30,* 751–756.

Ekström, M. (2012). Do watching eyes affect charitable giving? Evidence from a field experiment. *Experimental Economics, 15,* 530–546.

Erasmus, V., Daha, T. J., Brug, H., Richardus, J. H., Behrendt, M. D., Vos, M. C., & van Beeck EF. (2010). Systematic review of studies on compliance with hand hygiene guidelines in hospital care. *Infection Control & Hospital Epidemiology, 31,* 283–294.

Ernest-Jones, M., Nettle, D., & Bateson, M. (2011). Effects of eye images on everyday cooperative behavior: A field experiment. *Evolution and Human Behavior, 32,* 172–178.

Faul, F., Erdfelder, E., Buchner, A., & Lang, A.-G. (2009). Statistical power analyses using G*Power 3.1: Tests for correlation and regression analyses. *Behavior Research Methods, 41,* 1149–1160.

Green, L. R., Selman, C. A., Radke, V., Ripley, D., Mack, J. C., Reimann, D. W., ... Bushnell L. (2006). Food worker hand washing practices: An observation study. *Journal of Food Protection, 69,* 2417–2423.

Haley, K. J., & Fessler, D. M. T. (2005). Nobody's watching? Subtle cues affect generosity in an anonymous economic game. *Evolution and Human Behavior, 26,* 245–256.

Hayes, A. F. (2013). *Introduction to mediation, moderation, and conditional process analysis.* New York: The Guilford Press.

Judah, G., Donachie, P., Cobb, E., Schmidt, W., Holland, M., & Curtis, V. (2010). Dirty hands: Bacteria of faecal origin on commuters' hands. *Epidemiology and Infection, 138,* 409–414.

Kampf, G., Löffler, H., & Gastmeier, P. (2009). Hand hygiene for the prevention of nosocomial infections. *Deutsches Ärzteblatt International, 106,* 649–655.

Keller, J., & Pfattheicher, S. (2011). Vigilant self-regulation, cues of being watched and cooperativeness. *European Journal of Personality, 25,* 363–372.

King, D., Vlaev, I., Everett-Thomas, R., Fitzpatrick, M., Darzi, A., & Birnbach, D. J. (2016). "Priming" hand hygiene compliance in clinical environments. *Health Psychology, 35,* 96–101.

Leary, M. R., & Kowalski, R. M. (1990). Impression management: A literature review and two-component model. *Psychological Bulletin, 107,* 34–47.

Markus, H. R. (1978). The Effect of mere presence on social facilitation: An unobtrusive test. *Journal of Experimental Social Psychology, 14*, 389–397.

Maury, E., Moussa, N., Lakermi, C., Barbut, F., & Offenstadt, G. (2006). Compliance of health care workers to hand hygiene: Awareness of being observed is important. *Intensive Care Medicine, 32*, 2088–2089.

Meadows, E., & Le Saux, N. (2004). A systematic review of the effectiveness of antimicrobial rinse-free hand sanitizers for prevention of illness-related absenteeism in elementary school children. *BMC Public Health, 4*, 50.

Medeiros, C. O., Cavalli, S. B., Salay, E., & Proença, R. P. C. (2011). Assessment of the methodological strategies adopted by food safety training programmes for food service workers: A systematic review. *Food Control, 22*, 1136–1144.

Monk-Turner, E., Edwards, D., Broadstone, J., Hummel, R., Lewis, S., & Wilson, D. (2005). Another look at hand-washing behavior. *Social Behavior and Personality: An International Journal, 33*, 629–634.

Moyad, M. A., & Robinson, L. E. (2008). Lessons learned from the 2007–2008 cold and flu season: What worked and what was worthless. *Urologic Nursing, 28*, 145–148.

Munger, K., & Harris, S. J. (1989). Effects of an observer on hand washing in a public restroom. *Perceptual and Motor Skills, 69*, 733–734.

Murphy, K. S., DiPietro, R. B., Kock, G., & Lee, J. S. (2011). Does mandatory food safety training and certification for restaurant employees improve inspection outcomes? *International Journal of Hospitality Management, 30*, 150–156.

Naikoba, S., & Hayward, A. (2001). The effectiveness of interventions aimed at increasing handwashing in healthcare workers—A systematic review. *Journal of Hospital Infection, 47*, 173–180.

Nalbone, D. P., Lee, K. P., Suroviak, A. R., & Lannon, J. M. (2005). The effects of social norms on male hygiene. *Individual Differences Research, 3*, 171–176.

Nettle, D., Nott, K., Bateson, M., & Noë, R. (2012). 'Cycle thieves, we are watching you: Impact of a simple signage intervention against bicycle theft. *PLoS One, 7*, e51738.

Nicolle, L. (2007). Hygiene: What and why? *Canadian Medical Association Journal, 176*, 767–768.

Northover, S. B., Pedersen, W. C., Cohen, A. B., & Andrews, P. W. (2017). Artificial surveillance cues do not increase generosity: Two meta analyses. *Evolution and Human Behavior, 38*, 144–153.

Open Science Collaboration (2015). Estimating the reproducibility of psychological science. *Science, 349*, aac4716.

Pfattheicher, S. (2015). A regulatory focus perspective on reputational concerns: The impact of prevention-focused self-regulation. *Motivation and Emotion, 39*, 932–942.

Pfattheicher, S., & Keller, J. (2015). The watching eyes phenomenon: The role of a sense of being seen and public self-awareness. *European Journal of Social Psychology, 45*, 560–566.

Powell, K. L., Roberts, G., Nettle, D., & Fusani, L. (2012). Eye images increase charitable donations: Evidence from an opportunistic field experiment in a supermarket. *Ethology, 118*, 1096–1101.

Rosenthal, J. A. (1996). Qualitative descriptors of strength of association and effect size. *Journal of Social Service Research, 21*, 37–59.

Sax, H., Allegranzi, B., Uckay, I., Larson, E., Boyce, J., & Pittet, D. (2007). 'My five moments for hand hygiene': A user-centred design approach to understand, train, monitor and report hand hygiene. *Journal of Hospital Infection, 67*, 9–21.

Schnuerch, R., & Pfattheicher, S. (in press). Motivated malleability: Frontal cortical asymmetry predicts the susceptibility to social influence. *Social Neuroscience.*

Sparks, A., & Barclay, P. (2013). Eye images increase generosity, but not for long: The limited effect of a false cue. *Evolution and Human Behavior, 34*, 317–322.

Steinmetz, J., & Pfattheicher, S. (2017). Beyond social facilitation: A review of the far-reaching effects of social attention. *Social Cognition, 35*, 585–599.

Strohbehn, C., Sneed, J., Paez, P., & Meyer, J. (2008). Hand washing frequencies and procedures used in retail food services. *Journal of Food Protection, 71*, 1641–1650.

Van Bommel, M., van Prooijen, J., Elffers, H., & van Lange, P. A. M. (2014). Intervene to be seen: The power of a camera in attenuating the bystander effect. *Social Psychological and Personality Science, 5*, 459–466.

Wang, Z., Lapinski, M., Quilliam, E., Jaykus, L. A., & Fraser, A. (2017). The effect of hand-hygiene interventions on infectious disease-associated absenteeism in elementary schools: A systematic literature review. *American Journal of Infection Control, 45*, 682–689.

World Health Organization. (2009). *WHO guidelines on hand hygiene in health care: First global patient safety challenge. Clean care is safer care.* Geneva: World Health Organization.

Zajonc, R. B., Heingartner, A., & Herman, E. M. (1969). Social enhancement and impairment of performance in the cockroach. *Journal of Personality and Social Psychology, 13*, 83–92.

Section 2 Discussion Questions

1. Think about the article you've read in this section. Do you think the investigators used appropriate research methods?
2. Could this study have been designed differently to improve the overall results?
3. Discuss other research designs that could have been used to investigate this phenomenon.
4. Discuss how *surveys* could have been employed to collect data for this study. Would this make sense or be useful?
5. Consider how secondary data collection could have been used by these authors. Are there databases or archives that exist on this topic to examine?
6. How generalizable are the results of this study?
7. What elements of social life does this study reveal? Do you think the interpretation of the results the investigators present is trustworthy?
8. Discuss the possible ethical issues involved in how this study was carried out.

Section 2 Exercises

1. As humans, we are necessarily curious about others. On a daily basis, we wonder why others behave in the manner that they do ... we wonder why that driver did that, or we wonder why women/men do the things they do. The connection between research (collecting data or making observations) and theory (the attempt to explain various behaviors) needs to be understood.

    Theories need support (observations), and data/observations need organization (theories).

    So, I want you to make a series of observations this week. For example, you could sit and eat lunch at McDonald's and observe how the restaurant fills up: do people sit in a particular way? Do they maximize the space between them or sit close to others? This McDonald's example is just that—you may make observations on ANY human behavior. Be sure to make your observations over a period of time, at least two days; three or four days would be best. Once you finish your observations, you should then construct a theory (a sociological explanation) of why the people you observed behaved the way they did, then share a summary of your observations and your "mini" theory.

    Your work must include a description of where/when/whom you observed and a brief description of your findings. What were the patterns that you observed? (Include a "mini" theory that attempts to explain the patterns that you observed.

Remember, your little theory should employ the sociological perspective. That is, look for the social forces or social circumstances that influence people's behaviors.)
2. Think about your life and who you are: do you come from a wealthy family or one that is not so well-off? What is your gender? What is your ethnic background? Do you receive financial aid to attend college? Now, in terms of attending college, can you identify any ways in which the findings or results of social research have benefited you? Try to find three ways in which social research has influenced your ability to attend college. You might have to do a bit of research on this!
3. The next time you are discussing various social topics with people, try persuading them with two types of knowledge. With one person, try persuading them using tradition, intuition, or emotion. For example, tell them you *feel* that violent crime is on the rise, that it just *seems* that there is more violent crime than in the past. Note their reaction, then ask them if they feel your argument is strong or valid. Why or why don't they buy your argument? Do they *feel* the same way? Does this feeling reflect social reality? With the next person you encounter, tell them that violent crime in the United States has been on the decline since 1993, but let them know that this evidence is based on FBI crime statistics. Is this evidence more persuasive? Ask this person if they believe your argument. (FBI statistics show that violent crime has been on the decline since 1993.) Do people react differently to science- versus emotion-based evidence? Why or why not?
4. Visualizing large data sets. This exercise has two parts:
   Part 1:
   a. Go to https://www.gapminder.org/.
   b. Click on "Videos" at the top of the page, then scroll down to the video titled *Religions and Babies*. Watch the video.

   Part 2:
   Once you have watched the video, answer the following questions:
   a. What type of research does Hans Rosling use to develop his model that he showcases in this video?
   b. While it is popular to believe that countries need to get wealthy (a per capita income rise) in order to bring down the birth rate, Hans Rosling shows that this direct relationship is not necessarily true. What are the most important factors that must be present for national birth rates to fall?
   c. What does this research tell us about the relationship between religion and babies? This video illustrates the usefulness of social research. What benefits from social research are shown or implied in the video?
5. Locate at least five people you know, family or friends, who share a common experience—for instance, they were all in the military, lived in a foreign country, own dogs, or

grew up poor. Create an interview schedule—a document that contains all the questions you want to ask them. The questions should revolve around their accounts of that common experience; you should include at least ten questions with some having follow-up questions. Ask them if they would agree to sit down with you for an interview (be sure to get informed consent). As you conduct your interviews, try to notice not only what they are saying but *how* they are saying it (their tone). Do they seem reluctant, giddy, nervous, and so on? Let your analysis of the text begin as you collect it. You will probably start forming ideas about commonalities between stories. Record these ideas and insights. Once you have completed your interviews, transcribe them. By reading and rereading the transcribed interviews, conduct a rudimentary analysis by trying to identify five common words or phrases that all your participants used. Finally, identify at least one major theme that emerges from the text and ties all of the individual stories together. You should have five different stories, but some common theme(s) may emerge from your participants' shared common experience.

6. Over the years of teaching college-level classes, I have noticed that there seems to be a relationship between where students sit in the classroom and their grades. Generally, I find that students who sit near the front of the room tend to get better grades than those who sit in the back of the room. Imagine you have been asked to design three studies to examine this relationship.

Study 1: Create a true experiment to determine a cause-and-effect relationship between students' classroom seat locations and their grades in the course. How would you recruit participants? How would you randomly assign them to treatment and control groups? What is your independent variable? How would you manipulate the independent variable? What is your dependent variable? How would you measure your dependent variable? Diagram your experiment.

Study 2: Create a field experiment to examine the relationship between where students sit in a classroom and their grades. What would be the best design for this study if you wanted to maximize your internal validity? What key feature would you have to incorporate into your design to achieve this? How would you manipulate your independent variable? How could you increase generalizability of your results? Diagram your experiment.

Study 3: Construct a quasi-experiment to investigate the classroom location and course grade relationship. Specifically, design a nonequivalent groups pretest-posttest design. How would you create your treatment and control groups? What measures would you use to pre- and posttest your participants? What features of this design help increase internal validity compared to the nonequivalent groups design? Diagram your experiment.

CULTURE
DIFFERENT WAYS OF SEEING AND BEING

Culture is everything, everything is culture.[1]

—*Mark Plume*

If we think of culture in two distinct ways, we can see how the above quote can be supported. First, language and culture are indistinguishable. That is, culture is both developed and expressed through language. Culture could not emerge, evolve, or flourish without language. Second, everything created by humans is culture. Things, ideas, values, beliefs, worldviews, and practices are all created by humans and therefore are those things that comprise culture.

The attending social forces that emerge in various cultures influence the way that individuals think and behave, shaping their views of themselves, others, and the world. For example, in Chinese culture, there is considerable emphasis on the collective, whereas individualism is a central theme of American culture. While in general Americans expect people to achieve their goals based on their individual efforts, traditional Chinese culture emphasizes sacrificing one's own needs for the good of the group. Therefore, cultural

---

1 "Anything that is not culture—not created by humans—is ultimately co-opted by cultures."

themes can vary from society to society, but ultimately, they act as a sort of social gravity that everyone is subject to.

So, what is culture? Generally, we consider culture to be made up of two distinct parts: material culture consists of all those things that we make and use, like cars, houses, food, and laptops. Culture is also nonmaterial, which is expressed in our values, beliefs, and patterns of behavior. This nonmaterial, or symbolic, culture is of particular interest to sociologists because it provides the broad framework people use to interpret social life. Culture becomes the lens through which we see and interpret the world, how we construct reality and make decisions. Understanding this cultural orientation to the world is necessary to employing the sociological imagination.

However, because we are all so immersed in it, the processes and effects of our own culture generally remain imperceptible to us. This in turn can lead us to take our ways of being—language, values, beliefs and practices—for granted. Additionally, when we encounter other cultures or those from other cultures, we tend to judge them—their beliefs and behaviors—by our standards. Many times, we fail to recognize that other cultures are not inferior to ours, but rather they are just alternative ways of seeing and being in the world.

CHAPTER 3
CULTURE

The article in this section presents you with a dense description of the body rituals of a little-known people who live in North America. The author, an anthropologist who is apparently unfamiliar with these people and their ways, seems at times to struggle with understanding the ritualized acts of body purification. Ultimately, he delivers a fascinating account of a people somewhat obsessed with artifacts, spaces, and behaviors that revolve around body rituals. This article provides excellent instruction on describing the unfamiliar for any nascent anthropologist or field sociologist.

Some Things to Keep in Mind

As you read the following article about food and its cultural meanings, you might want to consider the following:

1. Are the Nacirema primitive or advanced?
2. What rituals are being described?
3. While reading the article, imagine in your mind's eye what the various artifacts and rituals might look like.
4. Why do these people seem so focused on body rituals?

BODY RITUAL AMONG THE NACIREMA

Horace Miner

The anthropologist has become so familiar with the diversity of ways in which different peoples behave in similar situations that he is not apt to be surprised by even the most exotic customs. In fact, if all of the logically possible combinations of behavior have not been found somewhere in the world, he is apt to suspect that they must be present in some yet undescribed tribe. This point has, in fact, been expressed with respect to clan organization by Murdock. In this light, the magical beliefs and practices of the Nacirema present such unusual aspects that it seems desirable to describe them as an example of the extremes to which human behavior can go.

Professor Linton first brought the ritual of the Nacirema to the attention of anthropologists twenty years ago, but the culture of this people is still very poorly understood. They are a North American group living in the territory between the Canadian Creel, the Yaqui and Tarahumare of Mexico, and the Carib and Arawak of the Antilles. Little is known of their origin, although tradition states that they came from the east. …

Nacirema culture is characterized by a highly developed market economy which has evolved in a rich natural habitat. While much of the people's time is devoted to economic pursuits, a large part of the fruits of these labors and a considerable portion of the day are spent in ritual activity. The focus of this activity is the human body, the appearance and health of which loom as a dominant concern in the ethos of the people. While such a concern is certainly not unusual, its ceremonial aspects and associated philosophy are unique.

The fundamental belief underlying the whole system appears to be that the human body is ugly and that its natural tendency is to debility and disease. Incarcerated in such a body, man's only hope is to avert these characteristics through the use of the powerful influences of ritual and ceremony. Every household has one or more shrines devoted to this purpose. The more powerful individuals in the society have several shrines in their houses and, in fact, the opulence of a house is often referred to in terms of the number of such ritual centers it possesses. Most houses are of

Horace Miner, "Body Ritual Among the Nacirema," *American Anthropologist*, vol. 58, no. 3, pp. 503-507, American Anthropological Association, 1956.

wattle and daub construction, but the shrine rooms of the more wealthy are walled with stone. Poorer families imitate the rich by applying pottery plaques to their shrine walls. While each family has at least one such shrine, the rituals associated with it are not family ceremonies but are private and secret. The rites are normally only discussed with children, and then only during the period when they are being initiated into these mysteries. I was able, however, to establish sufficient rapport with the natives to examine these shrines and to have the rituals described to me.

The focal point of the shrine is a box or chest which is built into the wall. In this chest are kept the many charms and magical potions without which no native believes he could live. These preparations are secured from a variety of specialized practitioners. The most powerful of these are the medicine men, whose assistance must be rewarded with substantial gifts. However, the medicine men do not provide the curative potions for their clients, but decide what the ingredients should be and then write them down in an ancient and secret language. This writing is understood only by the medicine men and by the herbalists who, for another gift, provide the required charm.

The charm is not disposed of after it has served its purpose, but is placed in the charm box of the household shrine. As these magical materials are specific for certain ills, and the real or imagined maladies of the people are many, the charm-box is usually full to overflowing. The magical packets are so numerous that people forget what their purposes were and fear to use them again. While the natives are very vague on this point, we can only assume that the idea in retaining all the old magical materials is that their presence in the charm-box, before which the body rituals are conducted, will in some way protect the worshipper.

Beneath the charm-box is a small font. Each day every member of the family, in succession, enters the shrine room, bows his head before the charm-box, mingles different sorts of holy water in the font, and proceeds with a brief rite of ablution. The holy waters are secured from the Water Temple of the community, where the priests conduct elaborate ceremonies to make the liquid ritually pure.

In the hierarchy of magical practitioners, and below the medicine men in prestige, are specialists whose designation is best translated "holy-mouth-men." The Nacirema have an almost pathological horror of and fascination with the mouth, the condition of which is believed to have a supernatural influence on all social relationships. Were it not for the rituals of the mouth, they believe that their teeth would fall out, their gums bleed, their jaws shrink, their friends desert them, and their lovers reject them. They also believe that a strong relationship exists between oral and moral characteristics. For example, there is a ritual ablution of the mouth for children which is supposed to improve their moral fiber.

The daily body ritual performed by everyone includes a mouth-rite. Despite the fact that these people are so punctilious about care of the mouth, this rite involves a practice which strikes the uninitiated stranger as revolting. It was reported to me that the ritual consists of inserting a small bundle of hog hairs into the mouth, along with certain magical powders, and then moving the bundle in a highly formalized series of gestures.

In addition to the private mouth-rite, the people seek out a holy-mouth-man once or twice a year. These practitioners have an impressive set of paraphernalia, consisting of a variety of augers, awls, probes, and prods. The use of these objects in the exorcism of the evils of the mouth involves almost unbelievable ritual torture of the client. The holy-mouth-man open the client's mouth and, using the above mentioned tools, enlarges any holes which decay may have created in the teeth. Magical materials are put into these holes. If there are no naturally occurring holes in the teeth, large sections of one or more teeth are gouged out so that the supernatural substance can be applied. In the client's view, the purpose of these ministrations is to arrest decay and to draw friends. The extremely sacred and traditional character of the rite is evident in the fact that the natives return to the holy-mouth-men year after year, despite the fact that their teeth continue to decay.

It is to be hoped that, when a thorough study of the Nacirema is made, there will be careful inquiry into the personality structure of these people. One has but to watch the gleam in the eye of a holy-mouth-man, as he jabs an awl into an exposed nerve, to suspect that a certain amount of sadism is involved. If this can be established, a very interesting pattern emerges, for most of the population shows definite masochistic tendencies. It was to these that Professor Linton referred in discussing a distinctive part of the daily body ritual which is performed only by men. This part of the rite involves scraping and lacerating the surface of the face with a sharp instrument. Special women's rites are performed only four times during each lunar month, but what they lack in frequency is made up in barbarity. As part of this ceremony, women bake their heads in small ovens for about an hour. The theoretically interesting point is that what seems to be a preponderantly masochistic people have developed sadistic specialists.

The medicine men have an imposing temple, or *latipso*, in every community of any size. The more elaborate ceremonies required to treat very sick patients can only be performed at this temple. These ceremonies involve not only the thaumaturge but a permanent group of vestal maidens who move sedately about the temple chambers in distinctive costume and head-dress.

The *latipso* ceremonies are so harsh that it is phenomenal that a fair proportion of the really sick natives who enter the temple ever recover. Small children whose indoctrination is still incomplete have been known to resist attempts to take them to the temple because "that is where you go to die." Despite this fact, sick adults are not only willing but eager to undergo the protracted ritual purification, if they can afford to do so. No matter how ill the supplicant or how grave the emergency, the guardians of many temples will not admit a client if he cannot give a rich gift to the custodian. Even after one has gained admission and survived the ceremonies, the guardians will not permit the neophyte to leave until he makes still another gift.

The supplicant entering the temple is first stripped of all his or her clothes. In everyday life the Nacirema avoids exposure of his body and its natural functions. Bathing and excretory acts are performed only in the secrecy of the household shrine, where they are ritualized as part of the body-rites. Psychological shock results from the fact that body secrecy is suddenly lost upon entry into the *latipso*. A man, whose own wife has never seen him in an excretory act, suddenly finds himself naked and assisted by a vestal maiden while he performs his natural functions into a sacred vessel. This sort of ceremonial treatment is necessitated by the fact that the excreta are used by a diviner to ascertain the course and nature of the client's sickness. Female clients, on the other hand, find their naked bodies are subjected to the scrutiny, manipulation and prodding of the medicine men.

Few supplicants in the temple are well enough to do anything but lie on their hard beds. The daily ceremonies, like the rites of the holy-mouth-men, involve discomfort and torture. With ritual precision, the vestals awaken their miserable charges each dawn and roll them about on their beds of pain while performing ablutions, in the formal movements of which the maidens are highly trained. At other times they insert magic wands in the supplicant's mouth or force him to eat substances which are supposed to be healing. From time to time the medicine men come to their clients and jab magically treated needles into their flesh. The fact that these temple ceremonies may not cure, and may even kill the neophyte, in no way decreases the people's faith in the medicine men.

There remains one other kind of practitioner, known as a "listener." This witchdoctor has the power to exorcise the devils that lodge in the heads of people who have been bewitched. The Nacirema believe that parents bewitch their own children. Mothers are particularly suspected of putting a curse on children while teaching them the secret body rituals. The counter-magic of the witchdoctor is unusual in its lack of ritual. The patient simply tells the "listener" all his troubles and fears, beginning with the earliest difficulties he can remember. The memory displayed by the Nacirema in these exorcism sessions is truly remarkable. It is not uncommon for the patient to bemoan the rejection he felt upon being weaned as a babe, and a few individuals even see their troubles going back to the traumatic effects of their own birth.

In conclusion, mention must be made of certain practices which have their base in native esthetics but which depend upon the pervasive aversion to the natural body and its functions. There are ritual fasts to make fat people thin and ceremonial feasts to make thin people fat. Still other rites are used to make women's breasts larger if they are small, and smaller if they are large. General dissatisfaction with breast shape is symbolized in the fact that the ideal form is virtually outside the range of human variation. A few women afflicted with almost inhuman hyper-mammary development are so idolized that they make a handsome living by simply going from village to village and permitting the natives to stare at them for a fee.

Reference has already been made to the fact that excretory functions are ritualized, routinized, and relegated to secrecy. Natural reproductive functions are similarly distorted. Intercourse is taboo as a topic and scheduled as an act. Efforts are made to avoid pregnancy by the use of magical materials or by limiting intercourse to certain phases of the moon. Conception is actually very infrequent. When pregnant, women dress so as to hide their condition. Parturition takes place in secret, without friends or relatives to assist, and the majority of women do not nurse their infants.

Our review of the ritual life of the Nacirema has certainly shown them to be a magic-ridden people. It is hard to understand how they have managed to exist so long under the burdens which they have imposed upon themselves. But even such exotic customs as these take on real meaning when they are viewed with the insight provided by Malinowski when he wrote:

"Looking from far and above, from our high places of safety in the developed civilization, it is easy to see all the crudity and irrelevance of magic. But without its power and guidance early man could not have mastered his practical difficulties as he has done, nor could man have advanced to the higher stages of civilization."

Section 3 Discussion Questions

1. Before you took this class, what did you think culture was? How did you define it, and what examples did you use to illustrate your understanding of culture?
2. Now that you have read about and discussed the concept of culture, do you have a different understanding of it? How does this view vary from your initial idea of culture? How similar was your original concept of culture to your new understanding?
3. Who do you think the Nacirema really are?
4. Discuss how the various elements of the Nacirema described in the article are identical to your own culture.
5. Discuss various elements of daily life described in the article. What is *really* being described?
6. What do you think is the value of using cross-cultural analysis? Discuss how this type of analysis is beneficial to not only acquiring a better understanding of other cultures, but also a better understanding of your own culture?
7. "Culture Is Everything, Everything Is Culture" is an idea presented by Plume (2017). What does this mean? Discuss ways in which this is true using examples from your own lived experiences.
8. Take a position against the argument that "Culture Is Everything, Everything Is Culture." Present examples that illustrate that culture is not everything. Develop an alternative position that presents a definition of culture that allows things and ideas to be outside of culture. Is this possible? Why or why not?

Section 3 Exercises

1. Your assignment is to observe an event, person, or social process as though you were someone from another culture and record that subject in a short paper. Over the next few days, I want you to closely observe some event such as a football game or a person like the minister of a church or some social process like a party, and report on that subject like you had traveled here from some distant culture to make these field observations. You may use the article "Body Ritual among the Nacirema" as a model for your paper.

    Remember, you are a sociologist who makes systematic observations. You are also a stranger to this culture and do not yet understand the customs and rules of our culture. Be *systematic, thorough, and detailed i*n your descriptions. You should end the paper by drawing some conclusion about the subject you chose.

Be sure to include details about your "field work." Include things such as why you chose this subject, how you made the observations, how you got access to the place or people, and describe your method of observation and how you took "field notes." Remember, you are in "the field," so you have to report back in a way that shows you were systematic in your work and complete in your descriptions.

Finally, I want you to comment on the efficacy of researching culture—that is, can someone from outside a culture truly come to know that culture? And suggest some other ways culture can be investigated, other than your "field work" done here.

2. Go to the URL provided below and watch the TED talk by the ethnobotanist Wade Davis. Then answer the questions below.

    https://www.ted.com/talks/wade_davis_on_endangered_cultures

    After you watch this Wade Davis video, answer the following questions:

    What does he mean when he talks about the ethnosphere?

    How does his discussion relate to the concepts of ethnocentrism and cultural relativism?

    What does Davis mean by "there are 'many ways of knowing and being?'"

3. For this exercise, you have to do a bit of online research. Find as much evidence as you can that zombies exist in Haiti and other parts of the world.

    What is the connection between Wade Davis and Haitian zombies? Explain this connection.

    Why does the threat of zombification work in the Haitian culture, but probably not in our culture?

    Now, do you believe in zombies?

4. For this assignment, first watch the TED talk on *What Explains the Rise of Humans?* using the URL below.

    https://www.ted.com/talks/yuval_noah_harari_what_explains_the_rise_of_humans

    After watching the TED talk on *What Explains the Rise of Humans?* from Yuval Noah Harari, complete parts I and II below.

Part I:

Discuss the connection between the talk and the idea of "culture."

Then answer these questions:

   a. What single element has allowed us to rise up to be the apex animal on the planet?
   b. What is the speaker describing when he mentions "fictions?"

Part II:

Using the talk as a starting point, discuss how humans have used "fictions" (culture) to become the only single species that can survive anywhere on this planet. In your opinion, what is the single greatest attribute of possessing culture and what is the single most detrimental element of possessing culture?

This exercise focuses on specific "relational settings"—subcultures. I want you to identify how your various subcultural identification/membership both creates your self-identity and is a reflection of the ideal self we all want to be.

Complete the following:
   a. Indicate those subcultures you identify with. Why do you identify with these groups?
   b. How has participation in these subcultures (relational settings) shaped your narrative-identity?
   c. How does membership in these groups reflect your attempt to "live up to deeper social and moral values?"

5. Click on the link below and watch the short video; then answer the following questions.
   http://www.ted.com/talks/shereen_el_feki_pop_culture_in_the_arab_world
   a. How do the examples in this video illustrate cultural diffusion?
   b. Why do you think some parts of culture become diffused but others don't?
   c. How is cultural diffusion linked to the idea of globalization?

CREATING ROUND PEGS FOR ROUND HOLES

SHAPING HUMANS AND THE INFLUENCE OF GROUPS

Newborn giraffes stand within thirty minutes of birth and are running alongside Mom within a few hours, and by eighteen months, they are hanging out in same-sex groups. Humans, on the other hand, require many years before they can run with the herd. Humans exist in complex social worlds, and as a result, we need many years of development in order to master the complex interplay between self and society. This lifelong process of learning how to fit into one's social world is called *socialization*.

I frequently tell anyone who will listen that "it takes people to make people." I don't mean that in a biological sense, but in the sociological sense. It takes *others* to shape and direct the development and social adjustment of individual humans. Take award acceptance speeches, for example; when people receive awards, they always thank others for their accomplishments, like their moms, spouses, coaches, families, and so on. It would be really weird for someone to win an Oscar and stand on stage and ramble on about how wonderful they are and how they did everything themselves with help from no one. So, at least on some level, we recognize the influence of others, but most of us fail to understand how profound the impact of others can be on our development and social adjustment, especially on things like our beliefs, behaviors, and decisions.

The social worlds in which we find ourselves shape each of us into social beings that are appropriately designed to navigate those social landscapes, which raises the question, "How does it happen?" All human collectives contain mechanisms like social rules, values, beliefs, groups, and social institutions. This *social structure,* or the way society is organized, is designed to shape our lives. Ultimately, others and social structure mold the vast majority of us into round pegs to fit into round holes—we become well adjusted, productive citizens capable of navigating our complex social worlds.

CHAPTER 4

SOCIALIZATION

In the following article, "Final Note on a Case of Extreme Isolation," Kingsley Davis shows us the power of others and contact with the social world on our development by reporting on someone who was deprived of such things. While we are all born *human*, it takes much more than our biology and genetic makeup to become functioning members of society: it takes others. This example, then, illustrates the tremendous influence that social contact has on the development and social adjustment of the individual.

Some Things to Keep in Mind

As you read through the article below about extreme social isolation, here are some things you might want to consider.

1. Think about the nature-versus-nurture debate as you read through this article.
2. Why do humans need others to develop "normally"?
3. What evidence does this case give for the importance of nature (biology and genes)?
4. What evidence does this article present for nurture (social contact with others)?
5. How important are primary groups and caregivers to our development and social adjustment?
6. Could even the way you walk be socially influenced?
7. Can severe deprivation like this be overcome? That is, can children who experience something like this ever recover fully?

FINAL NOTE ON A CASE OF EXTREME ISOLATION

Kingsley Davis

ABSTRACT

Anna, an extremely isolated girl described in 1940, died in 1942. By the time of her death she had made considerable progress, but she never achieved normality. Her slowness is probably explained by long isolation, poor training, and mental deficiency. Comparison with another case, a girl found in Ohio at the same age and under similar circumstances, suggests that Anna was deficient, and that, at least for some individuals, extreme isolation up to age six does not permanently impair socialization.

Early in 1940 there appeared in this *Journal* an account of a girl called Anna.[1] She had been deprived of normal contact and had received a minimum of human care for almost the whole of her first six years of life. At that time observations were not complete and the report had a tentative character. Now, however, the girl is dead, and, with more information available,[2] it is possible to give a fuller and more definitive description of the case from a sociological point of view.

Anna's death, caused by hemorrhagic jaundice, occurred on August 6, 1942. Having been born on March 1 or 6,[3] 1932, she was approximately ten and a half years of age when she died. The previous report covered her development up to the age of almost eight years; the present one recapitulates the earlier period on the basis of new evidence and then covers the last two and a half years of her life.

---

1 Kingsley Davis, "Extreme Social Isolation of a Child," *American Journal of Sociology*, XLV (January, 1940), 554–65.
2 Sincere appreciation is due to the officials in the Department of Welfare, Commonwealth of Pennsylvania, for their kind cooperation in making available the records concerning Anna and discussing the case frankly with the writer. Helen C. Hubbell, Florentine Hackbusch, and Eleanor Meckelnburg were particularly helpful, as was Fanny L. Matchette. Without their aid neither of the reports on Anna could have been written.
3 The records are not clear as to which day.

Kingsley Davis, "Final Note on a Case of Extreme Isolation," *American Journal of Sociology*, vol. 52, no. 5, pp. 432-437. Copyright © 1947 by University of Chicago Press. Reprinted with permission.

Early History

The first few days and weeks of Anna's life were complicated by frequent changes of domicile. It will be recalled that she was an illegitimate child, the second such child born to her mother, and that her grandfather, a widowed farmer in whose house her mother lived, strongly disapproved of this new evidence of the mother's indiscretion. This fact led to the baby's being shifted about.

Two weeks after being born in a nurse's private home, Anna was brought to the family farm, but the grandfather's antagonism was so great that she was shortly taken to the house of one of her mother's friends. At this time a local minister became interested in her and took her to his house with an idea of possible adoption. He decided against adoption, however, when he discovered that she had vaginitis. The infant was then taken to a children's home in the nearest large city. This agency found that at the age of only three weeks she was already in a miserable condition, being "terribly galled and otherwise in very bad shape." It did not regard her as a likely subject for adoption but took her in for a while anyway, hoping to benefit her. After Anna had spent nearly eight weeks in this place, the agency notified her mother to come to get her. The mother responded by sending a man and his wife to the children's home with a view to their adopting Anna, but they made such a poor impression on the agency that permission was refused. Later the mother came herself and took the child out of the home and then gave her to this couple. It was in the home of this pair that a social worker found the girl a short time thereafter. The social worker went to the mother's home and pleaded with Anna's grandfather to allow the mother to bring the child home. In spite of threats, he refused. The child, by then more than four months old, was next taken to another children's home in a near-by town. A medical examination at this time revealed that she had impetigo, vaginitis, umbilical hernia, and a skin rash.

Anna remained in this second children's home for nearly three weeks, at the end of which time she was transferred to a private foster-home. Since, however, the grandfather would not, and the mother could not, pay for the child's care, she was finally taken back as a last resort to the grandfather's house (at the age of five and a half months). There she remained, kept on the second floor in an attic-like room because her mother hesitated to incur the grandfather's wrath by bringing her downstairs.

The mother, a sturdy woman weighing about 180 pounds, did a man's work on the farm. She engaged in heavy work such as milking cows and tending hogs and had little time for her children. Sometimes she went out at night, in which case Anna was left entirely without attention. Ordinarily, it seems, Anna received only enough care to keep her barely alive. She appears to have been seldom moved from one position to another. Her clothing and bedding were filthy. She apparently had no instruction, no friendly attention.

It is little wonder that, when finally found and removed from the room in the grandfather's house at the age of nearly six years, the child could not talk, walk, or do anything that showed intelligence. She was in an extremely emaciated and undernourished condition, with skeleton-like legs and a bloated abdomen. She had been fed on virtually nothing except cow's milk during the years under her mother's care.

Anna's condition when found, and her subsequent improvement, have been described in the previous report. It now remains to say what happened to her after that.

Later History

In 1939, nearly two years after being discovered, Anna had progressed, as previously reported, to the point where she could walk, understand simple commands, feed herself, achieve some neatness, remember people, etc. But she still did not speak, and, though she was much more like a normal infant of something over one year of age in mentality, she was far from normal for her age.

On August 30, 1939, she was taken to a private home for retarded children, leaving the county home where she had been for more than a year and a half. In her new setting she made some further progress, but not a great deal. In a report of an examination made November 6 of the same year, the head of the institution pictured the child as follows:

Anna walks about aimlessly, makes periodic rhythmic motions of her hands, and, at intervals, makes gutteral and sucking noises. She regards her hands as if she had seen them for the first time. It was impossible to hold her attention for more than a few seconds at a time—not because of distraction due to external stimuli but because of her inability to concentrate. She ignored the task in hand to gaze vacantly about the room. Speech is entirely lacking. Numerous unsuccessful attempts have been made with her in the hope of developing initial sounds. I do not believe that this failure is due to negativism or deafness but that she is not sufficiently developed to accept speech at this time. ... The prognosis is not favorable. ...

More than five months later, on April 25, 1940, a clinical psychologist, the late Professor Francis N. Maxfield, examined Anna and reported the following: large for her age; hearing "entirely normal"; vision apparently normal; able to climb stairs; speech in the "babbling stage" and "promise for developing intelligible speech later seems to be good." He said further that "on the Merrill-Palmer scale she made a mental score of 19 months. On the Vineland social maturity scale she made a score of 23 months."[4]

Professor Maxfield very sensibly pointed out that prognosis is difficult in such cases of isolation. "It is very difficult to take scores on tests standardized under average conditions of environment and experience," he wrote, "and interpret them in a case where environment and experience have been so unusual." With this warning he gave it as his opinion at that time that Anna would eventually "attain an adult mental level of six or seven years."[5]

---

[4] Letter to one of the state officials in charge of the case.
[5] *Ibid*.

The school for retarded children, on July 1, 1941, reported that Anna had reached 46 inches in height and weighed 60 pounds. She could bounce and catch a ball and was said to conform to group socialization, though as a follower rather than a leader. Toilet habits were firmly established. Food habits were normal, except that she still used a spoon as her sole implement. She could dress herself except for fastening her clothes. Most remarkable of all, she had finally begun to develop speech. She was characterized as being at about the two-year level in this regard. She could call attendants by name and bring in one when she was asked to. She had a few complete sentences to express her wants. The report concluded that there was nothing peculiar about her, except that she was feebleminded—"probably congenital in type."[6]

A final report from the school, made on June 22, 1942, and evidently the last report before the girl's death, pictured only a slight advance over that given above. It said that Anna could follow directions, string beads, identify a few colors, build with blocks, and differentiate between attractive and unattractive pictures. She had a good sense of rhythm and loved a doll. She talked mainly in phrases but would repeat words and try to carry on a conversation. She was clean about clothing. She habitually washed her hands and brushed her teeth. She would try to help other children. She walked well and could run fairly well, though clumsily. Although easily excited, she had a pleasant disposition.

Interpretation

Such was Anna's condition just before her death. It may seem as if she had not made much progress, but one must remember the condition in which she had been found. One must recall that she had no glimmering of speech, absolutely no ability to walk, no sense of gesture, not the least capacity to feed herself even when the food was put in front of her, and no comprehension of cleanliness. She was so apathetic that it was hard to tell whether or not she could hear. And all this at the age of nearly six years. Compared with this condition, her capacities at the time of her death seem striking indeed, though they do not amount to much more than a two-and-a-half-year mental level. One conclusion therefore seems safe, namely, that her isolation prevented a considerable amount of mental development that was undoubtedly part of her capacity. Just what her original capacity was, of course, is hard to say; but her development after her period of confinement (including the ability to walk and run, to play, dress, fit into a social situation, and, above all, to speak) shows that she had at least this much capacity—capacity that never could have been realized in her original condition of isolation.

A further question is this: What would she have been like if she had received a normal upbringing from the moment of birth? A definitive answer would have been impossible in any case, but even an approximate answer is made difficult by her early death. If one assumes, as was

---

6 Progress report of the school.

tentatively surmised in the previous report, that it is "almost impossible for any child to learn to speak, think, and act like a normal person after a long period of early isolation," it seems likely that Anna might have had a normal or near-normal capacity, genetically speaking. On the other hand, it was pointed out that Anna represented "a marginal case, [because] she was discovered before she had reached six years of age," an age "young enough to allow for some plasticity."[7] While admitting, then, that Anna's isolation *may* have been the major cause (and was certainly a minor cause) of her lack of rapid mental progress during the four and a half years following her rescue from neglect, it is necessary to entertain the hypothesis that she was congenitally deficient.

In connection with this hypothesis, one suggestive though by no means conclusive circumstance needs consideration, namely, the mentality of Anna's forebears. Information on this subject is easier to obtain, as one might guess, on the mother's than on the father's side. Anna's maternal grandmother, for example, is said to have been college educated and wished to have her children receive a good education, but her husband, Anna's stern grandfather, apparently a shrewd, hard-driving, calculating farmowner, was so penurious that her ambitions in this direction were thwarted. Under the circumstances her daughter (Anna's mother) managed, despite having to do hard work on the farm, to complete the eighth grade in a country school. Even so, however, the daughter was evidently not very smart. "A schoolmate of [Anna's mother] stated that she was retarded in school work; was very gullible at this age; and that her morals even at this time were discussed by other students." Two tests administered to her on March 4, 1938, when she was thirty-two years of age, showed that she was mentally deficient. On the Stanford Revision of the Binet-Simon Scale her performance was equivalent to that of a child of eight years, giving her an I.Q. of 50 and indicating mental deficiency of "middle-grade moron type."[8]

As to the identity of Anna's father, the most persistent theory holds that he was an old man about seventy-four years of age at the time of the girl's birth. If he was the one, there is no indication of mental or other biological deficiency, whatever one may think of his morals. However, someone else may actually have been the father.

To sum up: Anna's heredity is the kind that *might* have given rise to innate mental deficiency, though not necessarily.

Comparison with Another Case

Perhaps more to the point than speculations about Anna's ancestry would be a case for comparison. If a child could be discovered who had been isolated about the same length of time as

---

7   Davis, *op. tit.*, p. 564.
8   The facts set forth here as to Anna's ancestry are taken chiefly from a report of mental tests administered to Anna's mother by psychologists at a state hospital where she was taken for this purpose after the discovery of Anna's seclusion. This excellent report was not available to the writer when the previous paper on Anna was published.

Anna but had achieved a much quicker recovery and a greater mental development, it would be a stronger indication that Anna was deficient to start with.

Such a case does exist. It is the case of a girl found at about the same time as Anna and under strikingly similar circumstances. A full description of the details of this case has not been published, but, in addition to newspaper reports, an excellent preliminary account by a speech specialist, Dr. Marie K. Mason, who played an important role in the handling of the child, has appeared.[9] Also the late Dr. Francis N. Maxfield, clinical psychologist at Ohio State University, as was Dr. Mason, has written an as yet unpublished but penetrating analysis of the case.[10] Some of his observations have been included in Professor Zingg's book on feral man.[11] The following discussion is drawn mainly from these enlightening materials. The writer, through the kindness of Professors Mason and Maxfield, did have a chance to observe the girl in April, 1940, and to discuss the features of her case with them.

Born apparently one month later than Anna, the girl in question, who has been given the pseudonym Isabelle, was discovered in November, 1938, nine months after the discovery of Anna. At the time she was found she was approximately six and a half years of age. Like Anna, she was an illegitimate child and had been kept in seclusion for that reason. Her mother was a deaf-mute, having become so at the age of two, and it appears that she and Isabelle had spent most of their time together in a dark room shut off from the rest of the mother's family. As a result Isabelle had no chance to develop speech; when she communicated with her mother, it was by means of gestures. Lack of sunshine and inadequacy of diet had caused Isabelle to become rachitic. Her legs in particular were affected; they "were so bowed that as she stood erect the soles of her shoes came nearly flat together, and she got about with a skittering gait."[12] Her behavior toward strangers, especially men, was almost that of a wild animal, manifesting much fear and hostility. In lieu of speech she made only a strange croaking sound. In many ways she acted like an infant. "She was apparently utterly unaware of relationships of any kind. When presented with a ball for the first time, she held it in the palm of her hand, then reached out and stroked my face with it. Such behavior is comparable to that of a child of six months."[13] At first it was even hard to tell whether or not she could hear, so unused were her senses. Many of her actions resembled those of deaf children.

It is small wonder that, once it was established that she could hear, specialists working with her believed her to be feebleminded. Even on nonverbal tests her performance was so low as to promise little for the future. Her first score on the Stanford-Binet was 19 months, practically at the zero point of the scale. On the Vineland social maturity scale her first score was 39, representing

---

9   Marie K. Mason, "Learning to Speak after Six and One-Half Years of Silence," *Journal of Speech Disorders*, VII (1942), 295–304.
10   Francis N. Maxfield, "What Happens When the Social Environment of a Child Approaches Zero." The writer is greatly indebted to Mrs. Maxfield and to Professor Horace B. English, a colleague of Professor Maxfield, for the privilege of seeing this manuscript and other materials collected on isolated and feral individuals.
11   J. A. L. Singh and Robert M. Zingg, *Wolf-Children and Feral Man* (New York: Harper & Bros., 1941), pp. 248–51.
12   Maxfield, unpublished manuscript cited above.
13   Mason, *op. cit.*, p. 299.

an age level of two and a half years.[14] "The general impression was that she was wholly uneducable and that any attempt to teach her to speak, after so long a period of silence, would meet with failure."[15]

In spite of this interpretation, the individuals in charge of Isabelle launched a systematic and skillful program of training. It seemed hopeless at first. The approach had to be through pantomime and dramatization, suitable to an infant. It required one week of intensive effort before she even made her first attempt at vocalization. Gradually she began to respond, however, and, after the first hurdles had at last been overcome, a curious thing happened. She went through the usual stages of learning characteristic of the years from one to six not only in proper succession but far more rapidly than normal. In a little over two months after her first vocalization she was putting sentences together. Nine months after that she could identify words and sentences on the printed page, could write well, could add to ten, and could retell a story after hearing it. Seven months beyond this point she had a vocabulary of 1,500–2,000 words and was asking complicated questions. Starting from an educational level of between one and three years (depending on what aspect one considers), she had reached a normal level by the time she was eight and a half years old. In short, she covered in two years the stages of learning that ordinarily require six.[16] Or, to put it another way, her I.Q. trebled in a year and a half.[17] The speed with which she reached the normal level of mental development seems analogous to the recovery of body weight in a growing child after an illness, the recovery being achieved by an extra fast rate of growth for a period after the illness until normal weight for the given age is again attained.

When the writer saw Isabelle a year and a half after her discovery, she gave him the impression of being a very bright, cheerful, energetic little girl. She spoke well, walked and ran without trouble, and sang with gusto and accuracy. Today she is over fourteen years old and has passed the sixth grade in a public school. Her teachers say that she participates in all school activities as normally as other children. Though older than her classmates, she has fortunately not physically matured too far beyond their level.[18]

Clearly the history of Isabelle's development is different from that of Anna's. In both cases there was an exceedingly low, or rather blank, intellectual level to begin with. In both cases it seemed that the girl might be congenitally feeble minded. In both a considerably higher level was reached later on. But the Ohio girl achieved a normal mentality within two years, whereas Anna was still marked inadequate at the end of four and a half years. This difference in achievement may suggest that Anna had less initial capacity. But an alternative hypothesis is possible.

One should remember that Anna never received the prolonged and expert attention that Isabelle received. The result of such attention, in the case of the Ohio girl, was to give her speech

---

14   Maxfield, unpublished manuscript.
15   Mason, *op. cit.,* p. 299.
16   *Ibid.,* pp. 300–304.
17   Maxfield, unpublished manuscript.
18   Based on a personal letter from Dr. Mason to the writer, May 13, 1946.

at an early stage, and her subsequent rapid development seems to have been a consequence of that. "Until Isabelle's speech and language development, she had all the characteristics of a feeble-minded child." Had Anna, who, from the standpoint of psychometric tests and early history, closely resembled this girl at the start, been given a mastery of speech at an earlier point by intensive training, her subsequent development might have been much more rapid.[19]

The hypothesis that Anna began with a sharply inferior mental capacity is therefore not established. Even if she were deficient to start with, we have no way of knowing how much so. Under ordinary conditions she might have been a dull normal or, like her mother, a moron. Even after the blight of her isolation, if she had lived to maturity, she might have finally reached virtually the full level of her capacity, whatever it may have been. That her isolation did have a profound effect upon her mentality, there can be no doubt. This is proved by the substantial degree of change during the four and a half years following her rescue.

Consideration of Isabelle's case serves to show, as Anna's case does not clearly show, that isolation up to the age of six, with failure to acquire any form of speech and hence failure to grasp nearly the whole world of cultural meaning, does not preclude the subsequent acquisition of these. Indeed, there seems to be a process of accelerated recovery in which the child goes through the mental stages at a more rapid rate than would be the case in normal development. Just what would be the maximum age at which a person could remain isolated and still retain the capacity for full cultural acquisition is hard to say. Almost certainly it would not be as high as age fifteen; it might possibly be as low as age ten. Undoubtedly various individuals would differ considerably as to the exact age.

Anna's is not an ideal case for showing the effects of extreme isolation, partly because she was possibly deficient to begin with, partly because she did not receive the best training available, and partly because she did not live long enough. Nevertheless, her case is instructive when placed in the record with numerous other cases of extreme isolation. This and the previous article about her are meant to place her in the record. It is to be hoped that other cases will be described in the scientific literature as they are discovered (as unfortunately they will be), for only in these rare cases of extreme isolation is it possible "to observe *concretely separated* two factors in the development of human personality which are always otherwise only analytically separated, the biogenic and the sociogenic factors."[20]

---

19 This point is suggested in a personal letter from Dr. Mason to the writer, October 22, 1946.
20 Singh and Zingg, *op. cit.*, pp. xxi–xxii, in a foreword by the writer.

CHAPTER 5

GROUPS

Conformity

The article below examines some of the reasons that lead to social conformity. The author shows that when the pressure is on us, most of us will conform to the group. What's interesting about this article is that it is easy to see yourself in the ideas the author presents about conformity, whether it be the peer pressure that our friends put on us on a regular basis or larger social pressures like going to college, pursuing a career, and getting married. The author argues that conformity and compliance are present in all cultures and are a necessary component of social order. However you view it, good or bad, we need people to conform to keep society chugging along.

Some Things to Keep in Mind

1. As you read about the Asch experiment, consider what you would do in this situation. Are you sure?
2. Have you ever been in a similar situation? If so, what did you do?
3. Have you ever been in a situation where you tried *not* to conform but ultimately conformed? Think about the factors that influenced your conformity.

4. Have you found yourself in a situation where you were expected to conform but you did *not*? What factors led to your nonconformity?
5. How are conformity and compliance beneficial to society?
6. What are some possible personal consequences of nonconformity?
7. What are some of the consequences for society if people don't conform to a certain degree?

WHY WE CONFORM
Rafael Narvaez

Human Beings Tend to Adapt to Social Circumstances

Even the most democratic societies constantly nudge people to conform to certain standards, ideas, values, fashion styles, to appropriate emotional styles (e.g., "boys don't cry"), often regardless of whether these are good or bad for us, or for our society, or for the future. In this chapter, we will study why people often comply, in different ways and by different degrees, with the broader demands of culture. We will examine research pertaining to how and why our decisions and aspects of our lifestyles may become manufactured by the broader array of social and cultural forces (not only by the market).

Solomon Asch (1951), one of the most prominent social psychologist of the twentieth century, was arguably the person who pioneered research pertaining, precisely, to how and why people conform to the norms and expectations of groups. Let us discuss one of his most illustrative experiments in some detail. It took place in the mid-1950s. Asch recruited 123 male study participants who were told that they were going to participate in an experiment about visual acuity. One by one, they entered a room where they encountered five or seven males who acted as though they were also participants in the experiment, though in reality they were confederates working for Asch. The experiment consisted of showing the participant and the confederates two large cards, A and B, and asking the group to compare the contents of these cards. Card A had three parallel and perpendicular lines, marked as lines one, two, and three; card B featured only one perpendicular line. All A and B cards in a stack were designed so as to make it immediately and unambiguously obvious that the single line on the B cards matched in length *only with one* of the lines on the A cards.

Rafael F. Narváez, "Why We Conform," *Reading the World: An Introduction*, pp. 25-30, 127-137. Copyright © 2015 by Cognella, Inc. Reprinted with permission.

One by one, the confederates and the real study participant were shown pairs of A and B cards drawn from the stack, and they were asked to state which of the three lines on card A matched in length with the single line on card B. For the first couple of trials, the confederates gave the obviously correct answer; but after the fourth trial, one by one the confederates began to give obviously incorrect answers. Let us say that it was obvious that the single line on card B matched in length with line *two* on card A, and yet the confederates were all in agreement that the line on card B actually matched with line *three* on card A. At this point in the experiment, something interesting began to happen. Save some exceptions, the actual participants also began to provide the obviously incorrect answers, following the cue of the confederates, even if the confederates were obviously wrong. Some participants went along with the wrong assessments of the group because they didn't want to rock the boat; they didn't want to stand out. But others, importantly, went along with the group by first denying the visual evidence provided by their own eyes; it was easier for them to think that their own eyes were conveying the wrong information, rather than to think that the group was conveying the wrong information. Solomon Asch showed that, on average, people not only tend to go along with the group but that in fact we may become blind to obvious aspects of reality simply to go along with the will of a group of peers or even strangers.

Asch's research suggests that human beings are, in general, strongly motivated by a will to conform. Human beings generally avoid transgressing the norms that govern their social surroundings. We are a very predatory species (indeed, we are responsible for the massive disappearance of other species) that, however, often acts like a herd species, often bowing to the will of the group, with individuals, in fact, often striving to dissolve themselves within the group.

Cultures That Encourage Individualism

All societies and all social groups elicit a degree of conformity from most social actors (save infants or people with socialization deficits, such as sociopaths). Indeed, as we will see in the next chapter, without a minimal degree of conformity, no society can exist. Yet, the idea that people normally tend to adapt to external demands is difficult to accept for many people, particularly for members of cultures that outwardly encourage self-reliance, self-determination, and a sense of uniqueness in individuals. So, beyond the laboratory conditions that frame Asch's research, let us begin by considering some everyday examples pertaining the phenomena of conformity and adaptation. Let us think of such occasions as weddings, funerals, parties, church functions, classrooms, your place of work, elevators—circumstances that demand a degree of conformity from all of us. It is clear that in these social environments people generally tend to abide by the expectations of the group; for example, by dress codes, codes of conduct, rules of speech, so that we behave and speak in ways that are more or less appropriate for the occasion. As many researchers have shown, we indeed tend to gesture within parameters that befit the situation, carry ourselves so as to signal a degree of agreement with the norms governing the interaction. In an elevator, for instance, people typically try to avoid displays of emotion, speak with an "appropriate" tone of voice, with appropriate manners and gestures. At a funeral we likewise tend to broadcast appropriate signals. At a job interview we tend to act and behave in a manner that generally befits the expectations of interviewers. When meeting acquaintances for the first time we yet again tend to display the version of ourselves that facilitates and eases the encounter. When on a date, we likewise tend to conduct ourselves in a manner befitting the occasion, and so forth.

To be sure, even members of groups who profess nonconformity—for instance, those who defy mainstream standards, values, or tastes—also tend to conform to the standards that govern their particular subcultures. Punks, Hippies, gang members, the Amish, and many other groups challenge mainstream codes. But members of these groups very much adhere to a subset of expectations and codes that govern their own subcultures. Similarly, members of highly individualistic cultures (that is to say, cultures that encourage individuals to see themselves as unique, independent, self-reliant, self-directed—cultures that value individual determination and perseverance) also tend to conform. The mainstream American culture, for example, is arguably the most individualistic in the world (Suh et al. 1998). Yet, Americans, much as members of any other society, also tend to conform and to adapt.

Bear in mind, firstly, that economic growth in the United States has historically hinged on consumption (among other factors, of course), which means that, as suggested, the personal desires and motives of consumers have to reflect, at least minimally, the needs of the market itself, the ideas and values engineered by it. But secondly, and more importantly, Americans undergo, much as members of any other society, a process of *socialization* whereby the person, from birth on, learns the social codes, how to display them, and what to expect if he or she violates them. Which teaches them how fit in, which allows them to partake in the social order and to become part of a larger and stronger (social) organism. Hence, as any member of any other society, Americans also undergo, and typically comply with, various mechanisms of *social control*: precisely, the social mechanisms that enforce collectively relevant beliefs, norms, and values, the mechanisms that typically punish those who infringe on these things. (If you go to a wedding wearing a t-shirt, for example, and thus infringe on the codes operant in this scenario, you will likely receive raised eyebrows and cold shoulders, be subjected to gossip, and so on, which are mechanisms of social control that keep people from infringing on the norm. And of course, the law is a mechanism of social control organized and enforced by the government itself.)

Perhaps, as some researchers have argued, Americans, much as the members of other individualistic cultures, conform less when compared to members of collectivistic cultures, that is to say, cultures that encourage individuals to see themselves not as unique but as active members of larger social order, cultures that value group accomplishment over individualistic perseverance, cultures that underscore the notion that fate is a collective accomplishment. But nevertheless the point to keep in mind is that all human beings, regardless of their culture, *must* conform to at least a minimum of social demands. To conform means to accept social norms and values, to abide by them, and thus conformity legitimizes these norms and values and helps society to sustain, enforce, and maintain a civic order. Conformity thus encourages social interconnection, cohesiveness, and stability (though we will further discuss the disadvantages of conforming soon, as well). And in this particular sense, conformity, and attendant mechanisms of social control, are not only helpful but also very desirable for any society.

The Risks of Noncompliance

Again, just as some people conform more readily than others, others resist social injunctions and demands more readily and frequently than others. But anyone who resists is likely to face retaliations from society itself. At a minimal level, these involve raised eyebrows and cold shoulders, as noted, but retaliations may also involve degrees of ostracism that can be injurious, psychologically and physically. Here is a telling example: a Saudi woman named Manal al-Shari was imprisoned and endlessly harassed by Saudi authorities *and* by fellow citizens—merely because she dared to drive a car. Her son at school was bullied and bruised on account of the "unfeminine" behavior of his mother. Her brother was detained twice for giving her the keys to his car and was subsequently harassed to the point of having to quit his professional job and having to leave the country with his wife and children. Her father had to endure sermons from the local Imam, who equated women who drive with prostitutes. Manal al-Shari insisted on defending her elemental right to drive; and thus, concerned Saudi citizens retaliated and used social media—to demand that she be flogged in public! As this courageous woman says, *fighting against oppressive societal norms is often harder than fighting against openly oppressive and tyrannical regimes*. More generally, persons who transgresses the codes of gender—that is to say, those who chose *not* to deploy the gestures, the sign language, the dress-codes that men and women are expected to deploy so that others can identify them as men and women "proper"—are likely to endure more than just disapproving looks. Hate crimes against gay men and lesbians—indeed the murdering of members of these communities—tragically illustrate this idea. (In general, those who transgress the codes of gender may suffer a disproportionate burden of mental health problems, such as stress and depression, as data pertaining to the health status of gay men and women clearly show [Meyer 2003]).

To be sure, sometimes noncompliers become cultural heroes, as the example of Manal al-Shari suggests, or as the Civil Rights Movement or feminist movements illustrate. But more often, people who transgress dominant norms, rather than thereby becoming cultural heroes, tend to become handicapped: socially, they are often ostracized or scorned rather than celebrated; politically they may become disenfranchised; economically, they may carry disproportionate burdens. Transsexual men and women, for example, have a much harder time finding adequate employment, adequate housing, adequate education, adequate health care, regardless of their skills and of their character.

Even the noncompliers who eventually emerge as cultural heroes—also tend to first pay the price of noncompliance. Some of the artists who opened entire new fields of aesthetic expression and experience—from the painter Vincent Van Gogh to the poet Charles Baudelaire—also experienced the sort of daily little miseries that often punctuate the existence of *true* outsiders (who are not merely fashionable eccentrics). Indeed, many of such artistic pioneers died forsaken, even despised. The case of Nelson Mandela, who spent twenty-seven years in prison, also illustrates this idea in the most sobering manner.

Compliance with Absurd or Belittling Social Rules

Indeed, it is important to underscore that the everyday existence of noncompliers is likely to be burdened—*even if the social codes that noncompliers violate are arbitrary, absurd, and even if these codes aim to dehumanize them.* The example of Manal al-Shari suggests that most Saudi women, save daring exceptions, had readily complied with the bizarre notion that driving was somehow unfeminine and embarrassing. As Thomas Paine, the eighteenth-century English-American revolutionary, argued, sometimes the will to follow "common sense" does not stem from the power of "commonsensical" ideas themselves, or from their intrinsic goodness, but simply from the fact that people tend to get used to inherited ideas, often unthinkingly abiding by the imaginations of dead generations.

The notion that people often comply with absurd or dehumanizing norms, or norms that damage their own existence, counterintuitive as it might be, warrants a full theoretical explanation, which I will provide in a subsequent chapter. But for now let us only consider a couple of additional examples closer to the United States.

In the 1950s, American girls and women were socialized, in general and save exceptions, to believe that they would find fulfillment primarily, or even exclusively, in their God-given role as nurturers (Friedan 2001). This particular belief system (which Betty Friedan, the leader of the second wave of feminism, termed the *feminine mystique*) postulated that women's natures had been intended for nurturing. Men and women often thought that women could therefore fulfill their biological fate primarily in the domestic sphere, nurturing the family, the children, the garden, the pets and taking care of the meals, the cleaning, and so on. This belief system postulated that women should exclude themselves from the public sphere, and from any life path that would drive them away from their role as nurturers. Hence, from a young age, women were discouraged from pursuing careers, businesses, or occupations with higher levels of responsibility (as these were seen as not feminine and indeed as unfeminine) and were thus discouraged from being financially, intellectually, and socially independent. Noncompliers—that is, "nonfeminine" women who strived to attain education and positions of power—often faced daily, petty retaliations from both men and women, from strangers and from kin. These outsiders brooked a disproportionate share of ego attacks, precisely because they went against the *arbitrary, absurdly limiting, and belittling* codes that governed femininity.

It is also worth taking a look at a contemporary example pertaining to gender. Let us turn to the work of Michael Kimmel, an American sociologist who has devoted most of his career to study masculinity in the United States. He has similarly shown that young American men today, for example, college students in their early twenties, often find themselves, much as their grandmothers in the fifties, unable to go against the codes of their gender, *however absurd and belittling these codes of masculinity might be*. Consider "bro codes" about drinking, for instance. Kimmel (2008) describes the following scene pertaining to drinking rituals:

> Nick starts his night by ingesting some vile concoction invented solely for the enjoyment of the onlookers. Tonight the drink of choice is a "Three Wise Men," a shot composed of equal parts Jim Beam, Jack Daniels, and Johnnie Walker. Other variations include the more ethnically diverse (substitute Jose Cuervo for the Johnnie Walker), or the truly vomit-inducing (add a little half-and-half and just a splash of Tabasco). The next drink comes at him fast, a Mind Eraser, another classic of the power hour [the time that Nick and buddies reserve for fun]. It's like a Long Island Iced Tea except more potent, and it is drunk through a straw as quickly as possible. Shot after shot after shot is taken, the guys become all the more loud and obnoxious, and the bar manager brings a trashcan over to Nick's side, just in case. [...] Not surprisingly, the trashcan comes in handy. Nick's body finally relents as closing time approaches. He spews out a stream of vomit and the other guys know it's time to go. Fun was had, memories were made, but most importantly ... he puked. His friends can rest easy: a job well done. (Kimmel 2008, 95–96)

For many of the Nicks who inhabit Guyland, getting sick in such a manner is clearly preferable to breaking the norms that govern Guyland. As Kimmel reports, doing fraternity pledges that involve cleaning vomit, walking around grabbing the penises of other pledges while being mocked and insulted, or indeed risking being killed in hazing rituals is also preferable to breaking these norms. Every year, as Kimmel notes, about 1,400 college students aged eighteen to twenty-four, almost four students per day, are in fact "killed as a result of drinking [and] nearly half a million suffer some sort of injury" (Kimmel 2008, 106).

Note also that, much as their grandmothers, these guys have not invented these norms, the codes and rules that often guide their behavior. They have merely inherited them, without thinking too much, it would seem, about whether these make sense, or whether, all things considered, they are good or bad for them. (For the most part, they are bad. A pile of data about shows that young American men, particularly the Nicks described by Kimmel, are failing in unprecedented ways in virtually every area of achievement that is important at their age: succeeding at school, moving away from the parental house, becoming financially independent, and so on. In comparison with women of their age, young American men are nearly twice as likely to live with their parents. In comparison to the previous generation, they are more likely to depend on parental money. The list is long. Philip Zimbardo, one of the most prominent contemporary social psychologists, has in fact describes this scenario as the "demise of guys.")

The examples above, in any case, illustrate the idea that men and women often fall prey to their own instinct, natural and useful as sometimes is, to follow the will of the larger (social) organism, not necessarily because this makes rational sense. This aspect of human nature is important for the life of a social species such as ours, but it also accounts for many of our troubles, much of our suffering, many of our delusions and humiliations. And it is therefore important for democratic societies to understand and to intervene in this aspect of social life. Let us conclude this chapter with Doris Lessing:

> Imagine saying to our children: "in the last fifty or so years, the human race has become aware of a great deal of information about its mechanisms [information provided particularly by sociologists and social psychologists]; how it behaves, how it must behave under certain circumstances. If this is to be useful, you must learn to contemplate these [social] rules calmly, dispassionately, disinterestedly, without emotion. It is information that will set people free from blind loyalties, obedience to slogans, rhetoric, leaders, group emotions. (1987, 61)

Though Lessing imagines a society where school children are encouraged to learn this sort of lesson, she also realizes that no government, no nation, no political party will actually design curricula to teach children "to become individuals able to resist group pressure" (1987, 62). Why? Because such groups often depend on group members who follow group thinking. Thus, she suggests, it is up to us: parents, teachers, friends—it is up to the civil society to nurse these ideas, to encourage *not* fashionable eccentricity or potentially dangerous deviance but a process of psychological decolonization.

References

Asch, Solomon. 1951. "Effects of Group Pressure upon the Modification and Distortion of Judgment." In *Groups, Leadership and Men*, edited by H. Guetzkow, 1951. Pittsburgh, PA: Carnegie Press.

Friedan, Betty. 2001. *The Feminine Mystique*. New York: W. W. Norton.

Kimmel, Michael. 2008. *Guyland: The Perilous World Where Boys Become Men*. New York: Harper Collins.

Lessing, Doris. 1987. *Prisons We Choose to Live Inside*. New York: Harper Collins.

Meyer, Ilan. 2003. "Prejudice, Social Stress and Mental Health in Lesbian, Gay, and Bisexual Populations." *Psychological Bulletin* 129: 674–97.

Suh, Eunkook, et al. 1998. "The Shifting Basis of Life Satisfaction Judgments Across Cultures: Emotions Versus Norms." *Journal of Personality and Social Psychology* 74 (2): 482–493.

Section 4 Discussion Questions

1. How does the example of extreme isolation of a child relate to the practice of isolation in prisons?
2. How does the case of extreme isolation relate to minor deprivations among children in poverty?
3. Is nature versus nurture a true dichotomy? Some argue it is a false dichotomy, not that we have a better understanding of the human genome and social influence. What do you think?
4. How is the process of socialization like a machine that produces compliant citizens?
5. Why is socialization so important to human societies?
6. Discuss ways in which you have influenced someone to conform in the context of a group.
7. List at least five ways that groups exert pressure on individuals to conform.
8. Think of a time in which you conformed to group/peer pressure. Why did you conform? Think about how you felt and what you were thinking and how those feelings and thoughts led to your conformity.

Section 4 Exercises

1. Socialization is a lifelong process. We are constantly being socialized into new statuses as we age and as we take on new roles associated with those new statuses. Write about a transition that you have recently made in life and how you had to adjust or be socialized into the new status that you transitioned into. For example, maybe you went from single person to married person, or maybe you went from employee to being unemployed. Tell how you had to adjust to this new status and take on new roles.
2. For this exercise, you need to interview three people who have recently made a transition in life and how they had to adjust or be socialized into the new status that they have transitioned into. For example, maybe you know someone who got their first job out of college, or maybe they went from married to divorced. Tell us how they had to adjust to this new status and take on new roles and how that has impacted their lives. Are there any similar themes about transition that emerge from their stories?
3. This exercise has two parts.

Part 1:

Watch the TED Talk (The Link between Unemployment and Terrorism) using the URL below.

https://www.ted.com/talks/mohamed_ali_the_link_between_unemployment_and_terrorism

Part 2:
   a. How does this video illustrate the concepts of social pressure and resocialization?
   b. What are the mechanisms that terrorist organizations use to convert civilians into terrorists? Give examples from the video.
   c. Why is this process necessary for these organizations?
   d. Think of how social circumstances and the application of social pressure can act to motivate individuals to join groups/organizations and commit certain acts. Describe how this could have happen in religions and political parties. Try to draw parallels to the pressures and practices described in the video.

4. If you want to see the effects of conformity, just take a look through some old high school yearbooks. Find some old high school yearbooks, maybe from your parents, grandparents, older siblings, friends, or even neighbors. Try to get a range of decades—get some from the 1960s, 1970s, 1980s, 1990s, and early 2000s. One highly visible sign of conformity is fashion. Now go through the books and look for similar clothing and hair fashions. You will probably notice a trend in the type of hairdos and clothing that the students are wearing in each of the different decades. I did this with my high school yearbook from the 1970s, and conformity to fashion was *very* evident! What kinds of trends do you see? Is it among both males and females? What else could you look for in terms of conformity? First names? Other fashion accessories?

STAYING WITHIN THE LINES
DEVIANCE AND SOCIAL CONTROL

When children first start coloring their parents typically encourage them to stay inside the lines. This advice represents the desire to have children conform to guidelines, just like when parents encourage their children to follow the rules of games. We are all encouraged to obey rules, and for the most part we do. By not doing so we risk appearing different or *deviant*, being embarrassed or even punished. Therefore, people are encouraged in many ways to stay within social lines in order to maintain social order. However, those who violate social rules risk suffering negative consequences.

Deviance is typically thought of as any violation of social norms that elicits negative responses. However, all societies have an array of social norms that range from the informal to taboos. Therefore, depending on the type of social norm that is violated, the consequences can vary broadly. So, broadly speaking, there are behaviors that violate any type of formal norm—**crime**—and behaviors that violate informal norms—**informal deviance**. Deviance, then, can range from something as minor as a social faux pas like close talking to the more serious crime of mass shooting.

Crime then would seem relatively straightforward in terms of being defined as deviant (deviance is the violation of social norms). Crime is the violation of formal social norms; therefore, crime is deviance. However, many times, deviance is not merely the clear violation of a social rule, but there is considerable nuance to understanding deviance at any given time or in any particular society. Think of deviance as the opposite of norms: while norms are the rules, deviance represents the violation of the rules. Consequently, because norms change over time and across cultures, definitions of deviance change over time and from place to place. Tattoos, for example, were once associated only with criminals and formal members of the military in the United States, but now suburban moms get their kids' names tattooed on their legs. You may even have a tattoo! And certainly, there is cultural variation in how deviance is interpreted. The Sambia (a pseudonym) People of Papua New Guinea require boys to fellate the single men of their village as part of their rite of passage ceremony, in order for the boys to become seen as men in their culture. While this is a necessary part of the passage to male adulthood for the Sambia, we would view it as pedophilia. Both these examples help illustrate the larger idea that there are *no* absolute deviant acts, only behaviors that have been determined at a certain time and/or place by a particular group of people to be deviant.

CHAPTER 6
DEVIANCE AND SOCIAL CONTROL

■ Is It Always Wrong to Eat People?

Not only place and time but social context can determine whether certain acts are normative or deviant. For example, eating human flesh is almost universally condemned as deviant. However, under certain social circumstances, it could become accepted behavior. In the article below, James M. Henslin shows us that even something as repugnant as cannibalism can become normalized given the right social conditions. The conditions that the people in this story encounter are extreme, but they highlight the processes societies use to construct reality—especially in terms of what is acceptable and what is deviant behavior. Be sure to pay attention to how the group of people described create a set of rules around their cannibalism in order to view themselves and others as "good" people who adhere to the newly constructed rules. As you read, you may want to ask yourself the following questions.

■ Some Things to Keep in Mind

1. How do the survivors construct new rules for their new reality?
2. How are these new norms enforced?
3. How does this story illustrate the idea that there are no absolutes when it comes to deviance?
4. What does this story tell us about norms and deviance in society at large?
5. What would it take for you to eat another human?

EATING YOUR FRIENDS IS THE HARDEST

THE SURVIVORS OF THE F-227
James M. Henslin

A theme running through our previous readings is that each culture provides guidelines for how to view the world, even for how we determine right and wrong. The perspectives we learn envelop us much as a fish is enveloped by water. Almost all the world's cultures uphold the idea that it is wrong to eat human flesh. (Some exceptions do apply, such as warriors who used to eat the heart or kidneys of slain enemies in an attempt to acquire the source of their strength or courage.) Thus it is safe to say that nowhere in the world is there a culture whose members regularly consume people as food. Yet, in the unusual situation recounted here, this is precisely what these people did.

Note how, even in the midst of reluctantly committing acts that they themselves found repugnant—and ones they knew that the world condemns—this group developed norms to govern their behavior. This was crucial for these survivors, because group support, along with its attendant norms, is essential for maintaining sanity and a sense of a "good" self. At the conclusion of the article, Henslin shows how this event is more than simply an interesting story—that it represents the essence of social life.

Located between Brazil and Argentina, near Buenos Aires, is tiny Uruguay. On October 12, 1972, a propeller-driven Fairchild F-227 left Uruguay's capital, Montevideo, bound for Santiago, Chile—a distance of about 900 miles. On board were 15 members of an amateur rugby team from Uruguay, along with 25 of their relatives and friends. The pilots, from the Uruguayan Air Force, soon became concerned about turbulence over the Andes Mountains. Winds blowing in from the Pacific were colliding with air currents coming from the opposite direction, creating a turbulence that could toss a plane around like a scrap of paper in a wind storm.

Since the threat was so great, the pilots decided to land in Mendoza, Argentina, where everyone spent the night. The next day, with the weather only slightly improved, the crew debated about turning back. Several of the rugby players taunted them, saying they were cowards. When

James M. Henslin, "Eating Your Friends is the Hardest: The Survivors of the F-227," *Down to Earth Sociology: Introductory Readings*, pp. 277-286. Copyright © 2007 by James Henslin. Reprinted with permission.

the captain of a plane which had just flown over the Andes reported that the F-227 should be able to fly over the turbulence, the Fairchild's pilots decided to continue the trip. Once again airborne, the young passengers laughed about its being Friday the 13th as some threw a rugby ball around and others played cards. Many of them still in their teens, and all of them from Uruguay's upper class (two were nephews of the president of Uruguay), they were in high spirits.

Over the Andes the plane flew into a thick cloud, and the pilots had to fly by instrument. Amid the turbulence they hit an "air pocket," and the plane suddenly plunged 3,000 feet. When the passengers abruptly found themselves below the cloud, one young man turned to another and said, "Is it normal to fly so close?" He was referring to the mountainside just 10 feet off the right wing.

With a deafening roar, the right wing sheared off as it hit the side of the mountain. The wing whipped over the plane and knocked off the tail. The steward, the navigator, and three of the rugby players still strapped in their seats were blown out of the gaping hole. Then the left wing broke off and, like a toboggan going 200 miles an hour, the fuselage slid on its belly into a steep, snow-covered valley.

As night fell, the survivors huddled in the wreckage. At 12,000 feet the cold, especially at night, was brutal. There was little fuel, because not much wood is used in the construction of airplanes. They had almost no food—basically some chocolate that the passengers had bought on their overnight stay in Mendoza. There were a few bottles of wine, and the many cartons of cigarettes they had purchased at a duty-free shop.

The twenty-seven who survived the crash expected to be rescued quickly. At most, they thought, they would have to spend the night on the mountain top. Seventy days later, only sixteen remained alive.

The chocolate and wine didn't go very far, and provided little nourishment. The plane, off course by a hundred miles or so and painted white, was not only difficult to track, but virtually invisible against the valley's deep layer of snow: Search planes were unable to locate the wreckage.

As the days went by, the survivors' spirits seemed to be sucked into a hopeless pit. Hunger and starvation began to bear down on them. They felt cold all the time. They became weaker and had difficulty keeping their balance. Their skin became wrinkled, like that of old people. Although no one mentioned it, several of the young men began to realize that their only chance to survive was to eat the bodies of those who died in the crash. The corpses lay strewn in the snow around the plane, perfectly preserved by the bitter cold.

The thought of cutting into the flesh of their friends was too ghastly a prospect to put into words. Finally, however, Canessa, a medical student, brought up the matter with his friends. He asserted that the bodies were no longer people. The soul was gone, he said, and the body was simply meat—and essential to their survival. They were growing weaker, and they could not survive without food. And what food was there besides the corpses? "They are no more human beings than the dead flesh of the cattle we eat at home," he said.

Days later, the topic moved from furtive discussion in a small group to open deliberation among all the survivors. Inside the plane, arguing the matter, Canessa reiterated his position. His three closest friends supported him, adding, "We have a duty to survive. If we don't eat the bodies, it is a sin. We must do this not just for our own sakes but also for our families. In fact," they continued, "God wants us to survive, and He has provided these bodies so we can live." Some, however, just shook their heads, the thought too disturbing to even contemplate.

Serbino pushed the point. He said, "If I die, I want you to eat my body. I want you to use it." Some nodded in agreement. In an attempt to bring a little humor to the black discussion, he added, "If you don't, I'll come back and give you a swift kick in the butt." Some said that while they did not think it would be wrong to eat the bodies, they themselves could never do it. The arguments continued for hours.

Four of the young men went outside. Near the plane, the buttocks of a body protruded from the snow. No one spoke as they stared at it. Wordlessly, Canessa knelt and began to cut with the only instrument he had found, a piece of broken glass. The flesh was frozen solid, and he could cut only slivers the size of matchsticks. Canessa laid the pieces on the roof of the plane, and the young men went back inside. They said that the meat was drying in the sun. The others looked mutely at one another. No one made a move to leave the plane.

Canessa decided that he would have to be the first. Going outside, he picked up a sliver of meat. Staring at it, almost transfixed, he became as though paralyzed. He simply couldn't make his hand move to his mouth. Summoning every ounce of courage, he forced his hand upwards. While his stomach recoiled, he pushed the meat inside his mouth and forced himself to swallow. Later, Serbino took a piece. He tried to swallow, but the sliver hung halfway down his throat. Quickly grabbing some snow, he managed to wash it down. Canessa and Serbino were joined by others, who also ate.

The next morning, on the transistor radio they had struggled so hard to get working, their hearts plunged when they heard that the air force had called off the search. The survivors knew that this announcement almost sealed their fate. The only way out, if there was one, was on their own. They held a meeting and decided that the fittest should try to seek help—even though no one knew where to seek it. But none was strong enough to try. With the snow's crust breaking under every step, even to walk was exhausting. There was only one way to regain strength, and, without giving words to the thought, everyone knew what it was.

Canessa and Strauch went outside. The corpse was in the same position as before. They took a deep breath and began to hack meat off the bone. They laid the strips on the plane to thaw in the sun. The knowledge that no rescuers were looking for them encouraged others to join in eating the human flesh. They forced themselves to swallow—their consciences, seconded by their stomachs, accusing them of extreme wrongdoing. Still, they forced the flesh down, telling themselves over and over that there was no other way to survive.

Some, however, could not. Javier and Liliana Methol, husband and wife, though they longed to return to their children, could not eat human flesh. They said that the others could do as they liked, but perhaps God wanted them to choose to die.

The survivors began to organize. Canessa took charge of cutting up the bodies, while a group of the younger ones had the job of preventing the corpses from rotting by keeping them covered with snow. Another group had the task of seeing that the plane was kept in order. Even the weakest had a job to do: They were able to hold pieces of aluminum in the sun to melt snow for drinking water.

The first corpses they ate were those of the crew, strangers to them.

One day, when it was too cold to melt snow, they burned wooden Coca-Cola crates that they had found in the luggage compartment. After they had water, they roasted some meat over the embers. There was only enough heat to brown the pieces, but they found the flavor better-tasting, like beef, they said, but softer. Canessa said they should never do this again, for heat destroys proteins. "You have to eat it raw to get its full value," he argued. Rejecting his advice, the survivors cooked the meat when they had the chance, about once or twice a week. Daily, the recurring question was, "Are we cooking today?"

Liliana told Javier that after they got back home she wanted to have another baby. He agreed. As they looked at one another, though, they saw eyes sunken into their sockets and bones protruding from their cheeks. They knew there was no hope, unless. ... Liliana and Javier shuddered as they picked up a piece of meat.

Some never could eat. Although the others argued with them, they never could overcome their feelings of revulsion. They continued to refuse, and so day by day grew weaker. Others, however, grew accustomed to what they were doing. They became able to cut meat from a body before everyone's eyes. They could even eat larger pieces, which they had to chew and taste.

As time went on, they developed a set of rules. They would not eat the women's bodies. No one had to eat. The meat would be rationed, and no one could eat more than his or her share. The three who were going to leave in search of help could eat more than the others. One corpse would always be finished before another would be started. (It was overlooked when those who had the disagreeable job of cutting the corpses ate a little as they cut.)

They refused to eat certain parts of the body—the lungs, the skin, the head, and the genitals.

There were some things they never could get used to, such as cutting up a close friend. When they dug a corpse out of the snow, it was preserved just as it had been at the moment of death. If the eyes had been open when the friend died, they were still open, now staring back at them. Everyone understood that no one had to eat a friend or relative.

Survival work became more organized. Those who could stomach it would cut large chunks from a body and pass them to another team, who would slice them with razor blades into smaller pieces. This was not as disagreeable a task, for, separated from the body, the meat was easier to deal with.

The sheets of fat from a body lay outside the rules. They were dried in the sun until a crust formed. Anyone could eat as much as they wished. But the fat wasn't as popular as the meat.

Also outside the rationing system were the pieces of the first carcasses they had cut up, before they developed the rules. Those pieces lay about the snow, and anyone who wanted could scavenge them. Some could never stomach the liver, others the heart or kidneys, and many could not eat the intestines of the dead. Three young men refused the red meat of the muscles.

The dead became part of their lives. One night, Inciarte reached up to get something from the hat rack and was startled when an icy hand brushed against his cheek. Apparently someone had sneaked it in as a late snack.

Constipation was an unexpected complication of their diet. As day after day went by without defecation, they began to worry that their insides would burst. Eventually they developed a sort of contest, wondering who would be the last hold-out. After 28 days, only two had not defecated. At 32, only one. Finally, on the 34th day, Bobby François joined the others.

The three who had been selected to go in search of rescuers had to solve the problem of preventing their feet from freezing. The skin of the dead provided the solution. By cutting an arm just above and below the elbow, and slowly pulling, the skin came away with its subcutaneous layers of fat. Sewing up the lower end made an insulated pair of socks.

Their bland diet became boring. As their bodies and minds cried out for variety, they began to seek new tastes. After eating the meat from a bone, they would crack it open and scoop out the marrow. Everyone liked the marrow. Some sought out the blood clots from around the heart. Others even ate parts of bodies that had started to rot. Many were revolted by this, but, as time went on, more of the survivors did the same.

Canessa, Parrado, and Vizintin were selected to go in search of help. Before they left, Parrado took aside a couple of friends and said that they might run short of food before help could arrive. "I prefer you don't," he whispered, "but I'll understand if you eat my mother and sister."

Ten days after the expeditionaries set out, they stumbled into a shepherd's hut. The news of their survival, long after they had been given up for dead, came as a shock to their friends and relatives. Those still waiting on the mountain were rescued by helicopter—just four days before Christmas.

Although the survivors felt a compulsive need to talk about what they had done, at first physicians and government officials kept the cannibalism a secret. When the news leaked out, however, it made headlines around the world. One survivor explained, "It was like a heart transplant. The dead sustained the living." Another said, "It was like holy communion. God gives us the body and blood of Christ in holy communion. God gave us these bodies and blood to eat."

All were Roman Catholics, and they asked forgiveness. The priests replied that they did not need forgiveness, for they had done nothing wrong. There was no soul in the bodies, the priests explained, and in extreme conditions, if there is no other way to survive, it is permissible to eat the dead. After consultation with relatives, it was decided to bury what was left of the dead at the crash site.

The young men, rejoining their families, became celebrities. They shunned the spotlight, however, banded together, and thought of themselves as special people. As persons who had survived the impossible, they felt that they had a unique purpose in life.

The world's reaction to the events in the Andes was shock and horror—mixed with fascination. As one Chilean paper asked in its headlines, "What would *you* have done?"

The Social Construction of Reality

I was going to let the story stop here, but I was told by a person very influential in my life that I really ought to make the sociology explicit. So let's see what sociological lessons we can derive from this tragedy in the Andes.

First, the main lesson, one from which the other points follow, comes from the symbolic interactionists, who stress that *our world is socially constructed.* By this, they mean that nothing contains built-in meanings. In other words, whatever meaning something has is arbitrary: We humans have given it a particular meaning, but we could just as well have given it a different meaning. *Second,* it is through a social process that we determine meanings; that is, people jointly decide on the meanings to assign events and objects. *Third,* because meanings (or what things symbolize to people) are arbitrary, people can change them. I am aware that these statements may sound extremely vague, but they should become clear as we look at how these survivors constructed their reality.

We might begin by asking what the meaning of a human body is. As with other aspects of life, a group can assign to a body any meaning that it wishes, for, by itself, a body has no meaning. These survivors did not begin to develop their definitions from scratch, however, for they brought to the Andes meanings that they had learned in their culture—basically that a body, while not a person, is still human, and must be treated with respect. A related meaning they had learned is that a human body is "not food." Such an understanding may seem natural to us because it matches our own cultural definitions—which obscures the arbitrary nature of the definition.

Fourth, when circumstances change, definitions can become outmoded—even definitions about fundamental aspects of life. *Fifth,* even though definitions no longer "work," changes in basic orientations do not come easily. *Sixth,* anyone who suggests such changes is likely to be seen as a threatening deviant. Shock, horror, or ridicule may be the reactions, and—for persons who persist on a disorienting course—shunning, ostracism, and violence may result. *Seventh,* the source of radical new ideas is extremely significant in determining whether or not they gain acceptance. *Eighth,* if an individual can drum up group support, then there exists a *social* basis for the new, competing definition. *Ninth,* if the group that offers the new definition can get enough others to accept it, then the common definition of reality will change. *Tenth,* changed circumstances make people more open to accepting new definitions of reality.

In this case, Canessa did not want to appear as a deviant, so he furtively proposed a new definition—entrusting it at first to only a few close friends. Even there, however, since it violated basic definitions acquired in early socialization, it was initially met with resistance. But the friends had high respect for Canessa, who had completed a year of medical school, and they were won over. This small group then proposed their new definition of human bodies to the larger group. Eventually, in the growing realization that death was imminent, this definition won out.

Eleventh, behavior follows definitions. That is, definitions of reality are not just abstract ideas; they also indicate the boundaries of what is allowable. We tend to do what our definitions allow. In this case, when the definition of human bodies changed, so did the survivors' behavior: The changed definition allowed them to eat human corpses.

Twelfth, definitions also follow behavior. That is, as people engage in an activity, they tend to develop ideas that lend support to what they are doing. In this instance, the eating of human flesh—especially since it was a group activity—reinforced the initial definition that had been held only tentatively, that the flesh was no longer human. Eventually, at least for many, the flesh indeed became meat—so much so that some people were even able to take a human hand to bed for a late-night snack.

Thirteenth, for their very survival, all groups must have norms. By allowing people to know what to expect in a given situation, norms provide a basic structure for people's relationships with one another. Without norms, anarchy and chaos would reign.

This principle also applies to groups that make deviance part of their activities. Although a superficial view from the outside may make such groups appear disorganized and without rules, they are in fact quite normative. Groups of outlaw motorcyclists, for example, share an elaborate set of rules about what they expect from one another, most of which, like those of other groups, are not in written form. In short, norms cover even deviant activities, for, without them, how can group members know what to expect of one another?

The Andes survivors developed a basic set of norms to provide order to their deviant activity. Some of those norms were:

1. No one had to violate his or her conscience. If someone did not wish to eat human flesh, no one would force them.
2. Some bodies were "off limits."
3. Meat was rationed, with a specified amount for each person:
   a. Fat was outside the rationing system, and
   b. Leftover parts from the first bodies were outside the rationing system.
4. Meat was distributed according to an orderly system, namely:
   a. Everyone who wished to could eat, and
   b. Designated parts of the body could be "wasted."

Fourteenth, human groups tend to stratify, that is, to sort themselves out on a basis of inequality, with some getting more of a group's resources, some less. A norm concerning eating human flesh that I did not mention above illustrates this principle: Those persons deemed most valuable to the group were allowed to eat more. These were persons who were going in search of rescue and those who performed the disagreeable task of cutting up the bodies. This unequal division of resources represents the formation of a basic system of social stratification.

Fifteenth, human groups tend to organize themselves. In this instance, the survivors did not just randomly cut away at the bodies, but specific tasks were assigned. Teamwork developed to coordinate tasks, with some individuals performing specialized jobs in making the meat edible. Even the weakest had a part to play. The incipient social stratification just mentioned is another example of organization, one that sociologists call the division of labor. *Sixteenth,* an essential part of the human tendency to organize is the emergence of leadership—to direct and coordinate the activities of others. In this case, Canessa stands out.

Seventeenth, people attempt to maintain a respectable sense of self. These survivors were conforming individuals in that they had accepted the norms of their society and were striving for a respectable place within it. They wanted to continue to think of themselves as good people. Yet, they had, to make a decision about doing an activity that went beyond the bounds of what they looked at as normal—one they even knew that "everyone" defined as wrong.

Eighteenth, it is possible to maintain a "good" self-image and still engage in deviant activities. Because the essence of human society is the social construction of reality, so the key to the self also lies in how reality is defined. If you can redefine an activity to make it "not deviant," then it does not threaten your sense of a "good" self. In this present instance, the Andes-survivors looked on eating human flesh as part of their "duty to survive." To do a duty is a good thing, and, accordingly, the acts required by it cannot be "bad." In fact, they must be "good." (The most infamous example of the use of this basic principle was Hitler's SS, who looked on killing Jews as necessary for the survival of the "Aryan" race and culture. They even termed the slaughter a "good" act and their participation in it as patriotic and self-sacrificing.)

This principle helps many people get through what otherwise would be excruciatingly painful nights—for they would toss sleeplessly owing to a gnawing conscience. Redefinition, by keeping one's sense of self intact, allows people to participate in a variety of acts condemned by society—even those disapproved by the self. For most people, redefinition involves much less dramatic acts than eating human flesh, such as a college student cheating on a test or a boss firing a worker.

Nineteenth, some people participate in deviant acts even though they remain unconvinced about such redefinitions. (Some do not even attempt to redefine them.) They may do so from a variety of motives—from what they consider "sheer' necessity" to the desire to reach a future goal. Liliana and Javier, who decided that they wanted a baby, are an example. Such persons have greater difficulty adjusting to their acts than those who redefine them as "good." (Even the latter may have difficulty, for redefinitions may be only partial, especially in the face of competing definitions.)

Twentieth, people feel they must justify their actions to others. This process of justifying the self involves clothing definitions of reality in forms thought to be acceptable to others. In order for definitions to be accepted, they must be made to fit into the others' already-existing definitional framework. In this case, the survivors first justified their proposed actions by redefining the bodies as meat and by saying that they had a duty to survive. After their rescue—speaking to a Roman Catholic audience—they used the analogy of holy communion to justify their act.

Twenty-first, to gain institutional support is to secure a broad, solid base for one's definitions of reality. Then one no longer stands alone, which is to invite insanity, nor is one a member of a small group, which is to invite ridicule and may require cutting off oneself from the larger group. In this case, institutional support was provided by the Roman Catholic Church, which, while not accepting the survivors' analogy of cannibalism as communion, allowed them to avoid the label of sin by defining their actions as allowable under the circumstances.

Finally, note that these principles are fundamental to human life. They do not simply apply to the Andes survivors—or to deviants in general—but they underlie human society. For all of us, reality is socially constructed, and the story of the Andes survivors contains the essence of human society.

Section 5 Discussion Questions

1. Discuss how the boundaries of what is considered deviant changes over time.
2. Why do behaviors considered to be deviant change across cultures?
3. What criteria do people use to determine if something is deviant?
4. How do ideas about what is deviant change over time?
5. Why are there no absolute deviant acts?
6. Is a man who prefers to hug those he meets rather than shake their hands deviant? Why or why not?
7. Can age be a deciding factor in judging someone's behavior as deviant or not?
8. Discuss the reasons that social control is important for society.
9. Get in a group in class and discuss the study presented above. How is social control achieved in your group?
10. List and describe at least twenty ways that society achieves social control.
11. What are the ways your college or university promotes social control on campus?

Section 5 Exercises

1. For this exercise, you need to go out in your community and be deviant in some NONCRIMINAL way. For example, wear your clothes inside out, carry a teddy bear around and treat it like a real human infant, or talk out loud to yourself. You may work in groups, say, if three people wanted to go on an elevator and face the wrong way and see what happens; watch for people's reactions, and be sure to ask people why they reacted the way they did and what they were thinking about you and the situation. Be creative in your deviance. Be sure that you do not violate any laws; do not harm yourself or others, and do not put yourself or anyone else at risk of harm.

    Whatever deviant act you engage in, do it for an entire day or repeat it at least three times. Then, in discussions, tell me the following:
    a. What you did to be deviant;
    b. Where you did it;
    c. What were the reactions of those around you or those who witnessed your deviance;
    d. Why you think people reacted in the ways they did (based on their input and your own ideas).

2. Go to the Death Penalty Information Center's online fact sheet (https://files.death-penaltyinfo.org/legacy/documents/FactSheet.pdf). Look over the fact sheet, and then answer the following questions:
   a. How does the total racial composition of America (White, 75.1 percent; Black, 12.3 percent; Hispanic, 12.5 percent*) compare with the racial composition of death row inmates?
   b. How does each region compare regarding its number of executions?
   c. Compare the support for a life sentence without parole with the support for the death penalty. Were you surprised? Why or why not?

   Now go to Amnesty International's website on the death penalty (https://www.amnesty.org/en/what-we-do/death-penalty/) and answer the following questions:
   a. Which countries committed the vast majority of executions?
   b. Compare these countries in terms of different sociological factors: that is, what economic, social, political, and religious differences are there between countries that put many people to death and those countries that put few or no people to death?

3. Try this field research to examine forms of social control: Take several bus, subway, or train trips, and violate some unspoken rule of riding that public transit system, such as don't give up your seat for an elderly person or ask an elderly person for their seat. Be sure to record the type of non-normative behavior you engaged in and the responses of your fellow riders. How was informal social control exercised? Note the different ways informal social control can be expressed. Was there a difference in the expression of informal social control between people? Were women more likely to express informal social control than men? Were there differences by age or race? Public transit is not unlike a lot of public places in which people feel the need to uphold the rules by using the power of informal social control. I see it in the classroom, in the audience at tennis matches, and in line at my favorite coffee shop. Where are some of the places you see people (maybe yourself) exercising informal social control? What are the most popular ways to express it? Is it effective? Why or why not?

TYPES OF INEQUALITY
SOCIAL CLASS, RACE, AND GENDER

All societies are unequal. Well, if we start here, all we have to determine is which groups in society are more privileged than others and *how* they are privileged. And in all societies, there are groups that have greater access to and possess more of the valuable social resources than other groups. In our society, most people believe that there is *equality of opportunity*—the idea that everyone has an equal chance at being successful, which is different from what sociologists refer to as *equality of condition*—the notion that all members of society have similar levels of income, education, wealth, power, and so on. It is fairly obvious that in the United States (and all other societies), there is an *inequality of condition*—that is, there is a tremendous discrepancy in levels of income, wealth, and power among social classes. Additionally, it is easy to see in today's world that there is also an *inequality of opportunity*, which is based primarily on what social groups you have membership in such as gender, race, ethnic identity, and age; but it is also influenced by one's level of education and the amount of various forms of capital. So, these conditions raise two important questions: What is the basis of systematic social inequality in society? How can social inequality be reduced?

Sociologists use the term **social inequality** to describe the unequal distribution of valuable social resources, rewards, and positions in a society. Social characteristics—differences, identities, and roles—are used to differentiate people and divide them into different categories, which have implications for social inequality. Social differentiation by itself does not necessarily imply a division of individuals into a hierarchy of rank, privilege, and power. However, when a social category like class, occupation, gender, or race puts people in a position in which they can claim a greater share of resources or services, then social differentiation becomes the basis of social inequality.

The term *social stratification* refers to an institutionalized system of social inequality. It refers to a situation in which the divisions and relationships of social inequality have solidified into a system that determines who gets what, when, and why. The term *stratification* may conjure up images of layers like you would see on the walls of the Grand Canyon or in a seven-layer dip. Society's layers, however, are made up of people, and society's resources are distributed unevenly throughout the layers. The people who have more resources represent the top layer of the social structure of stratification. Other groups of people, with progressively fewer and fewer resources, represent the lower layers of our society. Social stratification assigns people to socioeconomic strata based on factors like wealth, income, race, education, and power. In the United States, like many other countries, we call these strata *social classes*. Like all societies, the United States is unequal, but most Americans believe in a stratification of social class, and that there *should* be a ranking of individuals based primarily on achievement (Reynolds and Xian 2014). This system of *meritocracy*—a system that rewards effort and ability—or "work hard and get ahead" fuels the American ambition of social mobility. In general, Americans firmly believe that they can move up the ladder of success (move between social classes) by getting a college education and working hard. So, in the American psyche, those who combine the best abilities with the most effort, win.

This section highlights social inequality expressed through social class, race, and gender. Therefore, I have provided three articles that focus on those three dimensions of social inequality. In the first article, the author argues that economic inequality ruins everything we care about. The second examines White privilege, and the third article looks at gender inequality in the entertainment industry.

CHAPTER 7
SOCIAL CLASS

Social Mobility

In this article, Chuck Collins examines the detrimental effects that inequality has on social mobility, our health, our communities, and even our democratic system of government. He shows that the negative effects of economic inequality will lead to the loss of social mobility for nearly everyone, and the idea of working hard to get ahead is something that Americans hold sacred. As you read through the following article, consider your own social position and the real and potential effects it may have on your life. Also, you might want to ponder the ideas below.

Some Things to Keep in Mind

1. How does inequality affect social mobility?
2. Do you think your own social mobility will be influenced by growing economic inequality?
3. What are the ways that inequality impacts "life chances" like life expectancy, health, and other opportunities?
4. Which groups are more affected by social inequality?
5. Which groups are less affected or benefit from social inequality?

HOW INEQUALITY WRECKS EVERYTHING WE CARE ABOUT

Chuck Collins

> *The reality is that U.S. society is polarizing and its social arteries are hardening. The sumptuousness and bleakness of the respective lifestyles of rich and poor represents a scale of difference in opportunity and wealth that is almost medieval—and a standing offense to the American expectation that everyone has the opportunity for life, liberty and happiness.*
>
> —Will Hutton (b. 1951)

Inequality is wrecking the world. Not just poverty, which is destroying the lives of billions of people around the planet, but also inequality—the accelerating gap between the 99 percent and the 1 percent.

The Inequality Death Spiral

According to research in dozens of disciplines, the extreme disparities of wealth and power corrode our democratic system and public trust. They lead to a breakdown in civic cohesion and social solidarity, which in turn leads to worsened health outcomes.

Inequality undercuts social mobility and has disastrous effects on economic stability and growth. The notion of a "death spiral" may sound dramatic, but it captures the dynamic and reinforcing aspects of inequality. And these inequalities were a major contributing factor to the 1929 and 2008 economic downturns. What follows is the case against inequality.

Inequality Wrecks Our Democracy and Civic Life

Inequality is disenfranchising us, diminishing our vote at the ballot box and our voice in the public square. As dollars of the 1 percent displace the votes of the 99 percent as the currency of politics, the 1 percent wins. Not every time, but enough so that the tilt continues toward the agenda of the 1 percent.

The money of the 1 percent dominates our campaign finance system, even after efforts at reform. To run for U.S. Senate—or to win additional terms in the Senate after being elected—politicians must raise an estimated $15,000 a day in campaign contributions. To do this efficiently, politicians have to spend a lot of time courting people in the 1 percent, attending $1,000-a-plate fund-raising dinners and listening to their concerns and agenda. This means less time shaking hands in front of the Costco or Cracker Barrel. We all respond to the people we are surrounded by, and politicians are no different.

Elections do matter. Politicians care about votes on Election Day, and they campaign for those votes and work to get supporters to the polls. But candidates for the U.S. Congress know that every other day of the year they have to think about money.

The corporate 1 percent dominates the lobbying space around federal and state policies. In the last thirty years, the ranks of official lobbyists have exploded. In 1970, there were five registered lobbyists for every one of the 535 members of Congress. Today there are twenty-two lobbyists for every member.[1]

Who lobbies for the 99 percent? There are impressive organizations out there, such as Public Citizen and the Children's Defense Fund, that stand up, wave their arms, and say, "Hey, what about the 99 percent?" But they are severely underresourced, outgunned, and outmaneuvered by the organized 1 percent.

Inequality Makes Us Sick

The medical researchers have said it. And now a growing body of public health research is arriving at the same conclusion: inequality is making us sick.

The more inequality grows between the 1 percent and the 99 percent, the less healthy we are. Unequal communities have greater rates of heart disease, asthma, mental illness, cancer, and other morbid illnesses.

Of course, poverty contributes to all kinds of bad health outcomes. But research shows that you are better off in a low-income community with greater equality than you are in a community with a higher income but more extreme inequalities.

Counties and countries with lower incomes but less inequality have better health outcomes. They have lower infant mortality rates, longer life expectancy, and lower incidences of all kinds of diseases. Counties with higher average incomes but greater disparities between rich and poor have the opposite indicators. They are less healthy places to live.[2]

Why is this so? According to British health researcher Richard Wilkinson, communities with less inequality have stronger "social cohesion," more cultural limits on unrestrained individualism, and more effective networks of mutual aid and caring. "The individualism and values of the market are restrained by a social morality," Wilkinson writes. The existence of more social capital "lubricates the workings of the whole society and economy. There are fewer signs of antisocial aggressiveness, and society appears more caring."[3]

Inequality Tears Our Communities Apart

Extreme inequalities of wealth rip our communities apart with social divisions and distrust, leading to an erosion of social cohesion and solidarity. The 1 percent and the 99 percent today don't just live on opposite sides of the tracks—they occupy parallel universes.

New research shows that we're becoming more polarized by class and race in terms of where we live. A 2011 report based on U.S. Census data notes, "As overall income inequality grew in the last four decades, high- and low-income families have become increasingly less likely to live near one another. Mixed income neighborhoods have grown rarer, while affluent and poor neighborhoods have grown much more common."[4] As this distance widens, it is harder for people to feel like they are in the same boat.

High levels of inequality lead to the construction of physical walls. In many parts of the world, the members of the 1 percent reside in gated communities, surrounded by security systems and bodyguards. More than 9 million households in the United States live behind walls in gated communities, similar to the statistics in polarized societies such as Mexico and Brazil. Over a third of new housing starts in the southern United States are in gated communities.[5]

The relationship between the 1 percent and the 99 percent is characterized by fear, distance, misunderstanding, distrust, and class and racial antagonisms. As a result, there is less caring and a greater amount of individualistic behavior. Part of how people express care is support for public investments in health infrastructure and prevention that benefit everyone. As societies grow unequal, support for such investments declines.

Solidarity is characterized by people taking responsibility for one another and caring for neighbors. But for solidarity to happen, people must know one another and have institutions that transcend differences in class, culture, and race. In communities with great inequality, these institutions don't exist and solidarity is weakened.

Inequality Erodes Social Mobility and Equal Opportunity

Inequality undermines the cherished value of equality of opportunity and social mobility. Intergenerational mobility is the possibility of shifting up or down the income ladder relative to your parents' status. In a mobile society, your economic circumstances are not defined or limited by the economic origins of your family.

For many decades, economists argued that inequality in the United States was the price we paid for a dynamic economy with social mobility.[6] We didn't want to be like Canada or those northern European economies, economists would argue, with their rigid class systems and lack of mobility.

But here's the bad news: Canada and those European nations—with their social safety nets and progressive tax policies—are now more mobile than U.S. society. Research across the industrialized OECD countries has found that Canada, Australia, and the Nordic countries (Denmark, Norway, Sweden, and Finland) are among the most mobile. There is a strong correlation between social mobility and policies that redistribute income and wealth through taxation. The United States is now among the *least* mobile of industrialized countries in terms of earnings.[7]

Inequality Erodes Public Services

The 99 percent depends on the existence of a robust commonwealth of public and community institutions. As Bill Gates Sr., the father of the founder of Microsoft, wrote,

> The ladder of opportunity for America's middle class depends on strong and accessible public educational institutions, libraries, state parks and municipal pools. And for America's poor, the ladder of opportunity also includes access to affordable health care, quality public transportation, and childcare assistance.[8]

Historically, during times of great inequality, there is a disinvestment in the commonwealth.[9] There is less support provided for education, affordable housing, public health care, and other pillars of a level playing field. By contrast, in 1964, a time of relative equality, there was greater concern about poverty; in fact, we launched the War on Poverty to further reduce disadvantage.

Today, as the 1 percent delinks from our communities, it privatizes the services it needs. This leads to two bad outcomes. First, because the 1 percent does not depend on commonwealth services, it would rather not pay for them. They often prefer tax cuts and limited government, which leave them more of their money to spend on privatized services.

Second, the quality of life for the 99 percent suffers when the wealthy don't have a personal stake in maintaining quality public services. As we've seen, the 1 percent has tremendous clout. Its members have the ear of elected officials, command over charitable dollars, dominance of media ownership, and networking connections that are sometimes called "social capital." In a democratic society, good government and strong public institutions require civic engagement by everyone. But when those with the biggest amount of political power, largest number of connections, and greatest capacity don't have a stake, a cycle of disinvestment occurs.

The cycle of disinvestment begins when public services start to deteriorate after the withdrawal of tax dollars and the participation of the powerful. For example, if someone doesn't use the neighborhood public swimming pool because he or she belongs to a private club or spends summers at a private beach house, that person doesn't have a stake in ensuring that the public swimming pool is open all summer, clean and well maintained, and staffed with qualified lifeguards. When services deteriorate and the powerful no longer participate, it leads to a decline in political support and resources, which in turn leads to a cycle of further disinvestment.

This lack of stake is even more visible in terms of public education, where the withdrawal of the 1 percent and even the top 30 percent of families has contributed to severe disinvestment in some school districts. This triggers a vicious circle of budget cuts, stakeholders pulling out, and declining public support for education.

The cycle of disinvestment accelerates when it becomes rational to abandon public and community services if one can afford to do so. Those who can get out do so, in a rush-to-the-exits moment. Families in the 99 percent work extra hard to privatize the services they need until there is a wholesale withdrawal from the public sphere.

If you can't depend on the bus to get to work, you buy a car. If you can't rely on the local public schools to educate your child, then you stretch to pay for private schools. If you can't depend on the lifeguards to show up at the public pool, then you join the private pool. If you can't depend on the police to protect your neighborhood, you hire a private security service or move to a gated community. The cycle of disinvestment continues and the costs of privatized services rise, trapping the remaining families in poor schools and neighborhoods lacking services.

Inequality Undermines Economic Growth

Remember the last time in history that the 1 percent had such a large share of the wealth pie? It was 1929, the eve of the Great Depression. Economic historians argue that this was not a coincidence. Too much inequality contributes to economic instability.

The corollary is that periods of shared prosperity have greater economic growth and stability. The period after World War II, 1947 to 1977, is often cited as a case study of a high-growth and high-equality period.

Making such comparisons is fraught with danger—we're not just comparing apples and oranges, we're comparing bicycles and dump trucks. The period after World War II was unprecedented in terms of the dominant and unrivaled role the United States played in the global economy. But international comparative data that look at inequality and economic performance reinforce this story. More-equal societies do better on most indicators.

The conventional wisdom, espoused in the 1960s by economists such as Arthur Okun of the Brookings Institution, was that there was a trade-off between growth and equity: policies that increased equality would slow economic growth, and aggressive pro-growth policies would worsen inequality. But this thinking is now being turned on its head.

Research by the International Monetary Fund (IMF) and the National Bureau of Economic Research point to the fact that more-equal societies have stronger rates of growth, experience longer economic expansions, and are quicker to recover from economic downturns. According to Jonathan Ostry, an economist at the IMF, trends toward unequal income in the United States mean that future economic expansions will be just one-third as long as they were in the 1960s, prior to the widening of the income divide. Less-equal societies are more vulnerable to both financial crises and political instability.[10]

In volatile markets, investors become gun-shy, even those in the 1 percent. When they perceive that financial markets are rigged in favor of insiders and the politically connected, they take their money somewhere else. "You're going to lose a generation of investors," observed Barry Ritholtz, an investor researcher with Fusion IQ. "And that's how you end up with a 25-year bear market. That's the risk if people start to think there is no economic justice."[11]

Many economists have drawn parallels between 1929 on the eve of the Great Depression and the 2008 economic meltdown. Raghuram Rajan, a former chief economist for the IMF, argues that both depressions were preceded by periods of extreme inequality. In his book *Fault Lines: How Hidden Fractures Still Threaten the World Economy*, Rajan observes that during the decade prior to both economic downturns, the 1 percent captured a gigantic percentage of income gains and wages were stagnant for the majority of Americans. Meanwhile, government policies and private corporate practices encouraged easy access to credit and borrowing among the poor and middle classes. House hold debt nearly doubled during both periods.[12]

Did inequality play a role in the 2008 economic meltdown? The next chapter takes a closer look at this important question.

Notes

1. According to the Center for Responsive Politics, there were 12,220 registered lobbyists in 2011. This is 22.84 lobbyists for every one of the 535 members of Congress. Center for Responsive Politics, "Lobbying Database," www.opensecrets.org/lobby/index.php?ql3 (accessed January 3, 2012).

2. For a good overview of health and inequality issues, see Sam Pizzigati, *Greed and Good: Understanding and Overcoming the Inequality That Limits Our Lives* (New York: Apex Press, 2004), 311–30. Also see Dr. Stephen Bezruchka's website, Population Health Forum (http://depts.washington.edu/eqhlth), for information on global and U.S. health and inequality information. Also see Stephen Bezruchka and M. A. Mercer, "The Lethal Divide: How Economic Inequality Affects Health," in M. Fort, M. A. Mercer, and O. Gish, eds., *Sickness and Wealth: The Corporate Assault on Global Health* (Boston: South End Press, 2004), 11–18.

3. See Richard Wilkinson, *Unhealthy Societies: The Afflictions of Inequality* (London: Routledge, 1996).
4. Sean F. Reardon and Kendra Bischoff, "Growth in the Residential Segregation of Families by Income, 1970–2009," Stanford University, US 2010 Project, Russell Sage Foundation, and American Communities Project at Brown University, November 2011, www.s4.brown.edu/us2010/Data/Report/report111111.pdf (accessed January 3, 2012).
5. Edward J. Blakely and Mary Gail Snyder, *Fortress America: Gated Communities in the United States* (Washington, DC: Brookings Institution Press, 1997); and Justice Policy Institute study, as reported in Jesse Katy, "A Nation of Too Many Prisoners?" *Los Angeles Times*, February 15, 2000.
6. Wojciech Kopczuk, Emmanuel Saez, and Jae Song, "Earnings Inequality and Mobility in the United States: Evidence from Social Security Data Since 1937," *Quarterly Journal of Economics* 125, 1 (February 2010): 91–128, http://ideas.repec.org/a/tpr/qjecon/v125y2010i1p91-128.html (accessed January 3, 2012).
7. OECD, "A Family Affair: Intergenerational Social Mobility Across OECD Countries," *Economic Policy Reforms: Going for Growth*, www.oecd.org/dataoecd/2/7/45002641.pdf (accessed January 3, 2012). Also see the Pew Charitable Trust's Economic Mobility Project (www.economicmobility.org) and their study "Chasing the Same Dream, Climbing Different Ladders: Economic Mobility in the United States and Canada," January 2010, www.economicmobility.org/reports_and_research/other/other?id=0012 (accessed January 3, 2012).
8. Bill Gates Sr. and Chuck Collins, *Wealth and Our Commonwealth: Why American Should Tax Accumulated Fortunes* (Boston: Beacon Press, 2003).
9. Ibid., 19–22.
10. David Lynch, "How Inequality Hurts the Economy," *Business Week Insider*, November 16, 2011,www.businessweek.com/magazine/how-inequality-hurts-the-economy-11162011.html?campaign_id=rss_topStories (accessed January 3, 2012).
11. Ibid.
12. Raghuram G. Rajan, *Fault Lines: How Hidden Fractures Still Threaten the World Economy* (Princeton, NJ: Princeton University Press, 2010).

CHAPTER 8

RACE

White Privilege

This second piece investigates race inequality by examining "White privilege." The author, Peggy McIntosh, developed this article by thinking about her daily life in terms of her race and how she occupies various social spaces. She noticed how many activities of daily social life she took for granted because she is White. And after some reflection, she compiled a list of privileges. She uses the metaphor of a backpack (knapsack) to show that White people carry around the "baggage" of social privilege. She goes on to help the reader unpack and analyze the contents of that bag.

Some Things to Keep in Mind

As you read through the following article, try to think about how White privilege impacts the lives of both people of color and Whites. Think about the connection between White privilege and racism. How present is White privilege in most people's lives? Reflecting on your own life, think about how racism has touched it. Also, consider the ideas below.

1. What is White privilege?
2. How is your life (regardless of your racial identity) impacted by White privilege?

3. How are some people blind to White privilege?
4. Have you ever experienced someone who exploits their White privilege?
5. What are some of the unseen dimensions of racism in our society?

WHITE PRIVILEGE
UNPACKING THE INVISIBLE KNAPSACK
Peggy McIntosh

Through work to bring materials from Women's Studies into the rest of the curriculum, I have often noticed men's unwillingness to grant that they are over-privileged, even though they may grant that women are disadvantaged. They may say they will work to improve women's status, in the society, the university, or the curriculum, but they can't or won't support the idea of lessening men's. Denials which amount to taboos surround the subject of advantages which men gain from women's disadvantages. These denials protect male privilege from being fully acknowledged, lessened or ended.

Thinking through unacknowledged male privilege as a phenomenon, I realized that, since hierarchies in our society are interlocking, there was most likely a phenomenon of white privilege that was similarly denied and protected. As a white person, I realized I had been taught about racism as something that puts others at a disadvantage, but had been taught not to see one of its corollary aspects, white privilege, which puts me at an advantage.

I think whites are carefully taught not to recognize white privilege, as males are taught not to recognize male privilege. So I have begun in an untutored way to ask what it is like to have white privilege. I have come to see white privilege as an invisible package of unearned assets that I can count on cashing in each day, but about which I was "meant" to remain oblivious. White privilege is like an invisible weightless knapsack of special provisions, maps, passports, codebooks, visas, clothes, tools and blank checks.

Describing white privilege makes one newly accountable. As we in Women's Studies work to reveal male privilege and ask men to give up some of their power, so one who writes about white privilege must ask, "Having described it, what will I do to lessen or end it?"

After I realized the extent to which men work from a base of unacknowledged privilege, I understood that much of their oppressiveness was unconscious. Then I remembered the frequent charges from women of color that white women whom they encounter are oppressive.

Peggy McIntosh, "White Privilege: Unpacking the Invisible Knapsack," *Peace and Freedom Magazine*, pp. 10-12. Copyright © 1988 by Peggy McIntosh. Reprinted with permission.

I began to understand why we are justly seen as oppressive, even when we don't see ourselves that way. I began to count the ways in which I enjoy unearned skin privilege and have been conditioned into oblivion about its existence.

> I was taught to see racism only in individual acts of meanness, not in invisible systems conferring dominance on my group.

My schooling gave me no training in seeing myself as an oppressor, as an unfairly advantaged person, or as a participant in a damaged culture. I was taught to see myself as an individual whose moral state depended on her individual moral will. My schooling followed the pattern my colleague Elizabeth Minnich has pointed out: whites are taught to think of their lives as morally neutral, normative, and average, and also ideal, so that when we work to benefit others, this is seen as work which will allow "them" to be more like "us."

I decided to try to work on myself at least by identifying some of the daily effects of white privilege in my life. I have chosen those conditions which I think in my case *attach somewhat more to skin-color privilege* than to class, religion, ethnic status, or geographic location, though of course all these other factors are intricately intertwined. As far as I can see, my African American coworkers, friends, and acquaintances with whom I come into daily or frequent contact in this particular time, place and line of work cannot count on most of these conditions.

1. I can if I wish arrange to be in the company of people of my race most of the time.
2. If I should need to move, I can be pretty sure of renting or purchasing housing in an area which I can afford and in which I would want to live.
3. I can be pretty sure that my neighbors in such a location will be neutral or pleasant to me.
4. I can go shopping alone most of the time, pretty well assured that I will not be followed or harassed.
5. I can turn on the television or open to the front page of the paper and see people of my race widely represented.
6. When I am told about our national heritage or about "civilization," I am shown that people of my color made it what it is.
7. I can be sure that my children will be given curricular materials that testify to the existence of their race.
8. If I want to, I can be pretty sure of finding a publisher for this piece on white privilege.
9. I can go into a music shop and count on finding the music of my race represented, into a supermarket and find the staple foods that fit with my cultural traditions, into a hairdresser's shop and find someone who can cut my hair.
10. Whether I use checks, credit cards or cash, I can count on my skin color not to work against the appearance of financial reliability.

11. I can arrange to protect my children most of the time from people who might not like them.
12. I can swear, or dress in secondhand clothes, or not answer letters, without having people attribute these choices to the bad morals, the poverty, or the illiteracy of my race.
13. I can speak in public to a powerful male group without putting my race on trial.
14. I can do well in a challenging situation without being called a credit to my race.
15. I am never asked to speak for all the people of my racial group.
16. I can remain oblivious of the language and customs of persons of color who constitute the world's majority without feeling in my culture any penalty for such oblivion.
17. I can criticize our government and talk about how much I fear its policies and behavior without being seen as a cultural outsider.
18. I can be pretty sure that if I ask to talk to "the person in charge," I will be facing a person of my race.
19. If a traffic cop pulls me over or if the IRS audits my tax return, I can be sure I haven't been singled out because of my race.
20. I can easily buy posters, postcards, picture books, greeting cards, dolls, toys, and children's magazines featuring people of my race.
21. I can go home from most meetings of organizations I belong to feeling somewhat tied in, rather than isolated, out-of-place, outnumbered, unheard, held at a distance, or feared.
22. I can take a job with an affirmative action employer without having co-workers on the job suspect that I got it because of race.
23. I can choose public accommodations without fearing that people of my race cannot get in or will be mistreated in the places I have chosen.
24. I can be sure that if I need legal or medical help, my race will not work against me.
25. If my day, week, or year is going badly, I need not ask of each negative episode or situation whether it has racial overtones.
26. I can choose blemish cover or bandages in "flesh" color and have them more or less match my skin.

I repeatedly forgot each of the realizations on this list until I wrote it down. For me, white privilege has turned out to be an elusive and fugitive subject. The pressure to avoid it is great, for in facing it I must give up the myth of meritocracy. If these things are true, this is not such a free country; one's life is not what one makes it; many doors open for certain people through no virtues of their own.

In unpacking this invisible knapsack of white privilege, I have listed conditions of daily experience that I once took for granted. Nor did I think of any of these perquisites as bad for the holder. I now think that we need a more finely differentiated taxonomy of privilege, for some of these varieties are only what one would want for everyone in a just society, and others give license to be ignorant, oblivious, arrogant and destructive.

I see a pattern running through the matrix of white privilege, a pattern of assumptions that were passed on to me as a white person. There was one main piece of cultural turf; it was my own turf, and I was among those who could control the turf. *My skin color was an asset for any move I was educated to want to make.* I could think of myself as belonging in major ways and of making social systems work for me. I could freely disparage, fear, neglect, or be oblivious to anything outside of the dominant cultural forms. Being of the main culture, I could also criticize it fairly freely.

In proportion as my racial group was being made confident, comfortable, and oblivious, other groups were likely being made inconfident, uncomfortable, and alienated. Whiteness protected me from many kinds of hostility, distress and violence, which I was being subtly trained to visit, in turn, upon people of color.

For this reason, the word "privilege" now seems to me misleading. We usually think of privilege as being a favored state, whether earned or conferred by birth or luck. Yet some of the conditions I have described here work systematically to overempower certain groups. Such privilege simply *confers dominance* because of one's race or sex.

I want, then, to distinguish between earned strength and unearned power conferred systemically. Power from unearned privilege can look like strength when it is in fact permission to escape or to dominate. But not all of the privileges on my list are inevitably damaging. Some, like the expectation that neighbors will be decent to you, or that your race will not count against you in court, should be the norm in a just society. Others, like the privilege to ignore less powerful people, distort the humanity of the holders as well as the ignored groups.

We might at least start by distinguishing between positive advantages, which we can work to spread, and negative types of advantage, which unless rejected will always reinforce our present hierarchies. For example, the feeling that one belongs within the human circle, as Native Americans say, should not be seen as privilege for a few. Ideally it is an *unearned entitlement*. At present, since only a few have it, it is an *unearned advantage* for them. This paper results from a process of coming to see that some of the power that I originally saw as attendant on being a human being in the United States consisted in unearned advantage and conferred dominance.

The question is: "Having described white privilege, what will I do to end it?

I have met very few men who are truly distressed about systemic, unearned male advantage and conferred dominance. And so one question for me and others like me is whether we will be like them, or whether we will get truly distressed, even outraged, about unearned race advantage and conferred dominance, and, if so, what will we do to lessen them. In any case, we need to do more work in identifying how they actually affect our daily lives. Many, perhaps most, of our white students in the U.S. think that racism doesn't affect them because they are not people of color, they do not see "whiteness" as a racial identity. In addition, since race and sex are not the only advantaging systems at work, we need similarly to examine the daily experience of having age advantage, or ethnic advantage, or physical ability, or advantage related to nationality, religion, or sexual orientation.

Difficulties and dangers surrounding the task of finding parallels are many. Since racism, sexism, and heterosexism are not the same, the advantages associated with them should not be seen as the same. In addition, it is hard to disentangle aspects of unearned advantage which rest more on social class, economic class, race, religion, sex, and ethnic identity than on other factors. Still, all of the oppressions are interlocking, as the Combahee River Collective Statement of 1977 continues to remind us eloquently.

One factor seems clear about all of the interlocking oppressions. They take both active forms, which we can see, and embedded forms, which as a member of the dominant group one is taught not to see. In my class and place, I did not see myself as a racist because I was taught to recognize racism only in individual acts of meanness by members of my group, never in invisible systems conferring unsought racial dominance on my group from birth.

Disapproving of the systems won't be enough to change them. I was taught to think that racism could end if white individuals changed their attitudes. But a "white" skin in the United States opens many doors for whites whether or not we approve of the way dominance has been conferred on us. Individual acts can palliate, but cannot end, these problems.

To redesign social systems, we need first to acknowledge their colossal unseen dimensions. The silences and denials surrounding privilege are the key political tool here. They keep the thinking about equality or equity incomplete, protecting unearned advantage and conferred dominance by making these taboo subjects. Most talk by whites about equal opportunity seems to me now to be about equal opportunity to try to get into a position of dominance while denying that *systems* of dominance exist.

It seems to me that obliviousness about white advantage, like obliviousness about male advantage, is kept strongly inculturated in the United States so as to maintain the myth of meritocracy, the myth that democratic choice is equally available to all. Keeping most people unaware that freedom of confident action is there for just a small number of people props up those in power and serves to keep power in the hands of the same groups that have most of it already.

Although systemic change takes many decades, there are pressing questions for me and I imagine for some others like me if we raise our daily consciousness on the perquisites of being light-skinned. What will we do with such knowledge? As we know from watching men, it is an open question whether we will choose to use unearned advantage to weaken hidden systems of advantage, and whether we will use any of our arbitrarily awarded power to try to reconstruct power systems on a broader base.

CHAPTER 9

GENDER

Gender Inequality

In this final selection, Denise D. Bielby examines gender inequality in a specific occupation sector—the culture industries. This collection of film, television, music, and video game industries are commonly referred to as the "entertainment industry." The author gives us a historical overview of women in the culture industries in an attempt to remind us that while women have been involved in these industries from their beginnings, women remain a minority of the workers and celebrities. These industries, she argues, are microcosmic representations of society at large. On average, women are paid less than men in comparable positions and are systematically excluded from certain jobs.

Some Things to Keep in Mind

Most likely all of us have either been the victim of sexism, been a witness to it, or perhaps perpetrated sexism. So, as you read this article, reflect on your own life, and think about how sexism has touched it. Also, consider the ideas below.

1. Why are women underrepresented in many key positions in this industry?
2. What are some of the structural factors that contribute to gender inequality?

3. Why does gender inequality persist in these industries?
4. What conclusions does the author draw about the state of gender inequality in the culture industries?

GENDER INEQUALITY IN CULTURE INDUSTRIES

Denise D. Bielby

Gender inequality—the unequal distribution of pay between men and women or level of women's labor force participation relative to men's—can be found across occupations and professions in industrialized countries around the globe (Charles and Grusky 2004). Although the gender gap in pay and employment and in other job-related opportunities, resources, and rewards has lessened somewhat over time for the labor force as a whole, considerable gender inequality remains at the highest levels of management in paid labor (Blau et al. 2006).[1] Sex segregation, which is the concentration of men and women in different kinds of work because of the division of labor in which the delegation of tasks is determined by workers' sex, is the causal mechanism that underlies differences in women's and men's employment and pay. Sex segregation occurs because of societal beliefs about the appropriateness of activities for one sex or the other.[2] Jobs become gendered—perceived as more suitable for one sex than another—through employers' conscious and unconscious beliefs (i.e. sex stereotypes) about the characteristics that various jobs require and about what tasks women and men are capable of doing. These beliefs, in turn, affect how work is organized and workers produce (Padavic and Reskin 2002). Although the gender ideology that underlies occupational sex segregation is deeply entrenched within societies, the sex segregation it creates can change over time within occupations and industries and vary cross-nationally (Blau et al. 2006). Reskin and Roos' (1990) seminal research on the link between sex segregation and gender inequality was based upon the study of work throughout the American occupational structure as a whole, but less is known about the distinctive mechanisms at play within culture industries.

Denise D. Bielby, "Gender Inequality in Culture Industries," *The Routledge Companion to Media & Gender*, ed. Cynthia Carter, Linda Steiner and Lisa McLaughlin, pp. 137-146. Copyright © 2015 by Taylor & Francis Group. Reprinted with permission.

The Distinctiveness of Creative Industries

While gender inequality appears throughout the paid labor force, the cause of the unequal distribution of employment and earnings between men and women in the culture industries of film, television, and music, among others such as video games, is particularly complex because of the way in which creative industries and their markets are organized. Creative industries supply goods and services that we associate with cultural, artistic, or entertainment value; their products consist of symbolic forms that connote, suggest, or imply expressive elements that may be appropriated for creation of social meanings. Cultural economist Richard Caves (2000) defines creative industries (which also include book and magazine publishing, the visual arts, the performing arts, fashion, and toys) as possessing these economic properties: (1) demand for their products is very uncertain because it is driven by fads and fashions in popular taste; (2) their creative workers invest deeply in product originality but are unable to explain their aesthetic choices a priori, which problematizes workers' appropriate level of compensation; (3) production usually requires collaborative teams of creative workers that possess diverse and specialized skills and personal tastes, which makes organization of their labor through formal contracts infeasible; (4) no two creative products are identical, which results in an infinite variety of products from which consumers may choose; (5) cultural products vary in quality, which further increases uncertainty about product choice and the valuation of creative workers' contributions; (6) because of uncertainty about consumer tastes, the economic profitability of a cultural product depends on its timely completion; and (7) the ephemerality/durability of a cultural product affects what consumers will pay for it. How do these properties of creative industries translate into institutional dynamics that create gender inequality?

First, culture industries exist in environments with career systems and networks of worker relationships that form "cultures of production" (DuGay 1997) that include gender. Coordination of the different skill sets of industry workers—creative personnel as varied as actors, musicians, and directors, craft and technical workers such as sound engineers, camera operators, and film editors, creative managers such as television producers, and administrators, executives, and unskilled labor—necessitates shared understandings of artistic conventions (Becker 1982) that are informed by how the finished product ought to comport with culturally normative expectations, including gender. Second, the oversight of artistic origination, creation, and production is difficult to regulate bureaucratically because it relies upon intangible expertise, where the quality of the work cannot be unambiguously evaluated based on technical and measurable features of the finished product (see Stinchcombe 1959, on craft administration). Instead, the quality of the work and the competence of its creator, including the gendered competence of its creator, are evaluated post hoc based on the acceptance and success of the work within the marketplace. This arrangement significantly complicates the implementation of the rational bureaucratic organizational form and its control over the creative process and labor of its employees. Third, in the competitive environment of culture industries, "careers tend to be chaotic and foster cultural innovation, and career-building and market-sensing entrepreneurs enact careers from the bottom up by starting from the margins of existing professions and conventions" (Peterson and Anand 2004: 317). Thus, career paths are highly variable and can be influenced by normative expectations about gender. Fourth, the properties of a field's cultural product determine how that field's labor is organized; as Peterson and Anand (2004: 317) explain, "such structuring produces the need for specialized gatekeepers (Hirsch 1991 [1972]) such as talent agents (Bielby and Bielby 1999), who selectively favor a subset of producers over others, thereby magnifying distortions in age, gender, and other demographic characteristics (Tuchman 1989; Bielby and Bielby 1996)." Fifth, and finally, while most creative workers are legally employees of large organizations, their employment is similar to that of outside contractors hired for short-term projects (Christopherson 1996). As a result, the organizational structures and policies that create barriers to career advancement tend to remain invisible to the employees themselves, and the lines of authority for hiring and pay decisions are often blurred. For example, the producer who approves a project is likely to be reporting directly or indirectly to executives within his or her organization who are likely to demand input into the employee's hiring and compensation. Given these multiple authorities, it is not clear who would be responsible for monitoring gender inequality or implementing a policy to minimize it.[3]

Creative Industries and Gender Inequality: Film and Television

Although Hollywood has dominated domestic and global production of media images for a century, its success as an industry could hardly have been predicted from its disorganized beginnings. In the early decades of filmmaking, the industry lacked prestige, the lines dividing production roles were fluid, and the field was "empty." As a result, women who found work within it were able to move across its tasks of scenarist, editor, director, and producer with relative ease. Even though the industry began as a loose and rather chaotic collection of motion picture shooting activities, it quickly evolved between 1915 and 1930 into Hollywood's classic organizational form of the vertically integrated studio system—"a dense interlocking system of production companies, anchored in geographic space by its own virtuous circle of endogenous growth" (Scott 2005: 11). In the late 1940s, when the studios were dismantled as a result of the Supreme Court ruling against the studios' anti-competitive practices (Stanley 1978), the industry transformed once again and organized into production companies that oversaw short-term projects staffed by vast interconnecting networks of specialized personnel. By the 1980s, talent agencies emerged as powerful deal-makers, production companies came under corporate ownership and control, and distribution became crucial to profitability.

Despite women's visible presence in the early years of the industry, they were all but pushed out by the late 1920s when the studio system emerged and film production became bureaucratized. Women's representation behind the camera has been more or less flat ever since. Statistics from 2010 reveal women accounted for just 7 percent of directors, 10 percent of writers, 15 percent of executive producers, 24 percent of producers, 18 percent of editors, and 2 percent of cinematographers, or just 16 percent of important behind-the-scenes workers in film (Lauzen 2011). Their presence as creators, executive producers, producers, writers, directors, editors, and directors of photography in the television sector, which emerged in the 1950s, is not much better at 25 percent. Among directors of episodic television women are a mere 12 percent (Yi and Dearfield 2012).

Efforts to monitor gender representation in film and television can be viewed as the legacy of Gaye Tuchman's (1978) foundational essay on the symbolic annihilation of women by the mass media. Although Tuchman's analysis focused on the *visual images* used by mass media to depict women, it was highly influential in triggering scholarly interest in the *production* of images, especially for identifying *who* determines the images that appear onscreen and *how* decisions are made about what to depict. Of considerable interest in early research on gender inequality in onscreen representation was how the gender identity of lead characters was constructed narratively. Of primary concern was the extent to which characters were conventional representations and to what extent they transcended gender roles (Signorielli 1989; Fejes and Petrich 1993). Classic writings such as Mulvey's (1975) analysis of the relevance of the male gaze, developed in her essay "Visual Pleasure and Narrative Cinema," were instrumental to explaining how the dominant male gaze constructed gender onscreen; eventually this work shaped important analyses of television characterizations more broadly (Modleski 1982; D'Acci 1987). A subsequent focus by feminist media scholars on emotional authenticity in women's narratives and its relevance to women's lived experience led to important work on audience reception and fan practices (Ang 1985; Brown 1990; Harrington and Bielby 1995; Kuhn 1984; Stacey 1994). Ultimately, though, the importance of the focus on the who and the how behind the scenes launched scholarly interest in the cultural assumptions of industry decision-makers at work. Ethnographic studies that demonstrate how representativeness is constructed through the interpretative frames of reference deployed by producers and other key behind-the-scene decision-makers have been especially valuable (see, for example, Grindstaff 2002), although access to production sites can be difficult to achieve (Levine 2001).

Writers

Writers are crucial to film and television because without a script there is no product. Many of the most successful screenwriters of the silent film era were women—estimated at between 50 and 90 percent (Francke 1994; Martin and Clark 1987; McCreadie 1994; Mahar 2006). It is generally agreed that women screenwriters played a major role in establishing the narrative conventions of the film script. The process whereby screenwriting was transformed from a profession with substantial opportunities for women to one that became male dominated appears similar to that described by Tuchman in her account of the masculinization of authorship of the Victorian novel (Tuchman 1989). Like the occupation of novelist, screenwriting began as an "empty field" of low prestige. However, once film became more lucrative and men invaded the field, US filmmaking became industrialized, production became centralized and bureaucratized, and the skill requirements changed, pushing women out. By the late 1930s, membership statistics from the Writers Guild of America, West (Bielby and Bielby 1996) show that women accounted for less than 15 percent of those working as screenwriters. Of those employed, women were likely to be assigned to administrative or support roles such as reader or script supervisor (Francke 1994). In short, in a relatively brief period of time, women writers had become typecast by studio heads who applied sex role stereotypes about what jobs women writers were suited for and assigned them to scripting "women's films," writing dialog for female stars, and infusing the "woman's angle" into films (Francke 1994).

The decline of the studio system and the shift toward independent production in the 1950s, which theoretically should have created new opportunities for marginalized groups, had little positive impact on womens representation among screenwriters. Statistics from the Writers Guild of America, West (WGAW) reveal that in the 1950s and 1960s, which corresponds to the period when the studios were being dismantled and shifting to independent production, women constituted only about 12–13 percent of screenwriters; this persisted through the 1970s, the era of the women's movement (Bielby and Bielby 1996). When public calls for more enlightened images of women were raised during this period, women's groups within the WGA organized to advance their interests. Although these developments encouraged talented women writers to pursue careers in the industry, the early 1970s also marked the beginning of the blockbuster era, which greatly increased the financial risk involved in pursing projects with huge box office sales and ushered in a decline in the willingness of production heads to take chances. Over time, the blockbuster mentality of film production encouraged producers to seek out already established (i.e. men) directors, writers, and actors with track records of consistent success and to forgo serious consideration of unproven (i.e. women) writers.

Statistics computed from employment and earnings records of screenwriters show that these industry dynamics were highly consequential to cementing gender inequality for women writers in film. By the mid-1990s, the salaries of a small group of elite screenwriters were bid up to levels far in excess of the median earnings of women and men (Bielby and Bielby 1996: Figure 4), a pattern that persists to this day and contributes to the intractability of gender inequality in the industry. Statistical analyses over the past two decades of the earnings and employment of the vast majority of women screenwriters reveal that access to opportunity early in the career pays off more for men, causing women to experience *cumulative disadvantage* over time (Bielby and Bielby 1996).

Television was launched in the United States in the late 1940s, and by the mid-1950s the three major networks were established, dominated access to television production, and monopolized broadcast distribution. Early television programming consisted of live productions that were owned by commercial sponsors and produced at independent studios, but by a decade later ownership and control over production shifted to the networks and programming consolidated into genres (and scheduling) targeted to audience demographics (Meehan 2002). The television industry has always been dominated by men in key decision-making roles such as program procurement and financing, which is a pivotal factor in the persistence of gender inequality in this sector of the entertainment industry. The percentage of women in influential decision-making roles in the 2010–11 television season stood at 25 percent (Yi and Dearfield 2012). A report from 2007 indicates they filled less than 15 percent of the industry's high status executive producer positions (Writers Guild of America, West 2007: Figure 1). A second aspect of the television industry that places women at a disadvantage relative to men is the typecasting of writers by genre. Employment of women who defy convention by seeking to write "against type" is viewed as financially unsound by risk-averse industry executives. Executives' reliance on gender stereotypes to assess the creative capabilities of writers encapsulates writers, tying them to styles of writing that are susceptible to the cycles of popular taste that drive this industry. The combination of relative devaluation at career entry and typecasting makes women writers susceptible to continuous disadvantage (Bielby and Bielby 1992).

Actors

Scholars voiced concern early on about the unrealistic standards of beauty of the actresses who portray lead characters and whether the industry undermines potentially transcendent narratives about gender through the stereotypes created by its limited casting choices (see Dyer's 1979 classic essay on the role of stereotypes). The industry's overemphasis on conventional beauty (Levy 1990) came to be regarded as even more troubling when chronological age was shown to interact definitively with gender to yield vastly different career outcomes for actresses and actors (Bazzini et al. 1997). According to a Screen Actors Guild report, in 1999 men over 40 years of age received 37 percent of all male roles in film and television, while women over 40 received only 24 percent of all female roles in the two mediums combined. A statistical analysis (Lincoln and Allen 2004) of the career trajectory of leading film actors and actresses in Hollywood over a 70-year period found that while roles drop for both men and women over the course of their careers, the decline is much more precipitous for female stars than it is for male stars. Lincoln and Allen also analyzed gender differences in star presence, a statistical measure they created to assess the cumulative importance of an actor through the rank of an actor's billings in the credits over several films (the larger the presence, the bigger the star). Like the decline in the number of roles for women, Lincoln and Allen found that as actresses grew older their star presence declined precipitously; in short, although growing older negatively affects the careers of both men and women, age affects the careers of actresses far more greatly. Given aging's clearly gendered impact on women's careers,

Allen and Lincoln concluded that women face a double jeopardy in sustaining acting careers relative to men.

Writers and actors are just two of many occupations within creative industries that experience entrenched gender inequality. The music industry is well known for its gendered specialties; see, for example, Clawson's (1999) study of the overrepresentation of female electric bassists in alternative rock music. Other research (Schmutz and Faupel 2010) reveals that cultural assumptions about the "natural" intersection of gender and art shape the likelihood of a musician ever being recognized as an "all-time great," leaving female artists at a relative disadvantage in attaining such standing. The production of video games is another industry in which gender affects access to employment (Pham 2008; McKay and McKay 2010). Here, the not surprising nexus of men and technology has emerged much as it did in the computer industry, defining the work culture of video game production as male dominated for those considering entering the field (Stross 2008).

Conclusion

Given reliable evidence, observing gender inequality in culture industries can be relatively straightforward, but understanding the structural factors that account for inequality or the reasons why it is so entrenched and remains so persistent is more complicated. This is so for a couple of reasons. First, as sites that produce representations of gender, creative industries rely upon cultural idioms that embody cultural assumptions about gender. Not only do these givens shape the look of a finished product (see Mears' 2011 research on modeling and the fashion industry, for example), they are embedded in the labor of cultural production itself that creates the industry's culture(s) of production (DuGay 1997; see also Caldwell 2008; Peterson and Anand 2004). Cultures of production include shared beliefs among workers about gender enactment on the job (Ridgeway and Correll 2004), which, in turn, affects access to employment, earnings, and opportunities for advancement. Once in place, these systems are powerfully self-perpetuating. Second, the distinctive features of organizational practices in cultural industries sustain gender inequality. Sociologists have observed that making work assignments in an arbitrary and subjective manner, especially where accountability for equal employment opportunity is absent, allows stereotypes to influence personnel decisions. In the corporate world this happens when managers have unfettered discretion concerning whom to hire or promote, permitting them to make personal judgments about who best fits the job. More often than not, the "best" hire matches the gender, race, and age of those already doing the job. In such circumstances interpersonal ties can determine access to advancement.

Other research provides additional insight into how structural factors account for gender inequality in culture industries. Temporary organizations such as film projects, television series, concert tours, and the like are assumed to be ephemeral and unstable. However, organization scholars show that they are sustained in part by the informal social practices workers carry from one short-term project to the next, practices that contribute to organizational stability (Bechky 2006). This research suggests the importance of understanding how a contingent labor force informally manages the "revolving door" of temporary employment through reputation, and the role of gender in this process. Other research that analyzes actors' careers as social networks of professional experiences identifies the payoff that comes from the reputational accomplishments stemming from these opportunities and how those, in turn, contribute to cumulative advantage in project-based labor markets (Rossman et al. 2010). A network analysis that specifically took gender into account (Lincoln and Allen 2011) not only confirms the importance of studying network patterns of professional experience, it also reveals how career accomplishments can be differentially shaped by national context. This research points to the importance of cross-national comparisons in order to achieve a fuller understanding of the factors that account for gender inequality within culture industries in an increasingly globalized economy.

Notes

1. Gender inequality also persists in the division of unpaid labor.
2. More specifically, sex stereotypes (the socially shared beliefs that link various traits, attributes, and skills of one sex or the other), along with sex labeling of jobs (stereotypes about the characteristics that various jobs require) lead jobs to be labeled as either men's or women's work (Padavic and Reskin 2002: 42–4).
3. Hesmondhalgh (2007) takes some of these considerations a step further, arguing that culture industries have distinctive problems of production that include a high degree of risk and uncertainty in product success, an emphasis on creativity over commerce, high production costs and low reproduction costs, products that are semi-public goods, and the need to create scarcity. Typical organizational solutions include an overabundance of production to offset misses against hits, a reliance on publicity, the creation of artificial scarcity, formatting production through stars, genres, and serials, loose control of symbol creators, and tight control of distribution and marketing.

References

Ang, I. (1985) *Watching Dallas: Soap Opera and the Melodramatic Imagination*, London: Methuen.

Bazzini, D. G., W. D. McIntosh, S. M. Smith, S. Cook, and C. Harris (1997) "The Aging Woman in Popular Film: Underrepresented, Unattractive, Unfriendly, and Unintelligent," *Sex Roles* 36: 531–43.

Bechky, B. (2006) "Gaffers, Gofers, and Grips: Role-Based Coordination in Temporary Organizations," *Organization Science* 17(3): 3–21.
Becker, H. (1982) *Art Worlds*, Berkeley, CA: University of California Press.
Bielby, D. and W. Bielby (1996) "Women and Men in Film: Gender Inequality among Writers in a Culture Industry," *Gender & Society* 10: 248–70.
Bielby, W. and D. Bielby (1992) "Cumulative versus Continuous Disadvantage in an Unstructured Labor Market," *Work and Occupations* 19: 366–489.
——(1999) "Organizational Mediation of Project-based Labor Markets: Talent Agencies and the Careers of Screenwriters," *American Sociological Review* 64(1): 64–85.
Blau, F., M. Brinton, and D. Grusky (2006) *The Declining Significance of Gender?*, New York: Russell Sage Foundation.
Brown, M. E. (1990) *Television and Women's Culture: The Politics of the Popular*, London: Sage.
Caldwell, J. (2008) *Production Culture: Industrial Reflexivity and Critical Practice in Film and Television*, Durham, NC: Duke University Press.
Caves, R. (2000) *Creative Industries: Contracts Between Art and Commerce*, Cambridge, MA: Harvard University Press.
Charles, M. and D. Grusky (2004) *Occupational Ghettos*, Stanford, CA: Stanford University Press.
Christopherson, S. (1996) "Flexibility and Adaptation in Industrial Relations: The Exceptional Case of the U.S. Media Entertainment Industries," in L. S. Gray and R. L. Seeber (eds.) *Under the Stars: Essays on Labor Relations in Arts and Entertainment*, New York: ILR Press, pp. 86–112.
Clawson, M. A. (1999) "When Women Play the Bass," *Gender & Society* 13(2): 193–210.
D'Acci, J. (1987) "The Case of Cagney and Lacey," in H. Baehr and G. Dyer (eds.) *Boxed In: Women and Television*, London: Pandora, pp. 203–26.
DuGay, P. (1997) Production of Culture: Cultures of Production, London: Sage.
Dyer, R. (1979) "The Role of Stereotypes," in Jim Cook and Mike Lewington (eds.) Images of Alcoholism, London: British Film Institute, pp. 15–21.
Fejes, F. and K. Petrich (1993) "Invisibility, Homophobia and Heterosexism: Lesbians, Gays, and the Media," *Critical Studies in Mass Communication* 20: 396–422.
Francke, L. (1994) *Script Girls: Women Screenwriters in Hollywood*, Bloomington: Indiana University Press.
Grindstaff, L. (2002) *The Money Shot: Trash, Class, and the Making of TV Talk Shows*, Chicago: University of Chicago Press.
Harrington, C. L. and D. D. Bielby (1995) *Soap Fans: Pursuing Pleasure and Making Meaning in Everyday Life*, Philadelphia, PA: Temple University Press.
Hesmondhalgh, D. (2007) *The Cultural Industries*, 2nd edition, London: Sage Publications.
Hirsch, P. (1991 [1972]) "Processing Fads and Fashions: An Organization-Set Analysis of Cultural Industry Systems," in C. Mukerji and M. Schudson (eds.) *Rethinking Popular Culture*, Berkeley: University of California Press, pp. 313–34.

Kuhn, A. (1984) "Women's Genres: Melodrama, Soap Opera, and Theory," *Screen* 25(1): 18–28.

Lauzen, M. (2011) "Getting Real About Reel Employment. Women's Media Center Report." http://www.womensmediacenter.com/feature/entry/getting-real-about-reel-employment.

Levine, E. (2001) "Toward a Paradigm for Media Production Research: Behind the Scenes at *General Hospital*," *Critical Studies in Media Communication* 18: 66–82.

Levy, E. (1990) "Social Attributes of American Movie Stars," *Media, Culture & Society* 12: 247–67.

Lincoln, A. and M. Allen (2004) "Double Jeopardy in Hollywood: Gender and Age Effects on the Careers of Film Actors, 1926–99," *Sociological Forum* 19: 611–31.

———(2011) "Oscar et César: Deep Consecration in French and American Film Acting Careers," in C. Mathieu (ed.) *Careers in Creative Industries*, New York: Routledge, pp. 107–37.

Mahar, K. (2006) *Regendering the Movies*, Baltimore, MD: Johns Hopkins University Press.

Martin, A. and V. Clark (1987) "What Women Wrote: Scenarios, 1912–1929," *Cinema History Microfilm Series*, Frederick, MD: University Publications of America.

McCreadie, M. (1994) *Women Who Write the Movies*, New York: Birch Lane Press.

McKay, B. and K. McKay (2010) "So You Want My Job: Video Game Producer." http://artofmanliness.com/2010/09/29/so-you-want-my-job-video-game-producer/.

Mears, A. (2011) *Pricing Beauty: The Making of a Fashion Model*, Berkeley: University of California Press.

Meehan, E. R. (2002) "Gendering the Commodity Audience: Critical Media Research, Feminism, and Political Economy," in E. R. Meehan and E. Riordan (eds.), *Sex and Money: Feminism and Political Economy in the Media*, Minneapolis: University of Minnesota Press, pp. 209–22.

Modleski, T. (1982) *Loving with a Vengeance: Mass Produced Fantasies for Women*, London: Methuen.

Mulvey, L. (1975) "Visual Pleasure and Narrative Cinema," *Screen* 16(3): 6–18.

Padavic, I. and B. Reskin (2002) *Women and Men at Work*, 2nd edition, Thousand Oaks, CA: Pine Forge Press.

Peterson, R. and N. Anand (2004) "The Production of Culture Perspective," *Annual Review of Sociology* 30: 311–34.

Pham, A. (2008) "Women Left on Sidelines of Video Game Revolution," *Los Angeles Times*, October 21: C1–C9.

Reskin, B. and P. Roos (1990) *Job Queues, Gender Queues*, Philadelphia, PA: Temple University Press.

Ridgeway, C. and S. Correll (2004) "Unpacking the Gender System: A Theoretical Perspective on Gender Beliefs and Social Relations," *Gender & Society* 18(4): 510–31.

Rossman, G., N. Esparza, and P. Bonacich (2010) "I'd Like to Thank the Academy, Team Spillovers, and Network Centrality," *American Sociological Review* 75(1): 31–51.

Schmutz, V. and A. Faupel (2010) "Gender and Cultural Consecration in Popular Music," *Social Forces* 89(2): 685–707.

Scott, A. J. (2005) On *Hollywood*, Princeton, NJ: Princeton University Press.

Screen Actors Guild (1999) "Screen Actors Guild Casting Data Find Ageism Still a Critical Issue for American Performers," Press Release, April 21, 1999. http://www.asc.upenn.edu/gerbner/Asset.aspx?assetID=464.

Signorielli, N. (1989) "Television and Conceptions about Sex Roles: Maintaining Conventionality and the Status Quo," *Sex Roles* 21: 337–56.

Stacey, J. (1994) *Star Gazing: Hollywood Cinema and Female Spectatorship*, London: Routledge.

Stanley, R. (1978) *The Celluloid Empire*, New York: Hastings House.

Stinchcombe, A. (1959) "Bureaucratic and Craft Administration of Production," *Administrative Science Quarterly* 4: 168–87.

Stross, R. (2008) "What Has Driven Women Out of Computer Science?," *New York Times*, November 15. http://www.nytimes.com/2008/11/16/business/16digi.html.

Tuchman, G. (1978) "Introduction: The Symbolic Annihilation of Women," in G. Tuchman, A. Kaplan Daniels, and J. Benet (eds.) *Hearth and Home: Images of Women in the Mass Media*, New York: Oxford University Press, pp. 3–38.

———(1989) *Edging Women Out: Victorian Novelists, Publishers, and Social Change*, New Haven, CT: Yale University Press.

Writers Guild of America, West (2007) *The 2007 Hollywood Writers Report: Whose Stories Are We Telling?*, Los Angeles, CA: Writers Guild of America West.

———(2011) "Recession and Regression: The 2011 Hollywood Writers Report." http://www.wga.org/uploadedFiles/who_we_are/hwr11execsum.pdf.

Yi, R. and C. Dearfield (2012) "The Status of Women in the U.S. Media, 2012," Women's Media Center. www.womensmediacenter.com.

Section 6 Discussion Questions

1. Think about any family or friends that you know have experienced social mobility in their lifetime. What factors were most powerful in helping them move up the social ladder?
2. Discuss why you are in college. Is it connected to achieving the American dream and social mobility?
3. Who do you think lives longer on average: poor people or those in the upper middle class? Why?
4. Do you think White privilege exists, or is it a reaction to racism? Why or why not?
5. Think about ways in which you experience racism. You don't just have to be the target of it to experience it.
6. Discuss ways in which racism is expressed through laws, media, politics, and economics. Which ones are "unseen," and which ones are obvious? Which ones are more dangerous?
7. Create a list of "privileges" that would be associated with being male.
8. What mechanisms are used to maintain the gender inequality in the culture industries. Are they the same things that are used in other job sectors? Or are they different?
9. Do you think the #metoo movement has had an impact on gender inequality in these industries? If so, how?
10. The video gaming industry tends to be male dominated and commonly associated with gender inequality, from developers to gamers. Why do you think this is? Some researchers have compared the gaming industry culture to that of the male-dominated Silicon Valley coding culture. Do you think this is an accurate comparison? Why or why not?

Section 6 Exercises

1. With what social class do you identify? Think about how your social class will influence your future, specifically, how your social class can affect these two things: life expectancy and the types of disease/injury you may develop. Think about this example when discussing what sociological variables that are linked to social class influence your health and life expectancy.
2. Using the link below, view the video on social mobility and Legos. After viewing the video, list and describe at least three variables that influence social mobility in the United States. Why (sociologically) do you think these variables are so powerful in impacting social mobility? If you were a social engineer with unlimited power, what would you do

to reduce wealth inequality and increase social mobility vis-à-vis the variables described in this video?

https://www.youtube.com/watch?reload=9&v=t2XFh_tD2RA

3. Watch the video *I Am NOT Black, You Are NOT White* using the link below. Then, answer the following questions:

How does this video highlight the idea that race is a "social construction"? What is racism (your idea of racism, not a definition)? How does this video characterize racism? Do you think this video is advocating for a "colorblind" world, or is it attempting to articulate something else?

https://www.youtube.com/watch?v=q0qD2K2RWkc

4. In this exercise, you will use a research method called *content analysis*. Content analysis requires you to analyze the content of various media such as poems, TV shows, or radio shows. It is not simply watching shows and relaying your opinion of them or some overall evaluation. Content analysis requires you to analyze specific content of the target medium. For example, if someone did a content analysis study of violent behavior in TV cartoon shows, researchers would watch cartoon shows and watch for and record all the violent acts in each show. They would tally the number of acts in each show and determine whether there were overwhelming numbers of violent acts in those particular cartoons.

For this project, you need to watch at least five network TV sitcom shows or any shows that have as their focal situation the interaction between men and women (such as shows about married couples, families, or men and women in the workplace). You should watch five episodes of the same show. You may watch shows from Hulu, Netflix, cable television, prerecorded media (DVDs), or any other source of televised programming. The CONTENT that you will ANALYZE are negative and positive statements by one sex about the other sex.

So, for each show you watch, I want you to record four categories of comments: (1) all the negative things men say about a female character or women in general (for example, "Sally, you are so emotional. Are you PMS-ing?," or "Women are too emotional to be effective leaders."); (2) all the negative things women say about a male character or men in general (for example, "Mike, you are such a pig!," or "Men are such pigs."); (3) all the positive comments men make about a female character or women in general (for example, "Mary is a great parent." or "Women are the future of our society."); and (4) all the positive comments women make about a male character or men in general (for example, "Colin is a great dad." or "Men these days are much more involved as parents.").

After you finish watching all five shows and totaling up all the comments in each category, I want you to present three sections in your final report. Below I have outlined the three elements that should be included in your discussion to be complete.

Section 1 (description): A complete list of the five shows that you used for this content analysis project. You need to include the show's title, network on which you viewed it, and length of show (half-hour, hour, etc.). Also, include a brief description of the show's premise.

Section 2 (results/analysis): List each show and the negative/positive comment category totals. That is, for each show you watched, show me the total number of categories 1, 2, 3, and 4 comments. For each of the five shows you viewed, make sure to tell me which category was highest and which was lowest. Basically, I want you to tally the comments in each of the four categories and show which category had the greatest number of comments and which had the least.

Section 3 (conclusions): In this final section, I want you to use your comment category numbers to draw conclusions about the shows you watched. What did you notice while watching these shows and focusing on these types of comments? Why do you think writers use these comments? Do they use popular gender stereotypes to get laughs? Do they play on social biases to get laughs or set up situations? What other reasons do you think the shows use these sex-typed comments?

SOCIAL INSTITUTIONS
THE INVISIBLE HANDS OF SOCIAL STRUCTURE

All societies have structure or a shape—they *look* a certain way. American society doesn't look like Japanese society, which doesn't look like Egyptian society. If you had to describe *how* America looks different from Japan, you would most likely start with physical differences; for example, they drive on the left-hand side of the road, there are beer vending machines on street corners, and so on. You might then move onto social behaviors, such as the bow versus the handshake, differences in the amount of expected personal space, diet, and dress. You may acknowledge that collectivism is strongly encouraged in Japanese society, whereas in the United States, we stress individualism. Finally, you may go on to describe differences in other values, beliefs, customs, rituals, and so on. Whatever you may use to describe the differences in everyday life in America and Japan, they are all reflections of differences in **social institutions**—mechanisms and systems within society that pattern daily lives that are focused on meeting social needs.

The term *social institution* may seem daunting and a bit abstract at first glance. All societies have certain requirements that are necessary for survival. To meet these needs, societies develop major social institutions. For our discussion in this section, we will consider five such institutions: family, education, religion, economy, and government.

The truth is, our lives are influenced in fundamental ways by social institutions: they shape the way we see the world and how we interact with each other on a daily basis. Each day as we head out to work or school, we travel on roads that we expect to be maintained, which reflects our reliance on our government. When we purchase a new pair of shoes, buy groceries, or collect our paychecks, we engage with the economy. Just considering the amount of time each day and the number of years most of us spend in school and college shows how important education is in shaping lives and influencing society. Our families shape us into who we are and help us navigate our complex social worlds. And for many, religion is an important part in finding comfort and answering questions about their very existence. The characteristics of a society's institutions direct much of the interactions of everyday life, the side of the road we drive on, how we greet each other, the clothes we wear, what we eat, the families we form, and how we worship—and they ultimately shape what our society *looks* like.

To begin this section, I have selected a chapter from Stephanie Coontz's book *The Way We Never Were,* in which she challenges our commonly held ideas by describing how American family life in the past was quite unlike our romanticized images. Phil Zuckerman then asserts that religion, like nearly everything else in our lives, is learned from those around us and our limited social worlds. Then, John F. Covaleskie argues that solving inequality through education is a myth and ultimately harms society. Focusing on hipsters, Elizabeth Nolan Brown posits a new corporate form developed by hipsters who want to combine hippie ethics, with the next, new thing in order to get crazy rich. Finally, Ann Friedman challenges political correctness by putting the salient notion of identity politics right in our faces by asking "Aren't all politics identity politics?"

CHAPTER 10

THE BONDS THAT BIND

MARRIAGES AND FAMILIES

The Family and Change

In this reading, the author, Stephanie Coontz, argues that our romanticized ideas about the "traditional" family are far from the truth of the matter. In her brief historical overview of the family, she shows that we tend to project our modern ideas of family onto the family forms of previous time periods and bemoan the loss of "real" family ties. In fact, families of the past reflected, like modern families do, their adaptation to changing social, economic, and political environments. Our ideas of families throughout history are distorted—we have created a way we *wish* we were as families. Finally, she argues that we use those distorted, romanticized views of past families to lament the passing of a better time, leading us to believe that the modern family is in "crisis." Consider the following questions while reading this paper.

Some Things to Keep in Mind

1. What does the author mean by the "family crisis"?
2. Do you think the American family is in crisis?
3. Why is there no "traditional" family?
4. What major trends in families does the author identify?

5. Why are we seeing these trends?
6. Think about the family or families you grew up in and the changes in the family the author describes. Can you see your family in the writing?

THE WAY WE WISH WE WERE

DEFINING THE FAMILY CRISIS
Stephanie Coontz

When I begin teaching a course on family history, I often ask my students to write down ideas that spring to mind when they think of the "traditional family." Their lists always include several images. One is of extended families in which all members worked together, grandparents were an integral part of family life, children learned responsibility and the work ethic from their elders, and there were clear lines of authority based on respect for age. Another is of nuclear families in which nurturing mothers sheltered children from premature exposure to sex, financial worries, or other adult concerns, while fathers taught adolescents not to sacrifice their education by going to work too early. Still another image gives pride of place to the couple relationship. In traditional families, my students write—half derisively, half wistfully—men and women remained chaste until marriage, at which time they extricated themselves from competing obligations to kin and neighbors and committed themselves wholly to the marital relationship, experiencing an all-encompassing intimacy that our more crowded modern life seems to preclude. As one freshman wrote, "They truly respected the marriage vowels"; I assume she meant *I-O-U*.

Such visions of past family life exert a powerful emotional pull on most Americans, and with good reason, given the fragility of many modern commitments. The problem is not only that these visions bear a suspicious resemblance to reruns of old television series, but also that the scripts of different shows have been mixed up: June Cleaver suddenly has a Grandpa Walton dispensing advice in her kitchen; Donna Stone, vacuuming the living room in her inevitable pearls and high heels, is no longer married to a busy modern pediatrician but to a small-town sheriff who, like Andy Taylor of *The Andy Griffith Show*, solves community problems through informal, old-fashioned common sense.

Like most visions of a "golden age," the "traditional family" my students describe evaporates on closer examination. It is an ahistorical amalgam of structures, values, and behaviors that never coexisted in the same time and place. The notion that traditional families fostered intense

Stephanie Coontz, "The Way We Wish We Were: Defining the Family Crisis," *Way We Never Were: American Families and the Nostalgia Trap*, pp. 1-21, 428-432. Copyright © 2016 by Perseus Books Group. Reprinted with permission.

intimacy between husbands and wives while creating mothers who were totally available to their children, for example, is an idea that combines some characteristics of the white, middle-class family in the mid-nineteenth century and some of a rival family ideal first articulated in the 1920s. The first family revolved emotionally around the mother-child axis, leaving the husband-wife relationship stilted and formal. The second focused on an eroticized couple relationship, demanding that mothers curb emotional "overinvestment" in their children. The hybrid idea that a woman can be fully absorbed with her youngsters while simultaneously maintaining passionate sexual excitement with her husband was a 1950s invention that drove thousands of women to therapists, tranquilizers, or alcohol when they actually tried to live up to it.

Similarly, an extended family in which all members work together under the top-down authority of the household elder operates very differently from a nuclear family in which husband and wife are envisioned as friends who patiently devise ways to let the children learn by trial and error. Children who worked in family enterprises seldom had time for the extracurricular activities that Wally and the Beaver recounted to their parents over the dinner table; often, they did not even go to school full-time. Mothers who did home production generally relegated child care to older children or servants; they did not suspend work to savor a baby's first steps or discuss with their husband how to facilitate a grade-schooler's "self-esteem." Such families emphasized formality, obedience to authority, and "the way it's always been" in their childrearing.

Nuclear families, by contrast, have tended to pride themselves on the "modernity" of parent-child relations, diluting the authority of grandparents, denigrating "old-fashioned" ideas about child raising, and resisting the "interference" of relatives. It is difficult to imagine the Cleavers or the college-educated title figure of *Father Knows Best* letting grandparents, maiden aunts, or in-laws have a major voice in childrearing decisions. Indeed, the kind of family exemplified by the Cleavers, as we shall see in chapter 2, represented a conscious *rejection* of the Waltons' model.

The Elusive Traditional Family

Whenever people propose that we go back to the traditional family, I always suggest that they pick a ballpark date for the family they have in mind. Once pinned down, they are invariably unwilling to accept the package deal that comes with their chosen model. Some people, for example, admire the discipline of colonial families, which were certainly not much troubled by divorce or fragmenting individualism. But colonial families were hardly stable: High mortality rates meant that the average length of marriage was less than a dozen years. One-third to one-half of all children lost at least one parent before the age of twenty-one; in the South, more than half of all children aged thirteen or under had lost at least one parent.[1]

While there are a few modern Americans who would like to return to the strict patriarchal authority of colonial days, in which disobedience by women and children was considered a small form of treason, these individuals would doubtless be horrified by other aspects of colonial families, such as their failure to protect children from knowledge of sexuality. Eighteenth-century spelling and grammar books routinely used *fornication* as an example of a four-syllable word, and preachers detailed sexual offenses in astonishingly explicit terms. Sexual conversations between men and women, even in front of children, were remarkably frank. It is worth contrasting this colonial candor to the climate in 1991, when the Department of Health and Human Services was forced to cancel a proposed survey of teenagers' sexual practices after some groups charged that such knowledge might "inadvertently" encourage more sex.[2]

Other people searching for an ideal traditional family might pick the more sentimental and gentle Victorian family, which arose in the 1830s and 1840s as household production gave way to wage work and professional occupations outside the home. A new division of labor by age and sex emerged among the middle class. Women's roles were redefined in terms of domesticity rather than production, men were labeled "breadwinners" (a masculine identity unheard of in colonial days), children were said to need time to play, and gentle maternal guidance supplanted the patriarchal authoritarianism of the past.

But the middle-class Victorian family depended for its existence on the multiplication of other families who were too poor and powerless to retreat into their own little oases and who therefore had to provision the oases of others. Childhood was prolonged for the nineteenth-century middle class only because it was drastically foreshortened for other sectors of the population. The spread of textile mills, for example, freed middle-class women from the most time-consuming of their former chores, making cloth. But the raw materials for these mills were produced by slave labor. Slave children were not exempt from field labor unless they were infants, and even then their mothers were not allowed time off to nurture them. Frederick Douglass could not remember seeing his mother until he was seven.[3]

Domesticity was also not an option for the white families who worked twelve hours a day in Northern factories and workshops transforming slave-picked cotton into ready-made clothing. By 1820, "half the workers in many factories were boys and girls who had not reached their eleventh birthday." Rhode Island investigators found "little half-clothed children" making their way to the textile mills before dawn. In 1845, shoemaking families and makers of artificial flowers worked fifteen to eighteen hours a day, according to the New York *Daily Tribune*.[4]

Within the home, prior to the diffusion of household technology at the end of the century, house cleaning and food preparation remained mammoth tasks. Middle-class women were able to shift more time into childrearing in this period only by hiring domestic help. Between 1800 and 1850, the proportion of servants to white households doubled, to about one in nine. Some servants were poverty-stricken mothers who had to board or bind out their own children. Employers found such workers tended to be "distracted," however; they usually preferred young girls. In his study of Buffalo, New York, in the 1850s, historian Lawrence Glasco found that Irish and German girls often went into service at the age of eleven or twelve.[5]

For every nineteenth-century middle-class family that protected its wife and child within the family circle, then, there was an Irish or a German girl scrubbing floors in that middle-class home, a Welsh boy mining coal to keep the home-baked goodies warm, a black girl doing the family laundry, a black mother and child picking cotton to be made into clothes for the family, and a Jewish or an Italian daughter in a sweatshop making "ladies'" dresses or artificial flowers for the family to purchase.

Furthermore, people who lived in these periods were seldom as enamored of their family arrangements as modern nostalgia might suggest. Colonial Americans lamented "the great neglect in many parents and masters in training up their children" and expressed the "greatest trouble and grief about the rising generation." No sooner did Victorian middle-class families begin to withdraw their children from the work world than observers began to worry that children were becoming *too* sheltered. By 1851, the Reverend Horace Bushnell spoke for many in bemoaning the passing of the traditional days of household production, when the whole family was "harnessed, all together, into the producing process, young and old, male and female, from the boy who rode the plough-horse to the grandmother knitting under her spectacles."[6]

The late nineteenth century saw a modest but significant growth of extended families and a substantial increase in the number of families who were "harnessed" together in household production. Extended families have never been the norm in America; the highest figure for extended-family households ever recorded in American history is 20 percent. Contrary to the popular myth that industrialization destroyed "traditional" extended families, this high point occurred between 1850 and 1885, during the most intensive period of early industrialization. Many of these extended families, and most "producing" families of the time, depended on the labor of children; they were held together by dire necessity and sometimes by brute force.[7]

There was a significant increase in child labor during the last third of the nineteenth century. Some children worked at home in crowded tenement sweatshops that produced cigars or women's clothing. Reformer Helen Campbell found one house where "nearly thirty children of all ages and sizes, babies predominating, rolled in the tobacco which covered the floor and was piled in every direction."[8] Many producing households resembled the one described by Mary Van Kleeck of the Russell Sage Foundation in 1913:

> In a tenement on MacDougal Street lives a family of seven—grandmother, father, mother and four children aged four years, three years, two years and one month respectively. All excepting the father and the two babies make violets. The three year old girl picks apart the petals; her sister, aged four years, separates the stems, dipping an end of each into paste spread on a piece of board on the kitchen table; and the mother and grandmother slip the petals up the stems.[9]

Where children worked outside the home, conditions were no better. In 1900, 120,000 children worked in Pennsylvania mines and factories; most of them had started work by age eleven.

In Scranton a third of the girls between the ages of thirteen and sixteen worked in the silk mills in 1904. In New York, Boston, and Chicago, teenagers worked long hours in textile factories and frequently died in fires or industrial accidents. Children made up 23.7 percent of the 36,415 workers in southern textile mills around the turn of the century. When reformer Marie Van Vorse took a job at one in 1903, she found children as young as six or seven working twelve-hour shifts. At the end of the day, she reported, "They are usually beyond speech. They fall asleep at the tables, on the stairs; they are carried to bed and there laid down as they are, unwashed, undressed; and the inanimate bundles of rags so lie until the mill summons them with its imperious cry before sunrise."[10]

By the end of the nineteenth century, shocked by the conditions in urban tenements and by the sight of young children working full-time at home or earning money out on the streets, middle-class reformers put aside nostalgia for "harnessed" family production and elevated the antebellum model once more, blaming immigrants for introducing such "un-American" family values as child labor. Reformers advocated adoption of a "true American" family—a restricted, exclusive nuclear unit in which women and children were divorced from the world of work.

In the late 1920s and early 1930s, however, the wheel turned yet again, as social theorists noted the independence and isolation of the nuclear family with renewed anxiety. The influential Chicago School of sociology believed that immigration and urbanization had weakened the traditional family by destroying kinship and community networks. Although sociologists welcomed the increased democracy of "companionate marriage," they worried about the rootlessness of nuclear families and the breakdown of older solidarities. By the time of the Great Depression, some observers even saw a silver lining in economic hardship, since it revived the economic functions and social importance of kin and family ties. With housing starts down by more than 90 percent, approximately one-sixth of urban families had to "double up" in apartments. The incidence of three-generation households increased, while recreational interactions outside the home were cut back or confined to the kinship network. One newspaper opined, "Many a family that has lost its car has found its soul."[11]

Depression families evoke nostalgia in some contemporary observers, because they tended to create "dependability and domestic inclination" among girls and "maturity in the management of money" among boys. But, in many cases, such responsibility was inseparable from "a corrosive and disabling poverty that shattered the hopes and dreams of ... young parents and twisted the lives of those who were 'stuck together' in it." Men withdrew from family life or turned violent; women exhausted themselves trying to "take up the slack" both financially and emotionally, or they belittled their husbands as failures; and children gave up their dreams of education to work at dead-end jobs.[12]

From the hardships of the Great Depression and World War II and the euphoria of the postwar economic recovery came a new kind of family ideal that still enters our homes in *Leave It to Beaver* and *The Donna Reed Show* reruns. In the next chapter, I show that the 1950s were no more a "golden age" of the family than any other period in American history. For now, I argue that our recurring search for a traditional family model denies the diversity of family life, both past and present, and leads to false generalizations about the past as well as wildly exaggerated claims about the present and the future.

The Complexities of Assessing Family Trends

If it is hard to find a satisfactory model of the traditional family, it is also hard to make global judgments about how families have changed and whether they are getting better or worse. Some generalizations about the past are pure myth. Whatever the merit of recurring complaints about the "rootlessness" of modern life, for instance, families are *not* more mobile and transient than they used to be. In most nineteenth-century cities, both large and small, more than 50 percent—and often up to 75 percent—of the residents in any given year were no longer there ten years later. People born in the twentieth century are much more likely to live near their birthplace than were people born in the nineteenth century.[13]

This is not to say, of course, that mobility did not have different effects then than it does now. In the nineteenth century, claims historian Thomas Bender, people moved from community to community, taking advantage, as we shall see in chapter 4, of nonfamilial networks and institutions that integrated them into new work and social relations. In the late twentieth century, people move from job to job, following a career path that shuffles them from one single-family home to another and does not link them to neighborly networks beyond the family. But this change is in our community ties, not in our family ones.[14]

A related myth is that modern Americans have lost touch with extended-kinship networks or have let parent-child bonds lapse. In fact, more Americans than ever before have grandparents alive, and there is good evidence that ties between grandparents and grandchildren have become stronger over the past fifty years. In the late 1970s, researchers returned to the "Middletown" studied by sociologists Robert and Helen Lynd in the 1920s and found that most people there maintained closer extended-family networks than in earlier times. There had been some decline in the family's control over the daily lives of youth, especially females, but "the expressive/emotional function of the family" was "more important for Middletown students of 1977 than it was in 1924." More recent research shows that visits with relatives did *not* decline between the 1950s and the late 1980s.[15]

Today 54 percent of adults see a parent, and 68 percent talk on the phone with a parent, at least once a week. Fully 90 percent of Americans describe their relationship with their mother as close, and 78 percent say their relationship with their grandparents is close. And for all the family disruption of divorce, most modern children live with at least *one* parent. As late as 1940, 10 percent of American children did not live with either parent, compared to only one in twenty-five today.[16]

What about the supposed eclipse of marriage? Neither the rising age of those who marry nor the frequency of divorce necessarily means that marriage is becoming a less prominent institution than it was in earlier days. Ninety percent of men and women eventually marry, more than 70 percent of divorced men and women remarry, and fewer people remain single for their entire lives today than at the turn of the century. One author even suggests that the availability of divorce in the second half of the twentieth century has allowed some women to try marriage who would formerly have remained single all their lives. Others argue that the rate of hidden marital separation in the late nineteenth century was not much less than the rate of visible separation today.[17]

Studies of marital satisfaction reveal that more couples reported their marriages to be happy in the late 1970s than did so in 1957, while couples in their second marriages believe them to be much happier than their first ones. Some commentators conclude that marriage is becoming less permanent but more satisfying. Others wonder, however, whether there is a vicious circle in our country, where no one even tries to sustain a relationship. Between the late 1970s and late 1980s, moreover, reported marital happiness did decline slightly in the United States. Some authors see this as reflecting our decreasing appreciation of marriage, although others suggest that it reflects unrealistically high expectations of love in a culture that denies people safe, culturally approved ways of getting used to marriage or cultivating other relationships to meet some of the needs that we currently load onto the couple alone.[18]

Part of the problem in making simple generalizations about what is happening to marriage is that there has been a polarization of experiences. Marriages are much more likely to be ended by divorce today, but marriages that do last are described by their participants as happier than those in the past and are far more likely to confer such happiness over many years. It is important to remember that the 50 percent divorce rate estimates are calculated in terms of a forty-year period and that many marriages in the past were terminated well before that date by the death of one partner. Historian Lawrence Stone suggests that divorce has become "a functional substitute for death" in the modern world. At the end of the 1970s, the rise in divorce rates seemed to overtake the fall in death rates, but the slight decline in divorce rates since then means that "a couple marrying today is more likely to celebrate a fortieth wedding anniversary than were couples around the turn of the century."[19]

A similar polarization allows some observers to argue that fathers are deserting their children, while others celebrate the new commitment of fathers to childrearing. Both viewpoints are right. Sociologist Frank Furstenberg comments on the emergence of a "good dad–bad dad complex": Many fathers spend more time with their children than ever before and feel more free to be affectionate with them; others, however, feel more free simply to walk out on their families. According to 1981 statistics, 42 percent of the children whose father had left the marriage had not seen him in the past year. Yet studies show steadily increasing involvement of fathers with their children as long as they are in the home.[20]

These kinds of ambiguities should make us leery of hard-and-fast pronouncements about what's happening to the American family. In many cases, we simply don't know precisely what our figures actually mean. For example, the proportion of youngsters receiving psychological assistance rose by 80 percent between 1981 and 1988. Does that mean they are getting more sick or receiving more help, or is it some complex combination of the two? Child abuse reports increased by 225 percent between 1976 and 1987. Does this represent an actual increase in rates of abuse or a heightened consciousness about the problem? During the same period, parents' self-reports about very severe violence toward their children declined 47 percent. Does this represent a real improvement in their behavior or a decreasing willingness to admit to such acts?[21]

Assessing the direction of family change is further complicated because many contemporary trends represent a reversal of developments that were themselves rather recent. The expectation that the family should be the main source of personal fulfillment, for example, was not traditional in the eighteenth and nineteenth centuries, as we shall see in chapter 5. Prior to the 1900s, the family festivities that now fill us with such nostalgia for "the good old days" (and cause such heartbreak when they go poorly) were "relatively undeveloped." Civic festivals and Fourth of July parades were more important occasions for celebration and strong emotion than family holidays, such as Thanksgiving. Christmas "seems to have been more a time for attending parties and dances than for celebrating family solidarity." Only in the twentieth century did the family come to be the center of festive attention and emotional intensity.[22]

Today, such emotional investment in the family may be waning again. This could be interpreted as a reestablishment of balance between family life and other social ties; on the other hand, such a trend may have different results today than in earlier times, because in many cases the extrafamilial institutions and customs that used to socialize individuals and provide them with a range of emotional alternatives to family life no longer exist.

In other cases, close analysis of statistics showing a deterioration in family well-being supposedly caused by abandonment of tradition suggests a more complicated train of events. Children's health, for example, improved dramatically in the 1960s and 1970s, a period of extensive family transformation. It ceased to improve, and even slid backward, in the 1980s, when innovative social programs designed to relieve families of some "traditional" responsibilities were repealed. While infant mortality rates fell by 4.7 percent a year during the 1970s, the rate of decline decreased in the 1980s, and in both 1988 and 1989, infant mortality rates did not show a statistically significant decline. Similarly, the proportion of low-birth-weight babies fell during the 1970s but stayed steady during the 1980s and had even increased slightly as of 1988. Child poverty is lower today than it was in the "traditional" 1950s but much higher than it was in the nontraditional late 1960s.[23]

Wild Claims and Phony Forecasts

Lack of perspective on where families have come from and how their evolution connects to other social trends tends to encourage contradictory claims and wild exaggerations about where families are going. One category of generalizations seems to be a product of wishful thinking. For people overwhelmed by the difficulties of adjusting work and schools to the realities of working moms, it has been tempting to discern a "return to tradition" and hope the problems will go away. Thus in 1991, we saw a flurry of media reports that the number of women in the workforce was headed down: "More Choose to Stay Home with Children" proclaimed the headlines; "More Women Opting for Chance to Watch Their Children Grow."[24]

The cause of all this commotion? The percentage of women aged twenty-five to thirty-four who were employed dropped from 74 to 72.8 percent between January 1990 and January 1991. However, there was an exactly equal decline in the percentage of men in the workforce during the same period, and for both sexes the explanation was the same. "The dip is the recession," explained Judy Waldrop, research editor at *American Demographics* magazine, to anyone who bothered to listen. In fact, the proportion of *mothers* who worked increased slightly during the same period.[25]

This is not to say that parents, especially mothers, are happy with the pressures of balancing work and family life. Poll after poll reveals that both men and women feel starved for time. The percentage of women who say they would prefer to stay home with their children if they could afford to do so rose from 33 percent in 1986 to 56 percent in 1990. Other polls show that even larger majorities of women would trade a day's pay for an extra day off. But, above all, what these polls reveal is women's growing dissatisfaction with the failure of employers, schools, and government to pioneer arrangements that make it possible to combine work and family life. They do not suggest that women are actually going to stop working, or that this would be women's preferred solution to their stresses. The polls did not ask, for example, how *long* women would like to take off work, and failed to take account of the large majority of mothers who report that they would miss their work if they did manage to take time off. Working mothers are here to stay, and we will not meet the challenge this poses for family life by inventing an imaginary trend to define the problem out of existence.

At another extreme is the kind of generalization that taps into our worst fears. One example of this is found in the almost daily reporting of cases of child molestation or kidnapping by sexual predators. The highlighting of such cases, drawn from every corner of the country, helps disguise how rare these cases actually are when compared to crimes committed within the family.

A well-publicized instance of the cataclysmic predictions that get made when family trends are taken out of historical context is the famous *Newsweek* contention that a single woman of forty has a better chance of being killed by a terrorist than of finding a husband. The chance that a woman will reach age forty without ever having married has increased substantially since the 1950s. But the chance that a woman who postpones marriage will *eventually* marry has also increased substantially. A never-married woman over thirty-five has a better chance to marry today than she did in the 1950s. In the past twelve years, first-time marriages have increased almost 40 percent for women aged thirty-five to thirty-nine. A single woman aged forty to forty-four still has a 24 percent probability of marriage, while 15 percent of women in their late forties will marry. These figures would undoubtedly be higher if many women over forty did not simply pass up opportunities that a more desperate generation might have snatched.[26]

Yet another example of the exaggeration that pervades many analyses of modern families is the widely quoted contention that "parents today spend 40 percent less time with their children than did parents in 1965." Again, of course, part of the problem is where researchers are measuring from. A comparative study of Muncie, Indiana, for example, found that parents spent much more time with their children in the mid-1970s than did parents in the mid-1920s. But another problem is keeping the categories consistent. Trying to track down the source of the 40 percent decline figure, I called demographer John P. Robinson, whose studies on time formed the basis of this claim. Robinson's data, however, show that parents today spend about the same amount of time caring for children as they did in 1965. If the total amount of time devoted to children is less, he suggested, I might want to check how many fewer children there are today. In 1970, the average family had 1.34 children under the age of eighteen; in 1990, the average family had only .96 children under age eighteen—a decrease of 28.4 percent. In other words, most of the decline in the total amount of time parents spend with children is because of the decline in the number of children they have to spend time with![27]

Now I am not trying to say that the residual amount of decrease is not serious, or that it may not become worse, given the trends in women's employment. Robinson's data show that working mothers spend substantially less time in primary childcare activities than do nonemployed mothers (though they also tend to have fewer children); more than 40 percent of working mothers report feeling "trapped" by their daily routines; many routinely sacrifice sleep in order to meet the demands of work and family. Even so, a majority believe they are *not* giving enough time to their children. It is also true that children may benefit merely from having their parents available, even though the parents may not be spending time with them.

But there is no reason to assume the worst. Americans have actually gained free time since 1965, despite an increase in work hours, largely as a result of a decline in housework and an increasing tendency to fit some personal requirements and errands into the work day. And according to a recent Gallup poll, most modern mothers think they are doing a better job of communicating with their children (though a worse job of house cleaning) than did their own mothers and that they put a higher value on spending time with their family than did their mothers.[28]

Negotiating Through the Extremes

Most people react to these conflicting claims and contradictory trends with understandable confusion. They know that family ties remain central to their own lives, but they are constantly hearing about people who seem to have no family feeling. Thus, at the same time as Americans report high levels of satisfaction with their own families, they express a pervasive fear that other people's families are falling apart. In a typical recent poll, for example, 71 percent of respondents said they were "very satisfied" with their *own* family life, but more than half rated the overall quality of family life as negative: "I'm okay; you're not."[29]

This seemingly schizophrenic approach does not reflect an essentially intolerant attitude. People worry about families, and to the extent that they associate modern social ills with changes in family life, they are ambivalent about innovations. Voters often defeat measures to grant unmarried couples, whether heterosexual or homosexual, the same rights as married ones. In polls, however, most Americans support tolerance for gay and lesbian relationships. Although two-thirds of respondents to one national poll said they wanted "more traditional standards of family life," the same percentage rejected the idea that "women should return to their traditional role." Still larger majorities support women's right to work, including their right to use child care, even when they worry about relying on daycare centers too much. In a 1990 *Newsweek* poll, 42 percent predicted that the family would be worse in ten years and exactly the same percentage predicted that it would be better. Although 87 percent of people polled in 1987 said they had "old-fashioned ideas about family and marriage," only 22 percent of the people polled in 1989 defined a family solely in terms of blood, marriage, or adoption. Seventy-four percent declared, instead, that family is any group whose members love and care for one another.[30]

These conflicted responses do not mean that people are hopelessly confused. Instead, they reflect people's gut-level understanding that the "crisis of the family" is more complex than is often asserted by political demagogues or others with an ax to grind. In popular commentary, the received wisdom is to "keep it simple." I know one television reporter who refuses to air an interview with anyone who uses the phrase "on the other hand." But my experience in discussing these issues with both the general public and specialists in the field is that people are hungry to get beyond oversimplifications. They don't want to be told that everything is fine in families or that if the economy improved and the government mandated parental leave, everything would be fine. But they don't believe that every hard-won victory for women's rights and personal liberty has been destructive of social bonds and that the only way to find a sense of community is to go back to some sketchily defined "traditional" family that clearly involves denying the validity of any alternative familial and personal choices.

Americans understand that along with welcome changes have come difficult new problems; uneasy with simplistic answers, they are willing to consider more nuanced analyses of family gains and losses during the past few decades. Indeed, argues political reporter E. J. Dionne, they are *desperate* to engage in such analyses.[31] Few Americans are satisfied with liberal and feminist accounts that blame all modern family dilemmas on structural inequalities, ignoring the moral crisis of commitment and obligation in our society. Yet neither are they convinced that "in the final analysis," as David Blankenhorn of the Institute for American Values puts it, "the problem is not the system. The problem is us."[32]

Despite humane intentions, an overemphasis on personal responsibility for strengthening family values encourages a way of thinking that leads to moralizing rather than mobilizing for concrete reforms. While values are important to Americans, most do not support the sort of scapegoating that occurs when all family problems are blamed on "bad values." Most of us are painfully aware that there is no clear way of separating "family values" from "the system." Our values may make a difference in the way we respond to the challenges posed by economic and political institutions, but those institutions also reinforce certain values and extinguish others. The problem is not to berate people for abandoning past family values, nor to exhort them to adopt better values in the future—the problem is to build the institutions and social support networks that allow people to act on their best values rather than on their worst ones. We need to get past abstract nostalgia for traditional family values and develop a clearer sense of how past families actually worked and what the different consequences of various family behaviors and values have been. Good history and responsible social policy should help people incorporate the full complexity and the trade-offs of family change into their analyses and thus into action. Mythmaking does not accomplish this end.

Notes

1. Philip Greven, *Four Generations: Population, Land, and Family in Colonial Andover, Massachusetts* (Ithaca, N.Y.: Cornell University Press, 1970); Vivian Fox and Martin Quit, *Loving, Parenting, and Dying: The Family Cycle in England and America, Past and Present* (New York: Psychohistory Press, 1980), p. 401.
2. John Demos, *A Little Commonwealth: Family Life in Plymouth Colony* (New York: Oxford University Press, 1970), p. 108; Mary Ryan, *Cradle of the Middle Class: The Family in Oneida County, New York, 1790–1865* (New York: Cambridge University Press, 1981), pp. 33, 38–39; Carroll Smith-Rosenberg, *Disorderly Conduct: Visions of Gender in Victorian America* (New York: Oxford University Press, 1985), p. 24.
3. Frederick Douglass, *My Bondage and My Freedom* (New York: Dover, 1968), p. 48.
4. David Roediger and Philip Foner, *Our Own Time: A History of American Labor and the Working Day* (London: Greenwood, 1989), p. 9; Norman Ware, *The Industrial Worker, 1840–1860* (New York: Quadrangle, 1964), p. 5; Barbara Wertheimer, *We Were There: The Story of Working Women in America* (New York: Pantheon, 1977), p. 91; Sean Wilentz, *Chants Democratic: New York City and the Rise of the Working Class, 1788–1850* (New York: Oxford University Press, 1984), p. 126.
5. Faye Dudden, *Serving Women: Household Service in Nineteenth-Century America* (Middletown, Conn.: Wesleyan University Press, 1983), p. 206; Susan Strasser, *Never Done: A History of American Housework* (New York: Pantheon, 1982); Lawrence Glasco, "The Life Cycles and Household Structure of American Ethnic Groups," in *A Heritage of Her Own: Toward a New Social History of American Women*, ed. Nancy Cott and Elizabeth Pleck (New York: Simon & Schuster, 1979), pp. 281, 285.
6. Robert Bremner et al., eds., *Children and Youth in America: A Documentary History*, vol. 1 (Cambridge, Mass.: Harvard University Press, 1970), p. 39; Barbara Cross, *Horace Bushnell: Minister to a Changing America* (Chicago: University of Chicago Press, 1958); Ann Douglas, *The Feminization of American Culture* (New York: Knopf, 1977), p. 52.

7. Peter Laslett, "Characteristics of the Western Family over Time," in *Family Life and Illicit Love in Earlier Generations*, ed. Peter Laslett (New York: Cambridge University Press, 1977); William Goode, *World Revolution and Family Patterns* (New York: Free Press, 1963); Michael Anderson, *Family Structure in Nineteenth-Century Lancashire* (Cambridge: Cambridge University Press, 1971); Tamara Hareven, ed., *Transitions: The Family and the Life Course in Historical Perspective* (New York: Academic Press, 1978); Tamara Hareven, "The Dynamics of Kin in an Industrial Community," in *Turning Points: Historical and Sociological Essays on the Family*, ed. John Demos and S. S. Boocock (Chicago: University of Chicago Press, 1978); Linda Gordon, *Heroes of Their Own Lives: The Politics and History of Family Violence, 1880–1960* (New York: Viking, 1988).

8. Helen Campbell, *Prisoners of Poverty: Women Wage Workers, Their Trades and Their Lives* (Westport, Conn.: Greenwood Press, 1970), p. 206.

9. Rosalyn Baxandall, Linda Gordon, and Susan Reverby, eds., *America's Working Women* (New York: Random House, 1976), p. 162.

10. Rose Schneiderman, *All For One* (New York: P. S. Eriksson, 1967); John Bodnar, "Socialization and Adaption: Immigrant Families in Scranton," in *Growing Up in America: Historical Experiences*, ed. Harvey Graff (Detroit: Wayne State Press, 1987), pp. 391–92; Robert and Helen Lynd, *Middletown: A Study in Modern American Culture* (New York: Harcourt Brace Jovanovich, 1956), p. 31; Barbara Wertheimer, *We Were There: The Story of Working Women in America* (New York: Pantheon, 1977), pp. 336–43; Francesco Cordasco, *Jacob Riis Revisited: Poverty and the Slum in Another Era* (Garden City, N.Y.: Doubleday, 1968); Campbell, *Prisoners of Poverty* and *Women Wage-Earners* (Boston: Arnoff, 1893); Lynn Weiner, *From Working Girl to Working Mother: The Female Labor Force in the United States, 1829–1980* (Chapel Hill: University of North Carolina Press, 1985), p. 92.

11. For examples of the analysis of the Chicago School, see Ernest Burgess and Harvey Locke, *The Family: From Institution to Companionship* (New York: American Book Company, 1945); Ernest Mowrer, *The Family: Its Organization and Disorganization* (Chicago: University of Chicago Press, 1932); W. I. Thomas and F. Znaniecki, *The Polish Peasant in Europe and America*, 5 vols. (Boston: Dover Publications, 1918–1920). On families in the Depression, see Steven Mintz and Susan Kellogg, *Domestic Revolutions: A Social History of American Family Life* (New York: Free Press, 1988), pp. 133–49, quote on p. 136.

12. Glen Elder, Jr., *Children of the Great Depression: Social Change in Life Experience* (Chicago: University of Chicago Press, 1974), pp. 64–82; Lillian Rubin, *Worlds of Pain: Life in the Working-Class Family* (New York: Basic Books, 1976), p. 23; Edward Robb Ellis, *A Nation in Torment: The Great American Depression, 1929–1939* (New York: Coward McCann, 1970); Ruth Milkman, "Women's Work and the Economic Crisis," in *A Heritage of Her Own: Toward a New Social History of American Women*, ed. Nancy Cott and Elizabeth Pleck (New York: Simon & Schuster, 1979), pp. 507–41.

13. Rudy Ray Seward, *The American Family: A Demographic History* (Beverly Hills: Sage, 1978); Kenneth Winkle, *The Politics of Community: Migration and Politics in Antebellum Ohio* (New

York: Cambridge University Press, 1988); Michael Weber, *Social Change in an Industrial Town: Patterns of Progress in Warren, Pennsylvania, from the Civil War to World War I* (University Park: Pennsylvania State University Press, 1976), pp. 138–48; Stephen Thernstrom, *Poverty and Progress* (Cambridge, Mass.: Harvard University Press, 1964).

14. Thomas Bender, *Community and Social Change in America* (New Brunswick, N.J.: Rutgers University Press, 1978).

15. Edward Kain, *The Myth of Family Decline: Understanding Families in a World of Rapid Social Change* (Lexington, Mass.: D. C. Heath, 1990), pp. 10, 37; Theodore Caplow, "The Sociological Myth of Family Decline," *Tocqueville Review* 3 (1981): 366; Howard Bahr, "Changes in Family Life in Middletown, 1924–77," *Public Opinion Quarterly* 44 (1980): 51.

16. *American Demographics*, February 1990; Dennis Orthner, "The Family in Transition," in *Rebuilding the Nest: A New Commitment to the American Family*, ed. David Blankenhorn, Steven Bayme, and Jean Bethke Elshtain (Milwaukee: Family Service America, 1990), pp. 95–97; Sar Levitan and Richard Belous, *What's Happening to the American Family?* (Baltimore: Johns Hopkins University Press, 1981), p. 63.

17. Daniel Kallgren, "Women Out of Marriage: Work and Residence Patterns of Never Married American Women, 1900–1980" (paper presented at Social Science History Association Conference, Minneapolis, Minn., October 1990), p. 8; Richard Sennett, *Families Against the City: Middle Class Homes in Industrial Chicago, 1872–1890* (Cambridge, Mass.: Harvard University Press, 1984), pp. 114–15.

18. Mary Jo Bane, *Here to Stay: American Families in the Twentieth Century* (New York: Basic Books, 1976); Stephen Nock, *Sociology of the Family* (Englewood Cliffs, N.J.: Prentice Hall, 1987); Kain, *Myth of Family Decline*, pp. 71, 74–75; Joseph Veroff, Elizabeth Douvan, and Richard Kulka, *The Inner American: A Self Portrait from 1957 to 1976* (New York: Basic Books, 1981); Norval Glenn, "The Recent Trend in Marital Success in the United States," *Journal of Marriage and the Family* 53 (1991); Tracy Cabot, *Marrying Later, Marrying Smarter* (New York: McGraw-Hill, 1990); Judith Brown, *Sanctions and Sanctuary: Cultural Perspectives on the Beating of Wives* (Boulder, Colo.: Westview Press, 1991); Maxine Baca Zinn and Stanley Eitzen, *Diversity in American Families* (New York: Harper & Row, 1987).

19. Dorrian Apple Sweetser, "Broken Homes: Stable Risk, Changing Reason, Changing Forms," *Journal of Marriage and the Family* (August 1985); Lawrence Stone, "The Road to Polygamy," *New York Review of Books*, 2 March 1989, p. 13; Arlene Skolnick, *Embattled Paradise: The American Family in an Age of Uncertainty* (New York: Basic Books, 1991), p. 156.

20. Frank Furstenberg, Jr., "Good Dads-Bad Dads: Two Faces of Fatherhood," in *The Changing American Family and Public Policy*, ed. Andrew Cherlin (Washington, DC: Urban Institute Press, 1988); Joseph Pleck, "The Contemporary Man," in *Handbook of Counseling and Psychotherapy*, ed. Murray Scher et al. (Beverly Hills: Sage, 1987).

21. National Commission on Children, *Beyond Rhetoric: A New Agenda for Children and Families* (Washington, DC: GPO, 1991), p. 34; Richard Gelles and Jon Conte, "Domestic Violence and

Sexual Abuse of Children," in *Contemporary Families: Looking Forward, Looking Back*, ed. Alan Booth (Minneapolis: National Council on Family Relations, 1991), p. 328.

22. Arlene Skolnick, "The American Family: The Paradox of Perfection," *Wilson Quarterly* (Summer 1980); Barbara Laslett, "Family Membership: Past and Present," *Social Problems* 25 (1978); Theodore Caplow et al., *Middletown Families: Fifty Years of Change and Continuity* (Minneapolis: University of Minnesota Press, 1982), p. 225.

23. *The State of America's Children, 1991* (Washington, DC: Children's Defense Fund, 1991), pp. 55–63; *Seattle Post-Intelligencer*, 19 April 1991; National Commission on Children, *Beyond Rhetoric*, p. 32; *Washington Post National Weekly Edition*, 13–19 May 1991; James Wetzel, *American Youth: A Statistical Snapshot* (Washington, DC: William T. Grant Foundation, August 1989), pp. 12–14.

24. *USA Today*, 12 May 1991, p. 1A; Richard Morin, "Myth of the Drop Out Mom," *Washington Post*, 14 July 1991; Christine Reinhardt, "Trend Check," *Working Woman*, October 1991, p. 34; Howard Hayghe, "Family Members in the Work Force," *Monthly Labor Review* 113 (1990).

25. Morin, "Myth of the Drop Out Mom"; Reinhardt, "Trend Check," p. 34.

26. "Too Late for Prince Charming," *Newsweek*, 2 June 1986, p. 55; John Modell, *Into One's Own: From Youth to Adulthood in the United States, 1920–1975* (Berkeley: University of California Press, 1989), p. 249; Barbara Lovenheim, *Beating the Marriage Odds: When You Are Smart, Single, and Over 35* (New York: William Morrow, 1990), pp. 26–27; *U.S. News & World Report*, 29 January 1990, p. 50; *New York Times*, 7 June 1991.

27. William Mattox, Jr., "The Parent Trap," *Policy Review* (Winter 1991): 6, 8; Sylvia Ann Hewlett, "Running Hard Just to Keep Up," *Time* (Fall 1990), and *When the Bough Breaks: The Cost of Neglecting Our Children* (New York: Basic Books, 1991), p. 73; Richard Whitmore, "Education Decline Linked with Erosion of Family," *Olympian*, 1 October 1991; John Robinson, "Caring for Kids," *American Demographics*, July 1989, p. 52; "Household and Family Characteristics: March 1990 and 1989," *Current Population Reports*, series P-20, no. 447, table A-1. I am indebted to George Hough, Executive Policy Analyst, Office of Financial Management, Washington State, for finding these figures and helping me with the calculations.

28. John Robinson, "Time for Work," *American Demographics*, April 1989, p. 68, and "Time's Up," *American Demographics*, July 1989, p. 34; Trish Hall, "Time on Your Hands? You May Have More Than You Think," *New York Times*, 3 July 1991, pp. C1, C7; Gannett News Service Wire Report, 27 August 1991.

29. *New York Times*, 10 October 1989, p. A18.

30. E. J. Dionne, Jr., *Why Americans Hate Politics* (New York: Simon & Schuster, 1991), pp. 110, 115, 325; *Olympian*, 11 October 1989; *New York Times*, 10 October 1989; *Time*, 20 November 1989; *Seattle Post-Intelligencer*, 12 October 1990; Jerold Footlick, "What Happened to the Family?" *Newsweek Special Issue*, Winter–Spring 1990, p. 18.

31. Dionne, *Why Americans Hate Politics*.

32. David Blankenhorn, "Does Grandmother Know Best?" *Family Affairs* 3 (1990): 13, 16.

CHAPTER 11

PATHWAY TO THE AMERICAN DREAM?
EDUCATION

I grew up in a poor family with parents who did not graduate from high school, yet they both urged my siblings and me to get a college education. My parents, like most of their generation, viewed a college education as the pathway to the American dream—to the middle class. Here, John F. Covaleskie challenges this strongly held American belief. He argues that the link between educational attainment and economic success is more apparent than real. He argues further that reproduction of this "myth" masks serious injustices at the core of social life in the United States. Moreover, he insists, believing in this myth harms education. As you read through his paper, you might want to consider the questions presented below.

Some Things to Keep in Mind

1. Americans expect educational attainment to grant them social mobility. Is this a fair expectation?
2. Is there a subtext that's saying there needs to be educational inequality to maintain the value of education?

3. How has the definition of education shifted over time?
4. According to this article, what is it that schools cannot do?
5. What can individuals, organizations, or institutions do that schools cannot?

EDUCATIONAL ATTAINMENT AND ECONOMIC INEQUALITY

WHAT SCHOOLS CANNOT DO

John F. Covaleskie

It has long been an article of faith in the U.S. that education is the key to economic success. The faith works in two directions: (1) education is good for the economy in general and (2) education is good for the individual. The first article of faith is the assumption behind all the rhetoric connecting quality of education and international competitiveness. The second article is the reason teens are told, "stay in school."

Policy makers evidently know the first article is false: while schools are blamed when the economy is poor, they do not get the credit when things go well (Berliner & Biddle, 1995; Bracey, 2001). Regardless, the myth powerfully shapes the way schooling is thought about in the U.S. On the one hand, public schools are supported because the public believes the economy benefits when large numbers of an age cohort go to school for many years. On the other hand, individuals extend their schooling in the expectation of economic advantage. This appears to work to the advantage of schools, gaining both economic support and attendance.

However, the thesis of this paper is that the opposite is true. I will first make the argument that the relationship between educational attainment and economic success is more apparent than real. Then I will consider the ways in which these myths mask serious injustice at the core of U.S. national life. Finally, I will consider the implications of believing the myth and the ways the myth harms education. But before I begin the analysis, let me conduct a little thought experiment.

Imagine that U.S. schools were suddenly made perfect (whatever it is that one might mean by "perfect"). Imagine everyone obtains a perfect education in all areas. If the myth that equates good education with a good, well-paying job were true, everyone would now have a good, well-paying job.

We know these conditions would not follow. Service sector jobs would not pay a living wage or provide health insurance. If everyone were equally well educated, even perfectly so, the surplus of labor would still mean some jobs would pay less than a living wage. In a competitive economy,

---

John F. Covaleskie, "Educational Attainment and Economic Inequality: What Schools Cannot Do," *Journal of Thought*, vol. 45, no. 1, pp. 83-96. Copyright © 2010 by Caddo Gap Press. Reprinted with permission. Provided by ProQuest LLC. All rights reserved.

the educated reap economic benefits only from their education *relative to others'*. This claim will be elaborated below.

This paper will argue that what schools cannot do, should not be tasked with doing, and should not promise to do, is reduce inequality in the context of a broad socio-economic matrix designed to produce inequality; nor can it much reduce inequity when the means used to distribute inequality are themselves unjust.

However, this paper is not intended to update Coleman's (1966) argument that home effects overwhelm school effect. On Coleman's view, schools cannot produce equality of academic results. There is much evidence that this task, however difficult, is possible (Meier, 2002; Edmonds et al., 1977; Lezotte & Bancroft, 1985). The argument in this paper is: even when schooling does all it can do to educate those who begin life disadvantaged, this educational success will make a difference for only a chosen few; in the competitive life of a capitalist state, the rich and powerful will assure the success of their children over others', individual exceptions to the contrary notwithstanding.

The Argument

Many service-sector employers require a high school diploma or some years of post-secondary education. However, the job skills required are not particularly connected to these educational requirements, nor are wages simply related to the amount of schooling one has. Instead, wages are related to relative education. *It is not how much education one has that grants economic advantage in the job market; it is how much more education one has compared to others in that particular market.*

To understand why, we begin with what Tom Green (1980) called the Law of Zero Correlation:

> ... if there is a level within the system that everyone completes, then completing that level can have no bearing whatever upon any social differences that may subsequently arise within the population ... there is a point in the growth of the system at which there is no longer any correlation between educational attainment and ... the distribution of non-educational social goods associated with educational attainment. (90–91)

In other words, *at any level of educational attainment, when that level becomes virtually universal, there is no advantage to be gained by attaining that level.*

Further, as a corollary of the Law of Zero Correlation, once attainment of some level has become universal or nearly so, to fail to attain that level is a distinct disadvantage. As educational attainment expands, *the advantage gained as a consequence of that educational attainment decreases, but the price paid for not attaining that level of education increases*. When the vast majority of an age cohort graduates from high school, there is no real advantage to being a graduate, but there is a significant disadvantage to *not* being one. Employers are free to screen candidates out of most available jobs, but only because there is a persistent surplus of workers to jobs (Campbell, 1966). This appears to be the situation in which we find ourselves today.

The implications of this analysis for equity and justice issues lie in what Green refers to as the Law of Last Entry:

> It appears to be true that no society has been able to expand its total educational enterprise to include lower status groups *in proportion to their numbers in the population* until the system is "saturated" by the upper and middle status groups. (108)

Green's analysis gives us serious reason to be troubled: lower social status groups will always have the last access to whatever level of schooling that makes an economic difference; more seriously, *when those lower-status groups gain access, that level of the system will no longer confer any economic advantage.*

Green provocatively states: "The reason we have a drop out *problem* is not that we have too many drop-outs, but that we have too few" (99). That is, there are so few who drop out that they can be effectively written off as unemployable. What we fail to notice when we advocate decreasing the dropout rate is that, even if the dropout rate were zero, the number of jobs available would neither increase nor decrease. Dropouts are not given jobs precisely because there are no jobs to give them (Campbell, 1966).

Misdiagnosis of any problem leads predictably to ineffective solutions. The policy solution to the "dropout problem" has been to expand educational opportunity, to make at least a high school diploma universal, when the problem is great inequality of both wealth and opportunity. As a solution to the problem of economic inequality, expanded access to education is useless because the high school diploma becomes worthless when it is universal. Indeed, as economic policy, expanded educational opportunity is worse than useless, since it creates a simulacrum of justice while attaching more culpability to failure.

A further proposition to consider is what Green calls the Principle of the Moving Target. "As the group of last entry reaches its target of attainment at the nth level, the target will shift" (111). Hence, we now hear calls to extend free public education into the post-secondary level. This "solution" will eventually result in a reproduction of the problem, albeit at a slightly higher level of the system. The problem, however, is never simple unequal attainment at any level of the system; the problem is how to decouple consequences in the economic sphere from achievements in the educational sphere.

Economic inequality may result from differences in talent, skill, interest, ambition, or amount of time invested in one's career, to name but a few possibilities. Inequalities resulting from differences in any of these could be just (Walzer, 1983). On the other hand, economic inequalities might result from family wealth in prior generations, contacts, or preferences given for extraneous or inappropriate reasons. These causes of inequality would raise troubling issues of justice; we have the intuitive sense, rightly, that economic inequalities ought to be the result of one's own efforts and merits. The public's acceptance of inequality is grounded on the myths of equal opportunity and meritocracy; inequalities are earned and deserved, even chosen, and therefore just.

While we do not see inequalities in wealth or education as *prima facie* evidence of inequity, civic membership or citizenship is not like that. One of the premises of our constitutional form of democratic government is that we are all equal before the law, that we all have equal rights of citizenship, and that any form of second-class citizenship is a grave injustice, absent strong and specific justification (say, the disenfranchisement of felons). So, if one's wealth were to buy one privileges within the economic sphere, a newer, more luxurious automobile, for example, that would not be an injustice. On the other hand, if one's wealth enabled one to receive special treatment from the laws, either more favorable treatment in the courts, or success in having laws passed that favor you and yours, then that would be a clear injustice against others not so wealthy. The problem exists when inequalities in one sphere, where they are open and deserved, spill over into other spheres where our foundational mythologies say clearly they have no place.

The claim is that differential wealth should not lead to differences in educational attainment, *and* that differences in educational attainment should only lead to differences in wealth where those differences in wealth are the result of specific skills or knowledge obtained from one's education, not simply because one's educational experience gave access to wealthy and powerful friends.

There are two ways this frame of analysis points us to serious systematic injustice in our current situation: (1) the existence of a group of last entry, a group largely defined by circumstances of birth, wealth, and privilege—educationally irrelevant attributes—is a clear violation of the principle that differences in outcomes must be based on attributes relevant to the sphere of difference; and (2) the educational attainment target, while it has been a moving one, is perhaps becoming stable; it is clearly not possible for educational attainment to be raised infinitely. We are reaching the point where two things seem to be happening as the limits of expansion are reached. High school education is now effectively universal: 87.6% of the population have either a high school diploma or a GED by the time they are 24 years old (National Center for Educational Statistics, 2007); it has stopped being a means to screen prospective employees. As it is not likely that education beyond some college is ever going to be universal or anything like it, the Moving Target is approaching its limit. More to the point, the Law of Last Entry is likely to exclude the group of last entry permanently. We can see this happening already in the fact that attending college is no longer enough to give much advantage in the market place. The real advantage lies in attending an elite college. To these schools, the group of last entry will likely be permanently denied access in any numbers (Stevens, 2007).

Structure of the Myth

Consider the degree to which the myth relating education and economic progress, as pervasive as it is, is false. It is simply false at the social level, and in a more nuanced way it is also false at the individual level.

It is not one's level of educational attainment that contributes to one's economic advantage (one of what Green calls the "non-educational social goods associated with educational attainment" [42]); it is having more education than others. Having an eighth-grade education would suffice if people generally attained the sixth grade; having a high school diploma will not qualify for minimum wage if everyone else also has one.

Adam Smith and Karl Marx were correct on this point: it is surplus labor that keeps wages down at the bottom rungs of society, not any lack of educational attainment on the part of the workers. Rhetoric to the contrary notwithstanding, while the distribution of poverty is affected by educational attainment of individuals, the incidence of poverty is structural. The economy, quite without regard to the distribution of education among the populace, will determine how many individuals will be unemployed or employed in jobs that do not pay a living wage. If I am sufficiently educated, I increase my odds of escaping those jobs, but the jobs will exist and will go to those with less schooling than I.[1] My increased schooling does decrease statistically the likelihood of my living in poverty, but *it does nothing to reduce poverty generally*. It is not my educational attainment *per se* that helps me; it is my schooling in the *absence of others'*.

The second part of the myth is equally false, though not in quite the same way. The claim is, the quality of a nation's schooling determines (or at least strongly influences) a nation's wealth. *A Nation at Risk* (National Commission on Excellence in Education, 1983) is perhaps the most widely known policy document making this argument, and today functions as received wisdom. While nations with universal education tend to be the countries that are most economically advanced, there are two things that keep that analysis from being quite as straightforward as the report pretends. In the first place, there is the chicken-egg question: as nations improve their economies and have greater surplus wealth, they are able to support wider educational opportunity. Second, *sufficient* schooling is all a society really needs; once that is attained more does not equal better. The first point is obvious, but the second needs some clarification.

Schooling is necessary for a technological society; engineers, doctors, teachers, even lawyers, are needed for the society to function well. Bureaucrats must understand the nature of the work they are expected to do. And so on. What is interesting to ask is, why the constant emphasis on *more*? Once there are enough schooled people to staff the schools, once there are enough engineers to design the bridges and the buildings, once there are enough lawyers to allow the legal system to function and to serve the civil, corporate, and criminal justice needs of a society, what is the need for more?

It is instructive that those who attack public schools as responsible for economic downturns clearly do not believe their own rhetoric. In the 1980s, as a consequence of an oil shortage, macro-economic mismanagement rooted in the waste of Vietnam, and corporate management decisions to spend corporate wealth on leveraged buyouts and inflated executive salaries, there was a recession. Schools were blamed. The well-orchestrated campaign against public schools, distilled in the apocalyptic rhetoric of *A Nation at Risk*, claimed that the economic problems were due to the failure of the nation's schools ("unilateral educational disarmament"), which were responsible for putting the "nation at risk."

In the event, the nation's economy went on to outperform all others for the next decade and a half, and the workers who were then in those "failing" schools became the most productive in the world. The cynicism of the "reform" movement can be perceived by noting that, so far as I know, no one who claimed to see such a clear connection between the poor economic performance of the early 1980s and the low test scores of the era's schoolchildren (who were not, in any case, in the workforce at the time) could discern any possible relationship between the recovery and the quality of schools.

So, while attaining enough education to put one among the privileged is a good individual strategy, it does not alleviate the incidence of poverty in the society or improve the economy in general (beyond a minimal point). And so, as the policy designed to convince more people to stay in school longer succeeds, the only way for individuals to attain the benefits promised from more education is to get even *more* education.

Once, not really so very long ago, education was the province of the wealthy. Even after schools became free and universally available to the public, only a minority of families could afford to remove their children from the workplace; even free education had its opportunity cost, measured by what the student was not earning and not contributing to the family. At some point, people began to recognize that there was a strong and persistent relationship between the amount of education one received as a child and the amount of money one made as an adult. Over time, this relationship worked its way into the public consciousness, and a general perception developed that more schooling led to higher earnings. This is the set of circumstances that statisticians have in mind when they caution, "Correlation does not imply causation." Be that as it may, people will and do continue to infer causation from correlation. The connection between schooling and income is a reminder of that.

Additionally, there is just enough truth in the common impression to make it seem reasonable. As pointed out above, as a matter of individual choice, additional schooling likely *will* enhance earnings. As social policy, however, it is a Ponzi scheme.

Complex Justice

Walzer's (1983) concept of spheres of justice allows us to apprehend the significance of the extent to which our society bleeds influence and effect from one sphere to another, and which spheres dominate. We can begin to see that inequalities in the economic sphere, while not necessarily unjust in and of themselves, create and perpetuate inequalities in other spheres. This is the operational definition of injustice. Specifically, once we see that the power of money buys educational attainment and unearned economic advantage for one's offspring, we can no longer avoid seeing injustice. We may argue that injustice is inevitable in a fallen world, and that this form of injustice is both relatively benign and practically unpreventable, but that is not the same thing as arguing that the situation is just. When Jimmy Carter said, "… there are many things in life that are not fair, that wealthy people can afford and poor people can't" (Carter, July 12, 1977), the point he was conceding, often overlooked, is precisely that the policy under discussion was in fact unfair.[2]

There is a public virtue to be had in this sort of honesty, even when we decide for one reason or another not to act; the recognition that there is an injustice, even an incorrigible one, can lead to compensatory amelioration in other domains. For example, one might recognize that it is unjust that money buys educational opportunity and future economic advantage. We might also argue that for one reason or another it is not possible to prevent certain sorts of injustice. We might, for example, argue that the limitations on personal liberty needed to prevent this unjust reach from one social sphere to another are simply too great to justify on their own merits—what we might think of as a soft libertarian argument. However, once we have seen the injustice, we might be more open to policies of amelioration, such as progressive income taxes, near-confiscatory estate taxes, and generous funding for public education.

Such policies are more politically viable when they correct a recognized injustice than when they reduce justifiable inequality. Thus it is the mission of right-wing radio hosts to create the impression that progressives want equality of outcomes, not equality of opportunity. The assumption behind this argument is that we already have the latter, and the unequal outcomes are therefore just. In fact, to reduce the inequalities in our society, goes this argument, would be unjust, since it would require taking from the wealthy money they had earned and is rightfully theirs. This argument has traction only if one accepts the assumptions underlying it. Once the injustice of the class system we have produced in the U.S. becomes visible, different social policies to address it become possible, as happened during the New Deal.

The final consideration in this reflection is to consider the effect of these mythologies and realities on education.

Consequences

First we should note that a critically important social fact has been changed, largely without our being aware: while it used to be we understood that more wealth led to more schooling, today it is thought that more schooling leads to more wealth. This change in the relationship between the educational sphere and the economic sphere has dramatically changed the meaning of "education."

There was a time, not so very long ago, when a clear conceptual difference existed between "education" and "job training"; the latter was most commonly acquired outside school in some sort of internship, apprenticeship, or on-the-job training, either formal or informal; the former was connected not to job preparation, but to the use of leisure time. To quote Israel Scheffler (1976):

> [Education is] the formation of habits of judgment and the development of character, the elevation of standards, the facilitation of understanding, the development of taste and discrimination, the stimulation of curiosity and wondering, the fostering of style and a sense of beauty, the growth of a thirst for new ideas and vision of the yet unknown. (p. 206)

The rapidity of this fundamental shift is brought home by the fact that in my lifetime the term "vocational education" went from an oxymoron to a redundancy. This leaves Scheffler's question, "What is education?" not only unanswered, but unasked. Everyone knows what education is: it is schooling; it is preparation for a good job. That these answers miss the point is made clear if we stop for a moment and consider: we know a great deal about the economic value of education; we know a great deal about the personal value of education; we know a great deal about the civic value of education. It is instructive, then, to note that we hardly know what to make of the question: what is the *educational* value of education, in the sense Scheffler used the term? What are the *educational* goals of education—the goals *internal* to the practice? What do these questions even mean? These are difficult questions to ask in the current impoverished atmosphere. About the educational purposes of education—that is, the meaning of "education," we are not only silent; we are oblivious and seemingly content to be so.

Up until now I have argued that schools cannot solve the problem they have been assigned and accepted. Education can, at its best, be an instrument of social mobility, but that is not the same as saying that it will reduce either inequality or poverty. There are many consequences of any myth upon which social policy is based. Here I wish to point to some educational consequences of this one.

First, it has dramatically expanded educational access, providing the means for many from the working classes, myself included, to enter the middle and professional classes in American society. Because the public believed that expanded educational opportunity created economic success for the individual and society (see, for example, Levin & Bachman, 1972), educational access expanded during the 1950s and 1960s in a way that would have been inconceivable a generation earlier (Campbell, 1966; Schreiber, 1964). Other factors included: expansion of higher education opportunity resulting from the G.I. Bill (The Servicemen's Readjustment Act of 1944), the sheer weight of numbers of the Baby Boom generation who desired to go to college in the 1960s and 70s, the surplus resources a booming economy allowed to be put into schooling, and the desire to postpone entry into the labor force, among other factors.

However, the inequality predicted by the existence of a Group of Last Entry is pervasive and persistent through the post war period, as overall completion rates reach close to 90%, but those of racial and ethnic minorities lagging far behind (National Center for Educational Statistics, 1990, pp 18–23). As a result, the benefits resulting from the economic expansion and the resulting expansion of educational opportunity were unequally and inequitably distributed based on race, class, and ethnicity, not on merit.

Further, these post-war social conditions were so effective in expanding educational opportunity because of the education-equals-earnings myth. That is, the government might have created the G.I. Bill from a desire to reabsorb returning servicemen back into the workforce gradually in order to prevent economic instability following WWII or to reward "the greatest generation" for their service, but individuals did not take advantage of the G.I. Bill because of a desire to keep the economy stable or as a way of saying "You're welcome" to the society's "Thank you." Instead, individuals mostly chose to go to college because they believed it would give them an advantage as they re-entered the job market; they were there to get credentialed.

The government had expected only a small number of veterans to use the Bill, since such a small percentage of the population had gone to college prior to the War. An assumption of the lawmakers was that only the people who would have gone to college anyway would go under the G.I. Bill. This was not what happened, and the unanticipated consequences of the G.I. Bill are what made it such a socially transformative piece of legislation (Olson, 1973).

The consequences of the G.I. Bill echoed into the next generation. Colleges that had expanded to make room for the returning veterans now had extra seats to fill. In addition, given the expectation that more education leads to better jobs, the children of the baby boom decided in record and ever-expanding numbers to go to college. This combination of circumstances—excess capacity and increased demand—led to near-universalization of high school graduation and rapid expansion of higher education attendance. While the broader circumstances of the post-World War II economic boom had a great deal to do with why completing high school and/or attending college became more possible, they do not explain why such a rapidly increasing number of students chose to take advantage of the opportunity.

In a different vein, as educational access has become broader and more democratically distributed, its definition has fundamentally changed, as discussed in the previous section. As this shift accelerated over the past few decades, education stopped being anything different from training; "education" stopped meaning anything at all. Schools had changed so that they no longer had much of an independent mission apart from meeting the economic need of the society and affecting the economic prospects of their "customers," who used to be called students. We talk today of the civic purposes and functions of education and schooling even if we no longer take seriously what was once the central mission of schools: to produce good citizens (however one might define "good citizen"). We focus obsessively on the economic purposes and functions of education and schooling. Critics of this discursive focus so far have not helped clarify education's educational purposes much; instead of economic or civic functions, critical voices tend to be most concerned with schooling and educational objectives connected to social justice and equality.[3]

Now let me be clear: I firmly believe all of the above goals and purposes of education and schooling are both important and legitimate. Schools should help prepare children to take their place as productive and contributing members of their society. Schools should help prepare children to take their place as fully prepared and functioning members of the civic polity within which they will live. Schools should, in intimate connection with these tasks, help make society more just. Though these tasks are conceptually individuated, they are different facets of what full membership in a society means. Each task here, and others as well, is connected to a robust and relatively autonomous sphere of civic life, and that is as it should be. Different spheres of life should engage and make demands on each other where they overlap (Blacker, 2007).

If the above argument has validity, we come to the point of this paper: *society, educational policy makers in particular, needs to be more realistic, more modest, in setting our expectations of school effects*. One consequence of our focus on the civic, economic, and social justice functions of schooling means it has become almost unintelligible to speak about the *educational* purposes of education and schooling. To say schools should serve an educational function is not to deny that they serve other functions, but forgetting that is not the danger we face. We need to remember that, while schools have multiple functions, whatever else is going on, and whatever "education" means, *education is the central mission of schools*. That is what we are in danger of forgetting, "we" being both policy makers and educators themselves.

Further there are serious negative repercussions for educators to make promises they cannot keep, for this opens schools to charges of failure. We see this today in the many attacks on the very idea of public education (see, e.g., Friedman, 1955; Chubb & Moe, 1990). In addition to letting the very idea of democratic education be lost to our consciousness, defining the mission of schooling as the equalization of opportunity in an economic system in which inequality is woven into its very fabric means that such commitments set schools up to fail to reach an impossible goal. As argued above, even if schools were perfect, or, more realistically, even if schools were all that could be asked of them, inequality would still exist, people would still live on the margins of economic disaster, and the rich and powerful would still possess the social and cultural capital to give their children undeserved advantages in the competition that is capitalism.

Our goals must be more modest: policy makers must recognize that, while schools can and must be partners in ameliorating social injustices, they cannot do so while the broader cultural surround not only accepts but celebrates, under other names, the very injustices schools are supposed to reduce.

Until we understand the purposes and nature of education, we are unlikely to address them very effectively, public schools will remain unable to define or defend successfully their mission in the public square, and educators will be unable to fulfill the core purposes of their calling. Defining schooling only or primarily as a means to economic ends seriously distorts the process of schooling. In addition, until the problem of inequality is framed primarily as a *social* problem, not one of schooling, we are unlikely to be effective in making things better. Indeed, until the sort of persistent, inherited inequality that is endemic to our economic system as an inequity, we cannot even see it as a problem. And, consequently, we cannot properly conceive of the educational problems proper to schooling.

Notes

1. And the inequality is stabilized by the fact that both the winners and the losers in the competition sincerely believe that the outcomes are deserved and therefore just.
2. In this case, Carter was conceding the unfairness of denying poor women access to abortions that wealthier women already had access to, but the broader point is germane.
3. To see this sort of critique at its best, see just about anything by Michael Apple, Henry Giroux, or Joel Spring, to name perhaps the most eloquent critics.

References

Berliner, D. C., & Biddle, B. (1995). *The manufactured crisis: Myths, fraud, and the attack on America's schools*. New York: Perseus Books.

Blacker, D. J. (2007). *Democratic education stretched thin: How complexity challenges a liberal ideal*. Albany, NY: State University of New York Press.

Bracey, G. (2001). *The war against America's public schools: Privatizing schools, commercializing education*. Upper Saddle River, NJ: Allyn & Bacon.

Campbell, G. V. (1966). A review of the dropout problem. *Peabody Journal of Education, 44*(2), 102–109.

Carter, J. (1977, July 12). Press conference. The American Presidency Project. http://www.presidency.ucsb.edu/ws/index.php?pid=7786&st=fair&st1=abortion.

Chubb, J., & Moe, T. (1990). *Politics, markets, and America's schools*. Washington, DC: The Brookings Institute

Coleman, J. (1966). *Equality of educational opportunity study*. Washington, DC: Department of Health, Education, and Welfare. Available online: http://www.icpsr.umich.edu/cocoon/ICPSR/STUDY/06389.xml

Edmonds, R., Tatner, G., Frederiksen, J., Lezotte, L., Chang, C., & Mosher, F. (1977). *Search for effective schools: The identification and analysis of city schools that are instructionally effective for poor children*. ERIC Document ED 142 610. Available online: http://www.eric.ed.gov:80/ERICDocs/data/ericdocs2sql/content_storage_01/0000019b/80/39/f4/5f.pdf

Friedman, M. (1955). The role of government in education. In R. A. Solo (Ed.), *Economics and the public interest*. New Brunswick, NJ: Rutgers University Press.

Green, T. F. (1980). *Predicting the behavior of the educational system*. Syracuse, NY: Syracuse University Press.

Levin, H. M., & Bachman, J. G. (1972). *The effects of dropping out: The costs to the nation of inadequate education: A report prepared for the Select Committee on Equal Opportunity of the United States Senate*. Washington, DC: U.S. Government Printing Office. Available from ERIC, Accession Number ED072171.

Lezotte, L., & Bancroft, B. (1972). School improvement based on effective schools research: A promising approach for economically disadvantaged and minority students. *The Journal of Negro Education, 54*(3): 301–312.

Meier, D. (2002). *The power of their ideas: Lessons from a small school in Harlem*. Boston: Beacon Press.

National Center for Educational Statistics. (1990). *The condition of education: 1990, Vol 1: Elementary and secondary education*. Washington, DC: U.S. Department of Education, U.S. Government Printing Office.

National Center for Educational Statistics. (2007). *Dropout rates in the United States: 2005. Table A-3*. Washington, DC: U.S. Department of Education, U.S. Government Printing Office. http://nces.ed.gov/pubs2007/dropout05/tables/table_A3.asp#top

National Commission on Excellence in Education. (1983). *A nation at risk: The imperative for educational reform: A report to the nation*. Washington, DC: The Commission on Excellence in Education, U.S. Government Printing Office. http://www.ed.gov/pubs/NatAtRisk/risk.html.

Olson, K. W. (1973). The G.I. Bill and higher education: Success and surprise. *American Quarterly, 25*(Dec.), 596–610.

Scheffler, I. (1976). Basic mathematical skills: Some philosophical and practical remarks. *Teachers College Record, 78*(Dec.), 205–212.

Schreiber, D. (1964). The school dropout—A profile. *Educational Digest, XXX*(Sept.), 10–13.

Stevens, M. L. (2007). *Creating a class: College admissions and the education of elites*. Cambridge, MA: Harvard University Press.

Walzer, M. (1983). *Spheres of justice: A defense of pluralism and equality*. New York: Basic Books.

CHAPTER 12

FAITH, THE INDIVIDUAL AND SOCIETY

RELIGION

How We Come to Know Religion

In the article below, Phil Zuckerman presents ideas about how we learn religion. He shows that our families are important in learning religion as well as others in our social environments. This seems pretty straightforward. However, he goes on to argue that those "others" in our lives are far more powerful in shaping our view and acceptance of a particular religion because it is familiar to them and becomes familiar to us. This familiarity to a religion that is common among ourselves, family, and friends then becomes more powerful than exposure to alternative religions. Those and our surroundings shape our understanding, acceptance, and practice of any given religion. Below I have included some items you might want to keep in mind while you read through this article.

Some Things to Keep in Mind

1. Do you practice the same religion as your parents?
2. Do you think the historical time period in which you were raised influenced your ideas on religion?
3. Have you ever had a spiritual or mystical experience? Did it affect your view of religion?
4. Why do you think people who share the same religion have similar spiritual experiences in one culture but different experiences in another culture?

RELIGION IS SOCIALLY LEARNED
Phil Zuckerman

I remember noticing something peculiar when I was only in third grade: all my classmates were the same religion as their parents. All the Jewish kids had Jewish parents. All the Catholic kids had Catholic parents. All the Protestant kids had Protestant parents. And all the kids that "weren't religious" or "didn't have a religion" had parents of the same ilk. And then one day, a young girl named Emily joined our class midyear. What made Emily stand out—or, rather, *sit* out—was that she wouldn't stand and recite the Pledge of Allegiance along with the rest of us each morning. I was completely fascinated by this act of deviance. I thought that it took incredible chutzpah to sit each morning and not stand and recite the Pledge with the rest of the class. In the schoolyard, I quickly found out the reason for Emily's behavior: she was a Jehovah's Witness, and they don't believe in swearing their allegiance to anything but God. And it didn't take me long to find out that—surprise, surprise—Emily's parents were also Jehovah's Witnesses. "So that explains it," I thought to myself as I went to play handball with Stewart Stein.

Looking back now, I like to think that my awareness of parental influence over my fellow third graders' religious identities is evidence that I was simply destined to become a sociologist of religion. By age nine I had already realized a basic premise in the sociological perspective on religion: *it is socially learned.* People learn and acquire their religion from other people (Finney 1978; Chalfant and LeBeff 1991; Batson, Schoenrade, and Ventis 1993, 53).

In any decent introduction to sociology course, professors will spend some time talking about that good old sociological term "socialization." It gets defined a number of ways, but for me, it simply refers to the process of absorbing the infinite aspects of the culture around us. It is the process of informally learning and unconsciously internalizing the norms, beliefs, and values of our family, peer group, society, nation, and so on. So much of what we know, do, feel, think, and believe comes from how we were/are socialized. In sociology, we refer to the significant and influential people and institutions in our lives—the ones that informally "teach" us our culture—as

Phil Zuckerman, "Religion Is Socially Learned," *Invitation to the Sociology of Religion*, pp. 47-60, 131-149. Copyright © 2003 by Taylor & Francis Group. Reprinted with permission.

"agents of socialization." They include parents, friends, relatives, coaches, advertising executives, ministers, baby-sitters, neighbors, teachers, schools, politicians, rock stars, news anchors, and the like. These agents of socialization have an enormously strong and pervasive influence on much of our identities. I could go on and on discussing multiple levels and aspects of socialization, but this isn't the place—and I have already touched upon it in my discussion of Amala and Kamala in chapter 2. The point here is to emphasize that in addition to so many other aspects of ourselves, our religious identities also are often largely a result of basic socialization processes (Fowlkes 1988). Just as we learn our language from others—or what marriage means, or whether eating cow flesh is wonderful or horrible—so too do we learn our religion. More often than not, it is the "significant others" in our lives who play a major role in exposing us to religion and determining our specific religious identities (Batson, Schoenrade, and Ventis 1993).

Let's start with the profound influence the family unit has upon religious identity, particularly parents (Benson, Donahue, and Erickson 1989; Erickson 1992; Mosley and Brockenbrough 1988; Roof and McKinney 1987, 165–166). My experience back in third grade—where all my classmates' religious identities mimicked those of their parents—is quite common, and I would guess similar to the experience of you, the reader. But there are extensive data out there, in addition to our personal recollections. One hundred years ago, in his groundbreaking empirical study of black religious life in the South, W. E. B. Du Bois (2003 [1903]) surveyed over one thousand children and teenagers concerning their religious identity. When asked why they liked a certain church the best over others, the overwhelming majority cited "on account of parents or relatives." For nearly a century since, social scientists have observed the strong correlation between parents and their children in terms of religious identity (Hayes and Pittelkow 1993; Batson, Schoenrade, and Ventis 1993; Hyde 1990; Stark and Glock 1968; Ozorak 1989; Kleugel 1980; Greeley 1982; Hunsberger and Brown 1984; Nelsen 1981; Sherkat and Wilson 1995; Myers 1996). As Argyle and Beit-Hallahmi (1975, 30) conclude, after reviewing extensive literature on the subject, "there can be no doubt that the attitudes of parents are among the most important factors in the formation of religious attitudes." Potvin and Sloane (1985) found that teenagers whose parents are regular church attendees are five times more likely to be religiously active than teenagers whose parents are infrequent or non-church attenders. Stark and Bainbridge (1985) found a significant correlation between parents' beliefs in God and their children's beliefs in God, succinctly concluding that "believers tend to have believers for parents; nonbelievers tend to have nonbelievers for parents" (1985, 330). As cited in the previous chapter, more than 80 percent of Americans born Catholic stay Catholic, more than 90 percent of Americans born Protestant stay Protestant, and more than 90 percent of Americans born Jewish stay Jewish (Greeley 1991). Cornwall (1988) and Stott (1988) looked at Mormon religiosity, finding parental influence on religious identity to be empirically significant, with Stott concluding that his data "clearly support the belief that parents play a dominant role in the religious socialization of their offspring" (1988, 261). Concerning other specific Christian denominations in America, data analyzed and summarized by Spilka, Hood, and Gorsuch (1985) indicate that approximately 75 percent of children born to Baptist parents stay Baptist, approximately 76 percent of children born to Lutheran parents stay Lutheran, and approximately 62 percent of children born to Methodist or Episcopalian parents stay Methodist or Episcopalian, respectively. And it is important to keep in mind that those children who grow up and do not remain in the same specific Christian denomination as their parents will still most likely embrace some other form of Christian religious identity (Hadaway and Marler 1993; Stark and Finke 2000; Bibby and Brinkerhoff 1973; Sherkat 1993).

While the bulk of existing research does support the conclusion that parents clearly influence the religious beliefs and practices of their children, there is debate about the definite strength and actual time span of that influence (Kalish and Johnson 1972; Hoge, Petrillo, and Smith 1982; Bengston 1975; Dudley and Dudley 1986; Francis and Brown 1991). The fact is, of course, that it is not an absolute, air-tight causal relationship. Kids don't always and in every instance automatically adopt the exact same religion as their parents. Far from it. Although changing religions is a rarity in the United States—Stark and Finke (2000, 115) estimate that fewer than 1 percent of Americans convert to a completely new religion—most of us certainly know some people who didn't stick with their parents' religion and grew up to choose different religious paths.

Consider my friend Doug, who wrote that piece on prayer for the introduction to this book. Doug wasn't raised Mormon, but after his marriage to Michelle, he converted to the Church of Jesus Christ of Latter-day Saints. And what is interesting sociologically is that Doug's process of religious conversion/change following his marriage to Michelle is actually quite typical (Musick and Wilson 1995; Alba 1990; Hout and Greeley 1987; Bahr and Albrecht 1989; Hoge 1981). It fits one of the major patterns of religious switching: it is other people in our social world—usually those closest to us—who exert a strong influence over our religious choices/paths (Stark and Bainbridge 1985; Roberts and Davidson 1984; Richardson and Stewart 1977; Gaede 1976). As Stark and Finke (2000, 117) assert, "conversion is seldom about seeking or embracing an ideology; it is about bringing one's religious behavior into alignment with that of one's friends and family members." Our parents are the most influential in influencing our religious identity, as discussed above. And after parents come spouses and friends (Gunnoe and Moore 2002; Stark 1984; Hyde 1990; Willits and Crider 1989; Benson, Donahue, and Erickson 1989; Woodroof 1986; Potvin and Lee 1982; Stott 1988, Lenski 1963; Hoge, Petrillo and Smith 1978). That is, in the rare instances when people don't take on the same religious identity as their parents, they tend to take on the religious identity of their spouse or friends. And if it isn't a parent or spouse or friend, it will probably be a coworker or neighbor who sparks interest in the new faith. In sum, extensive sociological research reveals that people make religious choices and pursue religious paths which tend to follow neatly along lines of preexisting social networks, relational bonds, and personal attachments (Snow and Machalek 1984; Lofland and Stark 1965; Lofland 1966; Kox, Meeus, and t'Hart 1991; Leatham 1997).

All of this can be neatly summed up as follows: we generally acquire and absorb our religion from other people, usually those to whom we are personally close or are significantly attached. And what that ultimately means is that *while religion may have to do with a connection or attachment to God or some other Supreme Reality Out There, more significantly (and observably) it has to do with a connection or attachment to mom or dad or husband or wife or sibling or friend right here on planet Earth.*

Of course, recognizing this fact can be potentially threatening to the deeply religious individual. It suggests that the strong devotion of "Tom" to his religion or Jesus is quite arbitrary; if Tom's social location were different, or if he had had different parents or friends, he most probably would think some other religion was "true" and swear by it with equal passion. This thought always strikes me when I talk with passionate Christians who insist that they would still be Christian even if they had been born in Yemen three hundred years ago. They are so convinced of the eternal truth of their religion that they can't even entertain the notion that had they been born into a different community or country or family at a different time, they would most likely cling to a different religion and be equally convinced of its eternal truth. The fact of the matter is that had Tom been born and raised in Yemen three hundred years ago he would most certainly be a devout Muslim, convinced that Islam and the Qur'an were eternally true, not Christianity and the New Testament. Conversely, if "Mustafa," a devout Wahhabi Muslim of Saudi Arabia—who swears by the truth of the Qur'an and is vehemently certain that Muhammad is the greatest prophet of Allah—had been born and raised in northern Mississippi two hundred years ago, he would most likely be a Baptist or Methodist Christian, safe and secure in his Christian beliefs. Ultimately, religious identity and conviction aren't generally so much a matter of choice or faith or soul-searching as a matter of who and what one's parents, friends, neighbors, and community practice and profess.

It is important to remember that nonbelievers aren't necessarily exempt from this phenomenon, either. After all, I cannot escape the fact that I am a nonbeliever and—surprise, surprise—so are my folks, relatives, and most of my friends. I will be the first to admit that my skeptical agnosticism has its roots clearly in my social environment, and had I been born to devout Sikh parents and lived among other devout Sikhs, I'd most likely be writing a book on the Divine Wisdom and Eternal Truth of the Guru Granth Sahib right now, instead of this little book on the sociology of religion.

But perhaps you aren't convinced about the overwhelming impact of social location on religious identity. Maybe you just aren't sure that religion is so clearly something socially learned from the significant others in our lives. It is quite possible that you just happen to know a real rebel out there, someone who adopted a religion completely on her own. Perhaps your cousin became a pagan witch all by herself, without anyone directly influencing her. She just went out and looked into it, to the surprise and shock of all her friends and family. Such deviant things do happen, however rarely. I'll concede that some people do sometimes choose a religious path completely different from, or even at odds with, the significant others in their social world.

Take the case of John Walker Lindh, the young American found fighting with the Taliban in Afghanistan in the wake of the September 11 terrorist attacks on the United States. John Walker Lindh's parents were Catholic (although his mom, interestingly, converted to Buddhism when John was in adolescence). John had no Muslim relatives, neighbors, or friends, and yet at age sixteen he converted to Islam. On Friday nights, rather than hang out with his friends at the mall or go out on dates, he attended religious services, worshipping at a mosque on the other side of town. After graduating from high school, he left for the Middle East, where he completely committed himself to the study of Islam, roaming from Yemen to Pakistan and eventually up into Afghanistan.

How do we explain John Walker Lindh's religious choice? Clearly he wasn't socialized into Islam by his parents or lured into Islam by a friend or a girlfriend or even a neighbor or coworker. He did take classes on world religions, and his mother did expose him to various religious traditions. But that doesn't explain it. He did read *The Autobiography of Malcolm X,* which apparently got him interested in Islam. But the vast majority of teenagers who read Malcolm X don't convert to Islam. So what exactly was it? The only honest answer: we'll never really know for sure. As Marion Goldman (1999, 216) has eloquently acknowledged, "it is necessary for a blend of personal predispositions and social serendipity to combine at just the right moment in order for someone to join and remain part of a new faith."

But at least this much we can be sure of: his Islamic identity was still *socially learned.* Someone else—some other person or persons—had to teach John Walker Lindh about Islam and show him what it means to be Muslim. Those people may have been strangers from the other side of the city or from faraway lands, but he was still dependent upon other human beings in the formation of his religious identity. Somebody had to tell him about the Qur'an. Somebody had to tell him about the Hadith. Somebody had to tell him about Allah and Mecca and Medina and Muhammad and Ramadan. Someone had to teach him about *shahada, salat, zakat, sawm, Hajj,* and *jihad.* That person may have reached him in the form of a book or pamphlet or television show—but a book or a pamphlet or a television show still originates with somebody, somewhere.

Think about it: the main reason anyone alive today thinks that the Bible is divine (the revealed word of God) is that someone else told them it was. If a hypothetical individual who had never heard of the Bible or its contents found the Bible and read it—if such a person had never been taught about or even heard of God or Moses or Jesus or the Gospels and had never heard of or known of a Jew or a Christian and just found a Bible and read it—there is no reason to suppose that this person would conclude that it was any more holy or profound or divine than the works of Homer, the Tibetan Book of the Dead, the works of J. R. R. Tolkein, the Upanishads, the Qur'an, the Book of Mormon, or the writings of Plato.

Just as factors of time and place greatly affect our religious identities, equally crucial is our social world. We learn our religion—and all its significant particulars—from other people.

As with the contents of the last chapter, whenever I lecture on this chapter's contents, students have typical questions and challenges.

First question: "OK, it is easy to agree that the significant others in our social world teach us many details about religion. Our parents may teach us about the Bible and we probably learn the specific rituals, prayers, and dogmas of our faith from our parents, friends, Sunday school teachers, and so on. But what about people who actually have religious experiences? How can religious experiences be socially learned?"

As discussed in the introduction (see pages 7–9), people do have direct, personal "contacts" with the divine or otherworldly, and these are unavoidably important when trying to understand religion (Davis 1989). Consider this religious experience that a fellow sociologist recently reported to me via e-mail:

> One day, I went running, and I could see white bands of light that connected the trees to the houses to the grass to the sidewalk to people to dogs and cats walking around, birds flying around, even a few bugs. I have heard things about everything being interconnected, and when I saw these bands of light, I felt that all people were connected with one another, with the animals, with nature, and God, and that these bands were beaming visible manifestations of all of that interconnectedness. I considered this experience deeply spiritual and somehow religious.

When people claim to have religious experiences, it appears that something manifestly transcendental, mystical, and otherworldly is occurring which must be beyond mere social construction. However, I would still point out that even religious experiences can illustrate the determining influence of social learning. For, if nothing else, religious experiences are clearly socially patterned. Different cultures include within their religious rubric specific "religious experience scripts," and the members of such cultures tend to follow these religious experience scripts quite well, having the exact type of religious experience that is expected in their given culture (Lewis 1971).

Consider the religious experiences which take place in the temple of the goddess Bhadrakali, the patron Hindu deity of Kerala, in southern India (Caldwell 1999). During the *mutiyettu*—the dance-drama-performance offering which is enacted within the temples throughout Kerala—individual participants are believed to actually become possessed by the gods and goddesses, serving as literal human vehicles through which the deities become embodied:

> The drums pound relentlessly. The festival of the goddess is in full swing.
> Now it is the dead of night. The drama of Bhadrakali and Darika [her enemy] has been unfolding to the deep voices of the drums for several hours. As each scene begins, the actors dance and spin, carefully making offerings of prayers and flowers to the deity ...

It is the deepest part of the night of the most dangerous day of the week, the time when the ugly and bloodthirsty move abroad in search of their victims. It is a time when people should be safe and asleep in their beds ... But they are not in their beds. They are here, women, men, and children, in full view of the night sky, the unhealthy mists of evening, the frightening spirits of a Friday night, watching the battle of Bhadrakali and Darika on the dry, barren paddy fields of the village temple grounds. All night the actors and priests have been flirting with the dark powers at large. Everything has been calculated to call forth those powers and to invite them into the performance area, into the person of the actor himself, into the body of the Bhadrakali dancing mutiyettu.

And now it is time. Kali [the goddess] begins to veer madly into the audience, wildly waving her sickle-shaped iron sword in blood lust for Darika s head. People jump up from their seats and run for the safety of the shrine ... suddenly her heavy head-dress begins to slip, her steps falter, she swoons and begins to tremble violently, her eyes rolling up into her head, her arms flailing. She is helped to her seat near the flame, her head-dress removed, the energy temporarily contained and controlled, her body cooled. (Caldwell 1999, 65)

Consider this typical religious experience from an American Protestant Christian woman who was having doubts about the veracity of her faith (Brasher 1998, 97–98):

One night I said, "Lord if you are real, please reveal yourself to me." I went to sleep with that thought on my mind. The next morning, he woke me up early. I never get up early, but I woke up. There was a rainbow outlining the cross in my room. I have woken up morning after morning, year after year, looking at that cross and there was nothing unusual about it. I did not want to move from that spot. I felt as if I was being bathed in warmth right there. The presence of the Lord was so real and precious at that point that I felt as if I was lying in his arms.

Consider the religious experiences within the rubric of Haitian Vodou, wherein *Gede* spirits or divinities possess and inhabit the bodies of the living (McAlister 2000). As Karen McCarthy Brown (1991,5) explains:

Half a dozen times a year ... Alourdes [a Vodou priestess] holds "birthday parties" for her favorite spirits, or as they are also called. Clients, friends, and relatives gather around a decorated "niche," whose center-piece is a table laden with food. Here they pray, clap, and sing until the crowd is sufficiently "heated up" to entice a Vodou spirit to join the party, to "ride" Alourdes. In a trance state from which she will later emerge with little or no memory of what has transpired, her body becomes the "horse" of the spirit, her voice the spirit's voice, her words and behavior those of the spirit.

Among certain Christian Holiness religious groups throughout Appalachia, the physical handling of poisonous rattlesnakes can produce religious experiences, as this author recounts of his experience in one such snake-handling church (Covington 1995,175):

> So I got up there in the middle of the handlers ... Who was it going to be? Carl's eyes were saying, you. And yes, it was the big rattler, the one with my name on it, acrid-smelling, carnal, alive ... if I took it, I'd be possessing the sacred ... This was the moment. I didn't stop to think about it. I just gave in. I stepped forward and took the snake with both hands. Carl released it to me. I turned to face the congregation and lifted the rattlesnake up towards the light. It was moving like it wanted to get up even higher, to climb out of that church and into the air. And it was exactly as the handlers had told me. I felt no fear. The snake seemed to be an extension of myself. And suddenly there seemed to be nothing in the room but me and the snake. Everything else had disappeared. Carl, the congregation, Jim—all gone, all faded to white. And I could not hear the earsplitting music. The air was silent and still and filled with strong, even light. And I realized that I, too, was fading into the white. I was losing myself by degrees, like the incredibly shrinking man ... I knew then why the handlers took up serpents. There is power in the act of disappearing; there is victory in the loss of self. It must be close to our conception of paradise, what it's like before you're born or after you die ...
>
> I came back in stages ... I lowered the snake to waist level. It was an enormous animal, heavy and firm ... I extended it towards Carl. He took it from me, stepped to the side, and gave it in turn to J.L.
>
> "Jesus," J.L. said. "Oh, Jesus." His knees bent, his head went back. I knew it was happening to him too.

I could go on and on providing examples of various types of religious experiences found within different religious cultures: Native American vision quests, Buddhist meditative experiences, Catholic visions, and so on. But such a catalog of diverse religious experiences from around the world isn't necessary—such experiences need only be broached—to make my argument: social groups and cultures provide the contexts, symbols, triggers, and expectations for the religious experiences their members may have (Yamane and Polzer 1994). Religious experience scripts provide the specific, expected ways to have a religious experience and the contents thereof. Through cultural processes of socialization, people formally or informally learn the religious experience scripts of their culture or religious enclave and subsequently tend to have the exact kinds of religious experiences they are expected to have, in degree, form, shape, and substance. The Hindu worshippers of BhadraKali in Kerala have specific religious experiences involving bodily possession by deities. American Evangelical Protestants have their specific experiences, involving a profound sense of comfort or security and the felt presence of God or Jesus. In a Pentecostal church, speaking in tongues may be the expected experience. Within Haitian Vodou religious culture, bodily possession by spirits is what people expect and experience, with all the behavior and ceremony that go with it. In certain Christian Holiness groups in Appalachia, snake handling comes with its specific form of religious experience. In sum, though we can't write off religious experiences as being pure social constructions—something otherworldly may very well be occurring—we can still be sociologically confident that social learning is always a key ingredient and a determining, filtering factor. Even in the midst of dramatically personal and spiritual experiences of the otherworldly, cultural patterns and societal expectations are perpetual determining forces.

And now for the second common question that usually arises from students concerning religion being socially learned:

"Even though people obviously learn a lot about religion from those around them, this doesn't account for the genesis of a new religion. What about the people who start new religions? If you are arguing that we just learn our religion from others, well, then, how does the religion we are learning start in the first place? John Walker Lindh may have been taught about Islam by other people—but how did Islam originate? How do sociologists explain the birth of new religions?"

My first response to this important line of questioning is to begin by reminding students that successful new religions are excruciatingly rare. Sure, new religious groups pop up all the time, but how many of them actually flourish for multiple generations? How many new religions actually survive the death or disgrace of their charismatic leader? And of those that do, how many last more than one or two hundred years? The truth is, the overwhelming majority of new religions die relatively quickly. As Armand Mauss (1994, viiii) acknowledges, "history suggests that the overwhelming majority of [religious] movements fail to survive even one generation, to say nothing of enduring across the centuries." Of the religions that seem to have "made it" and are currently thriving on the planet, many don't have actual historical founders that we can point to (Hinduism, for instance). Some religions do have known historical founders, but these individuals are mind-numbingly rare. Just think of how many people have ever lived on this earth. Billions and billions. Now, of all the people who have ever lived, how many have started successful new religions? Twelve? Twenty? More than 99.99 percent of humanity doesn't found a successful new religion. So by arguing that religion is socially learned, that is, that people learn their religion from other people (which is the whole point of this chapter), I believe I am accurately accounting for the religious identities/experiences of more than 99.99 percent of humanity.

"But it does happen," the student rebuts. "Individuals do construct new religious traditions. You are avoiding the question."

My second response is to then remind students that "new" is a very relative and even questionable term when discussing the development of religious traditions. The fact is, every successful new religious tradition grows within a specific sociohistorical context, and thus unavoidably develops out of a preexisting religious culture. This means that every "new" religious tradition borrows from, reiterates, reinterprets, reflects, and straight-out plagiarizes from the religion or religions that have come before it. For instance, Christianity elaborates upon preexisting Judaism, Islam draws from preexisting Judaism and Christianity, Mormonism elaborates upon long-established Judaism and Christianity, Baha'ism grows out of Islam, Sikhism develops out of preexisting Hindu and Islamic traditions, and so on. OK, I'm still avoiding the question. The fact is, qualitatively new religions *do* arise, despite their dependence on preexisting traditions.

But I also can't help pointing out to students that in many instances of individuals starting new religions, the first converts to the new tradition are invariably family members and friends of that individual (Stark 1999)! The first converts to Islam were Muhammad's family and friends. The first converts to Mormonism were Joseph Smith's family and friends (Persuitte 2000). This further illustrates the importance of preexisting social relationships in (new) religious identities.

So when asked about the emergence of new religions I point out that (1) the successful creation of new religions is extremely rare, (2) no religion is completely "new," as all religions develop from preexisting religions, and (3) conversion to new religions seems to follow preexisting social networks. But I am still avoiding the ultimate question: How do we sociologically explain the birth of new religions?

I think most social scientists and historians of religion would subscribe to a sort of "right person, right time, right place" theory. This runs as follows: a highly motivated and inspired individual arises (such as Muhammad or Joseph Smith) who possess an abundance of charisma—a magnetic personal character trait made sociologically famous by Max Weber (1978). This individual formulates a clear religious vision which strongly resonates with the people receiving it on a variety of levels: psychologically, politically, economically, aesthetically, and, of course, theologically. The social circumstances are thus that the new religious vision is somehow able to grow and spread, despite persecution. And then, even after the disappearance of the remarkable individual who started it all, the tradition continues as a result of sound leadership, carefully crafted scriptures, and meaningful traditions and rituals. To be sure, sociologists and historians of religion have written and debated every single aspect of the above scenario, in abundance (Weber 1946; Moore 1986; Stark 1987; Wilson 1987; Bird 1993; Hammond and Machacek 1993; Miller 1991; Johnson 1992). But the overall point of this theoretical perspective is to assert that the emergence of successful new religions has to do with an exceedingly rare convergence of specific historical, personal, political, psychological, cultural, and theological circumstances.

In the end, the sociologist must also allow for the possibility that he or she simply can't explain everything. The sociological observer of religion must admit that maybe, just maybe, the founder of a new religion is indeed actually serving as a channel or voice or vehicle for the divine/otherworldly. Despite the lack of reliable data, we must entertain the possibility that when Muhammad recited the Qur'an, he really actually and literally was acting as the mouthpiece for Allah. Or when Joseph Smith was composing the Book of Mormon, he really was truly translating divinely inspired words. Or when Ann Lee of the Shakers was spreading her teachings, or when Paul was writing his epistles, or when the authors of the Upanishads were at work, they were actually and truly operating as loudspeakers for that great, mystical stereo in the sky. Personally, I think discerning whether such is the case is a matter of empirical evidence. Others, no doubt, would argue that it is a matter of personal faith. You will have to decide that one for yourself (but be forewarned: the significant others in your social world will most likely influence your decision!).

Bibliography

Alba, R. 1990. *Ethnic Identity.* New Haven: Yale University Press.

Argyle, M., and B. Beit-Hallahmi. 1975. *The Social Psychology of Religion.* London: Routledge and Kegan Paul.

Bahr, Howard, and Stan Albrecht. 1989. "Strangers Once More: Patterns of Disaffiliation from Mormonism." *Journal for the Scientific Study of Religion* 28 (2): 180–200.

Batson, C. Daniel, Patricia Schoenrade, and W. Larry Ventis. 1993. *Religion and the Individual: A Social-Psychological Perspective.* New York: Oxford University Press.

Bengston, V. L. 1975. "Generation and Family Effects in Value Socialization." *American Sociological Review* 40: 358–371.

Benson, Peter, Michael Donahue, and Joseph Erickson. 1989. "Adolescence and Religion: A Review of the Literature from 1970 to 1986." *Research in the Scientific Study of Religion* 1: 153–181.

Bibby, Reginald, and Merlin Brinkerhoff. 1973. "The Circulation of Saints: A Study of People Who Join Conservative Churches." *Journal for the Scientific Study of Religion* 12: 273–283.

Bird, Frederick. 1993. "Charisma and Leadership in New Religious Movements." In *Religion and the Social Order. The Handbook on Cults and Sects in America,* edited by David Bromley and Jeffrey Hadden. Greenwich, Conn.: JAI Press.

Brasher, B. 1998. *Godly Women.* New Brunswick, N.J.: Rutgers University Press.

Brown, K. M. 1991. *Mama Lola: A Vodou Priestess in Brooklyn.* Berkeley: University of California Press.

Caldwell, Sarah. 1999. *Oh Terrifying Mother: Sexuality, Violence, and Worship of the Goddess Kali.* New York: Oxford University Press.

Chalfant, Paul, and Emily LeBeff. 1991. *Understanding People and Social Life.* St. Paul: West Publishing.

Cornwall, Marie. 1988. "The Influence of Three Agents of Religious Socialization: Family, Church, and Peers." In *The Religion and Family Connection: Social Science Perspectives,* edited by Darwin Thomas. Provo, Utah: Religious Studies Center, Brigham Young University.

Covington, Dennis. 1995. *Salvation on Sand Mountain: Snake Handling and Redemption in Southern Appalachia.* Cambridge, Mass.: Perseus Publishing.

Davis, C. F. 1989. *The Evidential Force of Religious Experience.* Oxford: Clarendon Press.

Du Bois, W. E. B. 2003 [1903]. *The Negro Church.* Walnut Creek, Calif.: Alta Mira Press.

Dudley, R. L., and M. G. Dudley. 1986. "Transmission of Religious Values from Parents to Adolescents." *Review of Religious Research* 28: 3–15.

Erickson, J. A. 1992. Adolescent Religious Development and Commitment: A Structural Equation Model of the Role of Family, Peer Group, and Educational Influences. *Journal for the Scientific Study of Religion* 31: 131–152.

Finney, J. M. 1978. "A Theory of Religious Commitment." *Sociological Analysis* 39: 19–35.

Fowlkes, M. A. 1988. "Religion and Socialization." In *Handbook of Preschool Religious Education,* edited by D. Ratcliff. Birmingham, Ala.: Religious Education Press.

Francis, Leslie, and Lawrence Brown. 1991. "The Influence of Home, Church, and School Prayer among 16-Year-Old Adolescents in England." *Review of Religious Research* 33: 112–122.

Gaede, Stan. 1976. "A Causal Model of Belief-Orthodoxy: Proposal and Empirical Test." *Sociological Analysis* 37: 205–217.

Goldman, Marion. 1999. *Passionate Journeys: Why Successful Women Joined a Cult.* Ann Arbor: University of Michigan Press.

Greeley, Andrew. *Religion: A Secular Theory.* 1982. New York: The Free Press.

———. 1991. "American Exceptionalism: The Religious Phenomenon." In *Is America Different? A New Look at American Exceptionalism,* edited by Byron Shafer. Oxford: Clarendon Press.

Gunnoe, Marjorie, and Kristin Moore. 2002. "Predictors of Religiosity among Youth Aged 17–22: A Longitudinal Study of the National Survey of Children." *Journal for the Scientific Study of Religion* 41 (4): 613–622.

Hadaway, Kirk, and Penny Long Marler. 1993. "All in the Family: Religious Mobility in America." *Review of Religious Research* 35 (2): 97–111.

Hammond, Judith, Bettie Cole, and Scott Beck. 1993. "Religious Heritage and Teenage Marriage." *Review of Religious Research* 35 (2): 117–133.

Hayes, B., and Y. Pittelkow. 1993. "Religious Belief, Transmission, and the Family." *Journal of Marriage and the Family* 55: 755–766.

Hoge, Dean. 1981. *Converts, Dropouts, Returnees: A Study of Religious Change among Catholics.* New York: Pilgrim.

Hoge, D., G. Petrillo, and E. Smith. 1978. "Determinants of Church Participation and Attitudes among High School Youth." *Journal for the Scientific Study of Religion* 17: 359–379.

———. 1982. "Transmission of Religious and Social Values from Parents to Teenage Children." *Journal of Marriage and the Family* 44: 569–580.

Hout, M., and A. Greeley. 1987. "The Center Doesn't Hold: Church Attendance in the United States, 1940–1984." *American Sociological Review* 52: 325–345.

Hunsberger, Bruce, and L.B. Brown. 1984. "Religious Socialization, Apostasy, and the Impact of Family Background." *Journal for the Scientific Study of Religion* 23 (3): 239–251.

Hyde, Kenneth. 1990. *Religion in Childhood and Adolescence: A Comprehensive Review of the Research*. Birmingham, Ala.: Religious Education Press.

Johnson, Benton. 1992. "On Founders and Followers: Some Factors in the Development of New Religious Movements." *Sociological Analysis* 53: 1–13.

Kalish, R. A., and A. I. Johnson. 1972. "Value Similarities and Differences in Three Generations of Women." *Journal of Marriage and the Family* 34: 49–54.

Kleugel, James. 1980. "Denominational Mobility." *Journal for the Scientific Study of Religion* 19: 26–39.

Kox, Willem, Wim Meeus, and Harm t'Hart. 1991. "Religious Conversion of Adolescents: Testing the Lofland and Stark Model of Religious Conversion." *Sociological Analysis* 52: 227–240.

Leatham, Miguel. 1997. "Rethinking Religious Decision-Making in Peasant Millenarianism: The Case of Nueva Jerusalem." *Journal of Contemporary Religion* 12: 295–309.

Lenski, G. 1963. *The Religious Factor*. Garden City, N.Y.: Doubleday.

Lewis, I. M. 1971. *Ecstatic Religion: An Anthropological Study of Spirit Possession and Shamanism*. Baltimore, Md.: Penguin Books.

Lofland, John. 1966. *Doomsday Cult: A Study of Conversion, Proselytization, and Maintenance of Faith*. Englewood Cliffs, N.J.: Prentice Hall.

Lofland, John, and Rodney Stark. 1965. "Becoming a World-Saver": A Theory of Conversion to a Deviant Perspective." *American Sociological Review* 30: 862–875.

Mauss, Armand. 1994. *The Angel & The Beehive: The Mormon Struggle with Assimilation*. Urbana: U. of Illinois Press.

McAlister, Elizabeth. 2000. "Love, Sex, and Gender Embodied: The Spirits of Haitian Vodou." In *Love, Sex, and Gender in the World Religions*, edited by Joseph Runzo and Nancy Martin. Oxford: Oneworld.

Miller, Timothy, ed. 1991. *When Prophets Die: The Postcharismatic Fate of New Religious Movements*. Albany: State University of New York Press.

Moore, Laurence. 1986. *Religious Outsiders and the Making of Americans*. New York: Oxford University Press.

Mosley, R. J., and K. Brockenbrough. 1988. "Faith Development in the Preschool Years." In *Handbook of Preschool Religious Education,* edited by D. Ratcliff. Birmingham, Ala.: Religious Education Press.

Musick, Marc, and John Wilson. 1995. "Religious Switching for Marriage Reasons." *Sociology of Religion* 56 (3): 257–270.

Myers, Scott. 1996. "An Interactive Model of Religiosity Inheritance: The Importance of Family Context." *American Sociological Review* 61 (October): 858–866.

Nelsen, Hart. 1981. "Gender Differences in the Effects of Parental Discord on Preadolescent Religiousness." *Journal for the Scientific Study of Religion* 20: 351–360.

Ozorak, E.W. 1989. "Social and Cognitive Influences on the Development of Religious Beliefs and Commitment in Adolescence." *Journal for the Scientific Study of Religion* 28: 448–463.

Persuitte, David. 2000. *Joseph Smith and the Origins of the Book of Mormon.* Jefferson, N.C.: McFarland and Company.

Potvin, Raymond, and C. F. Lee. 1982. "Adolescent Religion: A Developmental Approach." *Sociological Analysis* 43 (2): 131–144.

Potvin, R.H., and D. M. Sloane. 1985. "Parental Control, Age, and Religious Practice." *Review of Religious Research* 27: 3–14.

Richardson, James, and Mary Stewart. 1977. "Conversion Process Models and the Jesus Movement." *American Behavioral Scientist* 20: 819–838.

Roberts, M. K., and J. D. Davidson. 1984. "The Nature and Source of Religious Involvement." *Review of Religious Research* 25: 334–350.

Roof, Wade Clark, and William McKinney. 1987. *American Mainline Religion.* New Brunswick, N.J.: Rutgers University Press.

Sherkat, Darren. 1993. "Theory and Method in Religious Mobility Research." *Social Scientific Research* 22: 208–227.

Sherkat, Darren, and John Wilson. 1995. "Preferences, Constraints, and Choices in Religious Markets: An Examination of Religious Switching and Apostasy." *Social Forces* 73: 993–1026.

Snow, David, and R. Machalek. 1984. "The Sociology of Conversion." *Annual Review of Sociology* 10: 167–190.

Spilka, Bernard, Ralph Hood, and Richard Gorsuch. 1985. *The Psychology of Religion: An Empirical Approach.* Engelewood Cliffs, N.J.: Prentice Hall.

Stark, Rodney. 1984. "Religion and Conformity. Reaffirming a Sociology of Religion." *Sociological Analysis* 45: 273–282.

———. 1987. "How New Religions Succeed: A Theoretical Model." In *The Future of New Religious Movements,* edited by David Bromley and Phillip Hammond, 11–29. Macon, Ga.: Mercer University Press.

———. 1999. "A Theory of Revelations," *Journal for the Scientific Study of Religion* 38 (2): 287–308.

Stark, Rodney, and William Sims Bainbridge. 1985. *The Future of Religion: Secularization, Revival, and Cult Formation.* Berkeley: University of California Press.

Stark, Rodney, and Roger Finke. 1993. "A Rational Approach to the History of American Cults and Sects." In *Religion and the Social Order: The Handbook on Cults and Sects in America,* edited by David Bromley and Jeffrey Hadden. Greenwich, Conn.: JAI Press.

———. 2000. *Acts of Faith.* Berkeley: University of California Press.

Stark, Rodney, and Charles Glock. 1968. *American Piety.* Berkeley: University of California Press.

Stott, Gerald. 1988. "Familial Influence on Religious Involvement." In *The Religion and Family Connection: Social Science Perspectives,* edited by Darwin Thomas. Provo, Utah: Religious Studies Center, Brigham Young University.

Weber, Max. 1946. *From Max Weber: Essays in Sociology,* edited by Hans Gerth and C. Wright Mills. New York: Oxford University Press.

———. 1978 [1922] *Economy and Society.* Berkeley: University of California Press.

Willits, Fern, and Donald Crider. 1989. "Church Attendance and Traditional Beliefs in Adolescence and Young Adulthood: A Panel Study." *Review of Religious Research* 31 (1): 68–81.

Wilson, Bryan. 1987. "Factors in the Failure of New Religious Movements." In *The Future of New Religious Movements,* edited by David Bromley and Phillip Hammond, 30–35. Macon, Ga.: Mercer University Press.

Woodroof, J. T. 1986. "Reference Groups, Religiosity and Premarital Sexual Behavior." *Journal for the Scientific Study of Religion* 25: 436–460.

Yamane, D., and Polzer, M. 1994. "Ways of Seeing Ecstasy in Modern Society." *Sociology of Religion* 55: 1–25.

CHAPTER 13

WORK, MONEY AND YOU

THE ECONOMY

Are Millennials Reshaping the Economy?

The term *hipster* itself is a bit elusive, mostly because hipsters are so varied in the expression of what the author of this reading, Elizabeth Nolan Brown, refers to as their "hippie ethics, yuppie consumerism, communal attitudes and capitalist practices." She argues that unlike their boomer parents, they aren't rebelling against another generation; rather, they are picking and choosing fashion, music, style, and other cultural modes from the past and keeping what they perceive as the hippest. Nolan Brown goes on to assert that hipsters are creating a kind of mash-up between their bohemian styles and the corporate boardroom—from boutique breweries to makerspaces. So, as you read this piece, you have to decide if hipsters have "sold out" to corporate America or created a whole new version of it, the hipster corporate model. As you read this interesting article, reflect on the questions I've included below.

Some Things to Keep in Mind

1. What does the author mean by *hipsters*?
2. What does she mean by "selling out"?
3. The author claims that most hipsters see themselves as entrepreneurs in the new "gig" economy. Do you agree with this statement?
4. Is there a real difference between being an entrepreneur and having several gigs?

RISE OF THE HIPSTER CAPITALIST

Elizabeth Nolan Brown

Popular WISDOM about millennials seems to come in two varieties: They are either an entitled, narcissistic group of basement-dwellers, gazing at their selfies while the world burns, or they're a perfectly upstanding young cohort who got a raw deal from the recession economy, Millennials make awful employees because their boomer parents gave them too many soccer trophies; or maybe they can't find jobs because those same boomer parents aren't exiting the workforce. The one thing everyone can agree on is that millennials are probably screwed.

If there is a single cultural avatar that has come to represent today's young adults, it's the *hipster*, a much debated and often reviled construction built on skinny jeans, music snobbery, and urban chicken coops. You can find them tending their beehives atop graffiti-covered warehouses in Brooklyn; opening craft breweries and Korean-taco food trucks in Portland; or ditching the cities to get back to the land—in a farmhouse with high-speed Internet service, six laptops, three iPhones, and a heavy-duty Vitamix blender.

The hipster mixes hippie ethics and yuppie consumer preferences, communal attitudes and capitalist practices. Unlike prior generational stand-ins—from flappers to beats, punks to slackers—hipsters aren't rebelling against their parents or prior generations; they're mixing and matching the best of what came before and abandoning the baggage that doesn't interest them.

The hipster ideal today is neither a commune nor a life of rugged individualism. It's the small, socially conscious business. Millennials are obliterating divisions between corporate and bohemian values, between old and new employment models—they're not the first to do this, but they are doing it in their own way. Armed with ample self-confidence but hobbled by stagnant prospects, millennials may be uniquely poised to excel in an evolving economy where the freelance countercultural capitalist becomes the new gold standard.

CHAPTER 13: WORK, MONEY AND YOU

"I think people used to be very wary of business, and still maybe are wary of business," says 26-year-old Mark Spera, who quit a corporate job with the Gap to launch an eco-friendly fashion company called BeGood Clothing with his college roommate. "But profit isn't seen as such an evil thing anymore. It's more about how that profit is used."

Beyond "Selling Out"

In the '90s musical *Rent,* a Disneyfied depiction of Gen X bohemians, a group of aimless artist/rebels coalesce around the AIDS crisis, a shared passion for "hating dear old Mom and Dad," and their widely held generational opposition to "selling out." From riot grrrl 'zine publishers to Nirvana's Kurt Cobain, anxiety over selling out to the mainstream dominated the cultural discourse of people who came of age in the '80s and '90s. Baked into the concern was an intrinsic sense that art and social change could only be corrupted by capitalism.

Millennials, generally considered to be those in the late teens to early 30s right now, simply do not wrestle with this issue. "Hipsters may be stylistically similar to earlier youth movements," wrote *The New Criterion's* James Panero in a 2012 New York *Daily News* story. But "they strip away the anti-social and anti-capitalist qualities of these groups and replace them with entrepreneurial drive."

William Deresiewicz, a Yale English professor turned Portland-based author and cultural critic, argues that the whole idea of a hipster "movement" is absurd, because modern youth culture lacks elements of radical dissent or rebellion. "The hipster world critique is limited. It's basically a way of taking the world we have now and tweaking it to make it better," he says. David Brooks' 2000 book *Bobos in Paradise* argued that two formerly distinct baby boomer classes—the hedonistic, artistic, and socially tolerant bohemians; and the conforming, capitalist bourgeoisie—had combined to form a new category he christened *bobos*. Hipsters, Deresiewicz argues, are the bobos' literal and metaphorical children.

"I suspect that a lot of these hipsters are going to be bobos in 20 years," he says." There's a symbiosis." Hipsters make and popularize the things, material and cultural, that bobos consume—from nitrate-free salami to the indie bands that make it into *Rolling Stone.*

"Millennials and boomers don't recognize how much they're like each other," he says, but this generation has "absorbed the values of the boomers." In a 2011 *New York Times* essay, Deresiewicz dubbed millennials "Generation Sell."

Much of this entrepreneurial spirit is born out of necessity. Older millennials were just entering the work force at the start of the Great Recession, and many lost their jobs or graduated from college with massive amounts of debt in a historically weak job market. As of spring 2014, the unemployment rate for 18- to 29-year-olds was still hovering around 16 percent, and millennials made up 40 percent of all unemployed Americans.

For those millennials who do have jobs, wages have stagnated or dropped. Since 2007, real wages have dropped 9.8 percent for high school graduates and 6.9 percent for young college graduates, according to data from the Economic Policy Institute, These trends predate the financial crisis: Since 2000, wages for high school graduates have declined 10.8 percent, and the wages of young college graduates have decreased 7.7 percent. (Compare that to Gen Xers from 1995 to 2000, when wages for young adults rose between 15 and 20 percent.)

Millennials have adjusted their expectations accordingly. Job security and retirement benefits seem as quaint and anachronistic as floppy disks and fax machines. And only 6 percent of millennials think full Social Security benefits will be available to them, according to a Pew Research poll from March 2014, compared to 51 percent who think they'll get nothing.

Yet members of Generation Y, as millennials were once known, are still remarkably optimistic about controlling their own destinies, despite the mess of 21st century America. Pew found that nearly half of millennials think the country's best years are ahead, and a majority expect to have enough money to lead the lives they wish. The recent Reason-Rupe poll of millennials found the three biggest factors they believe determine career and financial success are hard work, ambition, and self-discipline (followed by natural intelligence or talent, family connections, and a college degree). What do they think is the most important factor producing poverty? Poor personal decisions.

The very things seen as most portending of millennial doom—their overinflated sense of self-esteem and the stagnant economy—may have, when taken together, inspired a new paradigm. For millennials, when life gives you lemons, you make artisanal, small-batch beef jerky. Or start a cargo-bike delivery service. A yoga studio. A craft brewery. A combo cocktail and pie bar. An app-based laundry pickup service. Depending on which survey you consult, 30 to 80 percent of millennials aim to be self-employed at some point in their careers.

In the Reason-Rupe poll, 55 percent of millennials said they would like to own their own company someday. A 2011 poll from the Kauffman Foundation found that 54 percent of millennials had entrepreneurial ambitions, with higher levels among Latinos (64 percent) and blacks (63 percent). Sixty-five percent said that making it easier to start a business should be a priority for Congress.

More than a quarter of Gen Y is currently self-employed, according to the U.S. Chamber of Commerce Foundation. In 2011, nearly a third of all entrepreneurs were between the ages of 20 and 34. Millennials are also on the cutting edge of workplace flexibility. A 2011 poll from Buzz Marketing Group and the Young Entrepreneurs Council found that 46 percent of the cohort had done freelance work.

When people think of millennial entrepreneurs, their minds tend to go to tech giants like Facebook co-founder and CEO Mark Zuckerberg. Indeed, many of the most popular tech and social media startups of the past half-decade have been founded by young people, including Tumblr, Vimeo, Instagram, Dropbox, Lyft, Living Social, and AirBnB. But other sectors are benefitting from youthful creativity as well.

Millennial entrepreneurs are embracing publishing, from reimagined service-journalism (think Ezra Klein's *Vox*) to SEO-driven websites (Brian Goldberg's *Bleacher Report* and *Bustle*), publications directly targeting teens and 20-somethings (millennial news site *Mic*, Alexa von Tobel's *Learn Vest*, Tavi Gevinson's *Rookie*), and "small batch" niche magazines like the aspirational dinner party pub *Kinfolk*. They're founding socially conscious clothing companies such as BeGood (a San Francisco-based retailer that sells moderately priced, eco-friendly fashions such as bamboo tank tops and organic-cotton T-shirts) and Five Pound Apparel (which donates five pounds of food to Nepalese children for every T-shirt sold). And they're all over the craft alcohol and specialty food markets.

"Entrepreneurship has become *the* creative endeavor," says Deresiewicz. "It's not just a business endeavor, And even when you're engaged in a creative endeavor like music, it becomes sort of framed like an entrepreneurial act." In fact, "'selling out' as a category has disappeared, because everybody is selling out," he adds. "We're all inside the market system now."

Brooklyn Capitalism

Far from being a no-fly zone, cashing in is now the goal for many millennials. Molly Brolin, 26, is an "artist entrepreneur" who runs a small company, Muddy Boots Productions, from her living room in the hipster haven of Greenpoint, Brooklyn. When I lived across the street, in 2009 and 2010, I remember Molly—then a recent college graduate—having boundless enthusiasm for taking on new, unpaid creative work. "I used to do whatever inspired me," says Brolin."But now I'm more thinking about 'how is this going to make us money?' I feel like reality is really setting in right now. I can't keep doing things just for experience."

In another part of Brooklyn—Bushwick—I once lived in a warehouse that had been converted into a semi-legal residential space, populated largely by painters. My dozen or so roommates, which also included a D.J., a puppeteer/performance artist, an aspiring comedian, and an unemployed schizophrenic, were mostly in their twenties, socially liberal, ambitious, and poor. Our living space was rustic, with heat and Internet that frequently went out. (Guess which failure provoked more panic?) An area of the fridge was devoted to communal, dumpster-dived foods.

At one point, the painters decided we should use the front of the warehouse—which housed a skate ramp and a small purple school bus that served as a bedroom—to exhibit their paintings. Young, non-established artists have long used whatever space is available to them to showcase their work. But my roommates' planning from the get-go involved not merely showcasing their art for the local creative community but luring in wealthy buyers. They were dying to sell out.

"Ultimately, money is power, and if you have more power you can use that power for good things," says David Simnick, CEO and co-founder of SoapBox Soaps, which donates a bar of soap or a portion of proceeds to charity for every soap and body wash it sells.

But economic necessity is also at play. The concurrent rise in cultural capital and cost-of-living expenses in a handful of prominent U.S. metropolitan areas make them both vital and almost prohibitively expensive for young creative types. Tiny, lofted bedrooms in the aforementioned warehouse were still renting for $450 to $600 per month, plus utilities. Selling out means making rent.

In the Buzz Marketing Group/Young Entrepreneurs Council survey, 33 percent of the 18- to 29-year-old respondents had a side business. (This included activities like tutoring and selling stuff on eBay.) Platforms such as Etsy, an online emporium for handmade goods, and the ride-sharing service Uber put self-employment, of a sort, within millions of millennials' reach. Much is made of how the new "sharing economy" disrupts old business models and empowers consumers, but these businesses have a transformative effect for workers, too.

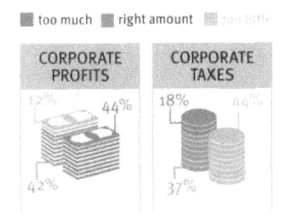

Fig. 13.1 Millennials Are Corporate Sellouts … And That's Ok
Source: Reason-Rupe Public Opinion Survey

Take Bellhops, a small-scale moving company founded by two college students in 2011. Bellhops now employs more than 8,000 part-time workers across 42 states. These student movers control their own jobs, choosing not just when and how much they work, but whether they want to take a "captain" or "wingman" role on a particular job.

Bellhops COO Matt Patterson told *Forbes* his motto is "Bellhops are entrepreneurs in their own rights." He's not exactly wrong: In a recent survey, 90 percent of working professionals defined being "an entrepreneur" as a mind-set, not just "someone who starts a company." In the new lexicon, Bellhops, Uber drivers, and AirBnB hosts are all entrepreneurs.

The flexibility and autonomy that comes with this small-scale entrepreneurship is ideal for millennials, who in survey after survey list these attributes among their most wanted from employers. Millennials are loathe to accept rigid work arrangements or stay at jobs they don't enjoy. "Our generation feels super entitled to live the way we want," says Brolin. She thinks "the American Dream has morphed," from the steady, practical careers of earlier generations to "making businesses as artists and creators." Because millennials are mostly unmarried and not tied to property, they're more willing to take risks to find a way to make a living that also inspires them creatively or creates some sort of social good.

"When my parents were growing up, providing came before playing," says Christopher "Tinypants" Dang, a 31-year-old designer whose latest clothing line is called As We Are. For Dang and his colleagues at Live Love Collective—a "lifestyle marketing agency" with the mono "Have Fun. Do Good. Live Love."—"money is part of the picture," but so is "excitement, awareness, responsibility and community," Dang says. The young entrepreneurs I talked to for this story kept coming back to the same narrative: They had launched businesses after becoming disillusioned by the corporate culture or lack of autonomy at a traditional job. Kalysa Alaniz-Martin, 26, opened her own hair salon in 2013 after working at several chain salons and disagreeing with their practices. At Kayos Studio in Lafayette, Indiana, Alaniz-Martin uses only ammonia-free and vegan hair care products and tries to be environmentally responsible in her product choices and water use.

BeGood co-founder Mark Spera was burned out on his corporate job at the Gap, "I couldn't imagine the idea of sitting at a desk all day, not having some autonomy over my workload," says Spera, who recalls being shocked when a vice president at the company scolded him for sitting barefoot at his desk. He and his business partner "were both sick of what we were doing and wanted to do something more impactful. I was considering getting into a nonprofit and he was considering traveling abroad."

Young do-gooders of generations past might have gone into the nonprofit world or the Peace Corps. Today, by contrast, many see themselves as able to do the most good via for-profit, socially conscious businesses. They do not see any inherent contradictions in that approach.

"You talk to people in the nonprofit world who say, 'You guys are doing a great thing, but why don't you donate all your money?'" says Spera, laughing. "Because then we'd be a nonprofit!" And BeGood is *not* a nonprofit. It's an example of a new dream, dubbed social entrepreneurship.

There are now at least 30 programs in social entrepreneurship at U.S. colleges and universities, according to Harvard Business School blogger Lara Galinsky; a decade ago, there were none. *Forbes* recently published its third annual list of "30 Under 30 Social Entrepreneurs." It included people like 38-year-old Joel Jackson, founder of Mobius Motors, which is making inexpensive SUVs to sell in Africa; and Kavita Shukla, the 29-year-old inventor of a cheap, compostable paper infused with organic spices that keeps produce fresh longer and ships to 35 countries.

Conscious Consumerism

Some social entrepreneurs—like Spera, a 2010 graduate of the University of Richmond's business school—come out of traditional undergraduate business or MBA programs. Many more have taken a more oblique path, turning hobbies like baking and gardening into full-time endeavors after corporate life proved unpalatable.

When her career in art administration proved unfulfilling, Allison Kave started selling pies at local food markets for extra cash and "creative satisfaction." When the pies proved a hit, she quit her art-world job and started selling them full time, supplementing her income with cooking classes and a bartending gig. Now Kave has a cookbook under her belt *(First Prize Pies,* 2014), and is working with friend Keavy Blueher to open a joint dessert and cocktail bar in Crown Heights, Brooklyn, called Butter & Scotch.

"A lot of my colleagues in the food world seem to have come to their businesses from previously established careers that were lucrative but not rewarding," says Kave, contrasting these entrepreneurs with previous generations. "They chose to take huge pay cuts to pursue their dreams and make a business out of their passions. I think about my grandfather, who owned Pepsi routes around Brooklyn, and his inclination toward self-employment seemed more driven by necessity than a particular love of carbonated beverages."

Consumer choices were also less value-laden then, but we're now squarely in the age of conscious consumerism. Any social entrepreneurs worth their (fair-trade, alder-smoked) sea salt will have an "our story" section on their website, explaining how a college trip to Guatemala or a grandmother's devotion to fresh produce inspired the company's current mission. "It's not just 'my candles are great', it's 'and then I went to Java and discovered this wax and this is a part of my journey, here's a picture,'" says Deresiewicz. "Goods now all have to be experiences."

BeGood founder Spera says conscious consumerism is what makes companies like his possible. "You have access to so much information now that companies that aren't doing the right things are going to get killed by companies who are."

America's appetite for organic, artisanal, locally sourced foodstuffs has put the gun in hipster entrepreneurs' hands. Critic and editor James Panero has called hipsters New York's "most active innovators." As traditional manufacturing has left Brooklyn and Queens, hipsters have taken up the slack.

In a few short years, an array of Brooklyn companies founded by millennials have gone from passion projects to national powerhouses. Erica Shea, 29, and Stephen Valand, 38, quit their jobs in 2009 to start Brooklyn Brew Shop, a line of easy-to-brew beer kits designed for kitchen stove tops. They are now sold in over 2,500 retailers globally. In 2010, Kings County Distillery was founded by two millennials who use local grain and traditional distilling methods to make small-batch spirits; the duo have won multiple craft distiller awards and distribute regionally and in California. Laena McCarthy started selling Anarchy in a Jar jam at indie food markets in 2009, and now makes handmade, all-natural jams, marmalades, chutneys, and mustards for stores from Portland, Maine, to San Francisco. The Brooklyn Salsa Company started as an underground taco delivery service run from a Bushwick loft and now sells locally sourced, direct-trade organic salsas around the country.

"In post-industrial capitalist society, 'work' has come to be disconnected from any conception of directly producing something or contributing work with any specific content," the socialist mag *Jacobin* complained recently. But for hipster entrepreneurs, this couldn't be further from the truth. Adam Davidson, co-founder of NPR's *Planet Money,* asserts that hipsters are classical capitalists in the Adam Smith model.

Today's niche startups and craft businesses aren't a rejection of modern industrial capitalism, Davidson wrote in a *New York Times* piece titled "Don't Mock the Artisanal-Pickle Makers." Rather they're "something new" entirely, "a happy refinement of the excesses of the industrial era plus a return to the vision laid out" by Smith. They also highlight a potential bright spot in U.S. manufacturing: small American producers succeeding by avoiding direct competition with cheap commodities from low-wage countries and instead providing hyper-specialized technological and lifestyle products. Perhaps "the fracturing of the manufacturing industry, however painful, has helped prepare parts of the economy for this new course," Davidson suggested.

"If hipsters are to evolve into anything meaningful, they will adhere to no historical pattern," journalist Ilie Mitaru predicted in *Adbusters* back in 2009. "Every journalist, politician, and organizer works with an assumed vision of our sociopolitical future—be it partisan reform, fringe uprising or global revolution. This vision blinds us to the potentiality of it happening another way, one with no historical precedent."

As we enter the post-crisis period, the business and economic contexts we knew pre-recession are increasingly unlikely to re-materialize. In their willingness to embrace new ideas and new work models, millennials may turn out to be revolutionary in ways altogether different from generations past.

CHAPTER 14

POWER, POLITICS AND AUTHORITY

GOVERNMENT

The Age of Identity Politics

After reading this article by Ann Friedman, you will no doubt have a very good sense why she titled it *"All Politics Are Identity Politics."* She is very bold in her assertion that people see the world, and their politics, through the lens of who they are—their identity. She argues further that it is unfair to ask any single group to not vote based on their identity. Friedman goes on to claim that ultimately identity groups and their political action can be good for politics and society because they want to be part of something bigger: a larger identity as a better country. As you read this paper, think about the questions below.

Some Things to Keep in Mind

1. What are identity politics?
2. Do you agree that all politics are identity politics? If not, why not?
3. How are identity politics good for society?
4. How are they damaging to society?

ALL POLITICS IS IDENTITY POLITICS

Ann Friedman

Are there two political forces more vilified than interest groups and identity politics? No matter what your ideology or political party, if you want to prove that you are truly committed to the betterment of our nation, you are almost required to speak out against these pernicious influences. Organizing with other people who share your particular identity and interests? That's selfish. Practically anti-democratic. And, many have argued in this magazine and in other progressive venues over the past 20 years, it's harmful to liberalism.

Kathleen M. Sullivan, writing in the *Prospect* in 1998, summarized Nancy Rosenblum's book, *Membership and Morals:* "Rather than socializing members for democracy, groups are likely to be exclusionary, snobbish, and competitive vis-à-vis others. The internal cooperation they foster in no way guarantees that they will be … civic, virtuous, or deliberative in relation to the larger polity." In 2004, Michael Lind argued in these pages that, in order to regain the majority, the Democratic Party should attempt to dissociate itself from "identity-politics groups—blacks, Latinos, feminists, gays, and lesbians—and economic-interest groups, like unions"—and instead organize itself by geography. And perhaps most notably, in a 2006 *Prospect* cover story Michael Tomasky decried the "million-little-pieces, interest-group approach to politics" and stated that "citizens should be called upon to look beyond their own self-interest and work for a greater common interest."

Barack Obama's adoption of the "Yes we can!" slogan—"we" being the operative word—tested the greater-good thesis on the campaign trail. Although pundits like Andrew Sullivan praised what they saw as Obama's attempt to distance himself from identity politics, his appeal to the common good was also packaged within a historic narrative: the promise of the first black president. Exit-poll analysis shows that race was a significant factor in his victory—Obama won 95 percent of black votes and 67 percent of Hispanic votes, compared to Kerry's 88 percent and 53 percent, respectively. But the increased support among minority voters for Obama was not due solely to his race. As John Halpin and Ruy Teixeira have been pointing out for years, African Americans, Hispanics, and Asians are the most reliable Democratic voters—no matter what the candidate's ethnicity. Indeed, as we head into what looks to be a difficult midterm election for Democrats, the Democratic National Committee is again turning to its nonwhite base. In a DNC video released this spring and directed at minority voters, Obama says, "It will be up to each of you to make sure that the young people, African Americans, Latinos, and women who powered our victory in 2008 stand together once again."

While identity is not the sole predictor of ideology, at least today, for many groups it is a strong indication. In an 18,000- word research paper published in the *Prospect* in 2006, Halpin and Teixeira identified racial and ethnic minorities as "the single strongest element of the progressive coalition,"

Party Faithfuls: The May 2006 cover story called for citizens to "work for a greater common interest."

followed by "single, working, and highly educated women." In other words, the people most likely to identify with the liberal worldview are those who have experienced some lack of freedom and opportunity themselves.

Progressives love identity in the voting booth—it's how we knew our long-awaited majority was going to emerge. But when it comes time to govern, these constituencies quickly transform

   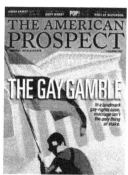

Whose Ideology? Identity politics are our politics say covers from November/December 1996, April 2005, March 2009, and December 2009.

from the very lifeblood of progressivism into a perceived burden. You would think that, because minorities and women are the keys to progressives' demographic success at the polls, their particular concerns would be of utmost importance to leaders and lawmakers. Instead, "identity groups" agitating for equality and their place at the table have often been told to sit tight and trust movement leaders to do what's best for everyone. We might all agree that gay couples deserve marriage rights, and women must have access to reproductive health care, but when it comes to devising a political strategy and policy agenda, these are inevitably the issues that slide quietly to the back burner. It is painfully clear that in reality we do not all take on the same level of responsibility for securing the rights in which we claim to believe.

Calls to reject identity and adopt a "greater good" approach never make clear who defines that greater good. Who decides which issues have to wait and which are of utmost importance? Think back on some of the biggest steps this country has taken toward equality. Without the existence of groups specifically advocating for their rights, would women, African Americans, or LGBT people have made any progress? Would Lyndon Johnson actually have signed the Civil Rights Act absent pressure from the NAACP, the Student Nonviolent Coordinating Committee, and other racial-justice oriented groups? Would the Family and Medical Leave Act have passed without the insistence of feminists? If it weren't for the gay-rights movement, would the federal government still be denying the existence of AIDS?

The problem is not the presence of identity groups within the progressive coalition. The problem is the party and movement structure that make them necessary. Despite their nominal commitment to equality and opportunity, the Democratic Party and progressive movement reflect the biases and hierarchies of the rest of the country. The president may be black and the speaker of the House a woman, but as I argued in these pages shortly after Hillary Clinton dropped out of the 2008 Democratic primary, a handful of leaders who break the mold are not enough to actually, well, break the mold. Until the progressive-movement leadership actually reflects the members that make up its core constituencies, pressure from identity groups will be necessary to ensure those constituencies are given a voice, that their concerns are addressed.

The common good is a laudable goal, but asking progressives to subsume their identities and interests is not the way to achieve it. Allowing people to organize based on their identities and deeply held beliefs is just smart politics. Those groups can—and do—work together to craft policies and organizing strategies that lift all members of the coalition, not just those who are white, heterosexual, economically advantaged, and male. Until we can trust the movement's standard-bearers to include the top-tier concerns of women, people of color, and gay Americans in that common good, identity-based groups will remain necessary.

The progressive movement will only ensure its survival by deepening its commitment to these people, not taking their votes for granted. If we continue to compromise on their concerns, or dismiss them as "special interests" working against a nebulous greater good, we will ultimately render our shared concept of liberalism totally meaningless. After all, if each group within the coalition is actually just in it alone, what's the point of subscribing to a common ideology at all?

Critiques of identity politics fail to acknowledge that people join social-justice and political groups because they actually do want to look beyond themselves and make our country a better place. Amy Gutmann writes in her 2003 book, *Identity in Democracy,* that members of the sorts of identity groups that make up the progressive coalition "don't usually join because they want some instrumental goods from the group that they could not otherwise obtain. ... Shared identity is connected to identification with a group and, as a large body of psychological literature demonstrates, is independent of the pursuit of self-interest." This holds true with what I know about people who came to progressive politics by way of identity—including myself. I didn't become a feminist to ensure my own access to contraception or a salary equal to that of my male peers. In a view typical of women of my generation, I don't want to believe I personally need feminism for that. However, these are issues with which I have direct experience, and I can connect that experience to the broad, societal ways sexism and gender discrimination persist. I can safely say that if I hadn't initially seen politics through the lens of gender, I would not work at a progressive magazine today. I was a feminist before I was a liberal.

I'm certainly not alone. Most political acts—even those done under the auspices of "special interests" like immigrant rights, abortion rights, or racial justice—are done in service of a greater good. Most activists don't become clinic escorts or agitate to get racist shock jocks fired or cancel their vacations to Arizona *for themselves.* Identity groups are made up of people who want to be part of something bigger, people who recognize personal injustices and want to channel their indignation into a greater quest for a better country. That sentiment is the very fuel of progressivism.

After all, as Tomasky wrote in his cover story, we're all in it together. Labor rights are tied to gay rights are tied to women's rights are tied to immigrants' rights. If what binds us together as progressives is our vision for a more just society, it is our commitment to *all* of these issues that will define us. This doesn't mean everyone must be an advocate for every single issue. Each of us has a different metric for separating the political negotiables from the nonnegotiables. But I do expect the liberal coalition, particularly its leaders, to be sensitive to whose greater good our agenda is serving. Until the leaders of the progressive movement and Democratic Party reflect the core constituencies that support them, interest and identity groups will remain powerful and necessary. And I wouldn't have it any other way. After all, my identity is why I'm a liberal in the first place.

Section 7 Discussion Questions

1. List and describe the types of social forces that have been instrumental in changing the structure and function of the American family over the past sixty years.
2. How significant has the women's movement been to the changes we have seen in families over the past six decades?
3. In general, what kinds of changes in attitudes/beliefs toward marriage do you think millennials are expressing? What impact will these attitudes have on marriage and families in the United States?
4. Do you think your religious beliefs and rituals reflect larger social values and beliefs? If so, why do you think they are connected? If not, why are they divergent?
5. In what ways do you think that religion in our society is interconnected with other institutions like education and family? Are these interactions necessary? Do you think they are socially helpful or harmful?
6. Discuss both the most socially beneficial aspects of religion and the most damaging.
7. How do you think different educational settings, experiences, and resources influence students' futures, both educationally and economically?
8. Have your own educational experiences influenced the opportunities you have experienced?
9. In what ways have public schools attempted to address the issue of equal opportunity? What solutions have been tried in the schools you attended? Were you aware of differences between schools in your community in terms of resources and facilities? If so, what were the differences?
10. Consider your economic future. What are your greatest economic fears for your future? What are your greatest economic hopes and ambitions?
11. Do you think the types of jobs/careers that you want to pursue will be available to you when you enter the workforce? Why or why not?
12. Some economists have shown that many millennials prefer the "gig" economy to a single job in the "mainstream" economy. Would you consider having several "gigs" instead of one job so you could feel you had more autonomy?
13. Discuss the basic elements of a free democratic society. How is America doing in terms of supporting all those elements?
14. Recent research shows that there has been a "de-democratization" happening globally. That is, there has been a drop in the number of liberal democratic governments worldwide in the past decade. What forces do you think can be identified in creating such changes?
15. In the United States, compared to many developed nations, we have an unusual two-party political system. Do you think having more than two major political parties would be good for our country? If so, why? If not, why not?

Section 7 Exercises

1. Families are primary groups and are influential in our development and social adjustment. Think about the family you grew up in. Also, think about the families you knew as you were growing up. Tell me the changes you have seen in the American family (or families where you were raised) in your lifetime. What forces/attitudes/economics have created these changes? Additionally, why do you think the family is such an important agent of socialization? (This is one of the key functions of family in society.) Be honest—but also think sociologically!
2. Although frequent claims are made in the media about the family's decline and impending demise as a social institution, most sociologists see the family as a changing institution, not a declining one. The internet is a place to find the latest data on these changes. It is also a place where families find resources and support and where advocates of alternative conceptions of the family argue their case and seek support.
3. Revitalization movements are one indicator of religion's power to adapt to contemporary life and the changing cultural, political, and economic environments. One new religious movement that has increasingly caught the attention of the US public consciousness is Scientology. Go to http://www.scientology.org/ and explore the history of this religion.
    a. Why has its membership base increased dramatically?
    b. Why are numerous groups challenging its legitimacy?
4. For this exercise, you will be engaging in some ethnographic work. You will be looking for the connection between religion and other social institutions. Specifically, you will be investigating whether religious sermons promote social integration through participation in the economy, family, and community.

    Choose several places of worship in your community that you can visit. Try to select two locations for each of the three major Abrahamic religions: two churches, two temples, and two mosques. (If there are not enough places of worship to attend in your community, try to visit as many different kinds that you can. Also, you can go to other places like shrines, Buddhist temples, etc.) Visit each location at least once, more often if possible. Pay attention to the messages that the clergy at each location are transmitting to their respective congregations—look for common messages of family, work, community, and financial responsibility. You will most likely hear messages that encourage congregants to be hard workers, good parents or children, good members of their communities, and to be financially responsible. Be sure to take good "field notes" so you can identify what types of messages these religious leaders are relaying to the members of their congregations. How do the leaders of the various religions frame their messages? That is, you will most likely hear similar messages across religions (be good people) but framed in different contexts using different stories. Why would different religions use different frameworks to send the same message? Why would religious leaders encourage their followers to be "good citizens?" Do you think these religious messages, in general, are good for society? What other things did you notice about the various messages you heard?

5. Some people have referred to the "hidden curriculum" in our public schools, things that are learned but not openly intended. A hidden curriculum refers to the unspoken or implicit values, behaviors, procedures, and norms that exist in the educational setting. While such expectations are not explicitly written, hidden curriculum is the unstated promotion and enforcement of certain behavioral patterns, professional standards, and social beliefs while navigating a learning environment (Miller and Seller 1990). For instance, if you attend an elementary school where all the teachers are female (not unrealistic) and all the administrators (deans, vice principal, and principal) are all male, you may learn that men have power over women and that men occupy more powerful positions than women. You get the idea. Now I want you to think back on your educational experiences. Are there things that you learned in school that were not necessarily part of any lesson plan? Looking back on your educational experiences, what types of things could you identify as being part of the hidden curriculum in your schools? Are those lessons still being taught? What changes do you think can be made to our public education system that would reduce the impact of the hidden curriculum? Is the hidden curriculum necessarily bad? Why or why not?

6. Considering that a large segment of the workforce in today's economy takes part in what has been termed the "gig economy" and may not be as fully employed as they would like to be, how are employment, underemployment, and unemployment measured in the United States? Do some research by visiting the Bureau of Labor Statistics website (bls.gov) and determine how unemployment is defined and measured. How does this measure allow for "discouraged" workers, part-time workers who would like to be full-time, workers who are full-time but on short-term contracts, workers whose skills are not fully utilized, and others (like those in the "gig economy")? And what does it mean to be "fully employed"? Do you think these measures fully capture the state of the workforce in the United States? Why or why not? What are the limitations of the current measure of unemployment? Now try to devise an "ideal" measure of unemployment. What elements would you discard? What elements would you include?

7. The term *autocratization* refers to the decline in the attributes of the democratic style of government. Contemporary autocratization has happened more slowly and inconspicuously than before. Instead of coups conducted by military officers, democratically elected incumbents have been responsible for more than two-thirds of all episodes of contemporary autocratization. These elected officials *erode* democracy gradually by gaining control of media outlets, restricting civil society, and undermining the autonomy of election management bodies, among other tactics. They generally do so clandestinely without

abolishing key democratic institutions such as multiparty elections or legislative bodies (Aydin-Duzgit et al. 2019). Considering this definition/description of autocratization, do you think the process is taking place in the United States? What examples could you point to in order to argue that there is minor autocratization happening in the United States? If you don't think it is happening in this country, do you think it could in the future? Why or why not? How could you argue that this process could never happen in the United States?

REFERENCES

Bertrand, Marianne, and Sendhil Mullainathan. "Are Emily and Greg More Employable than Lakisha and Jamal? A Field Experiment on Labor Market Discrimination." *The American Economic Review* 94.4 (2004): 991–1013.

Bhopal, Kalwant. *The Experiences of Black and Minority Ethnic Academics: A Comparative Study of the Unequal Academy.* New York: Routledge, 2016.

McIntosh, P. "White Privilege: Unpacking the Invisible Knapsack." In S. Plous (Ed.), *Understanding Prejudice and Discrimination* (pp. 191–196). McGraw-Hill, 2003.

Pfattheicher, S., Strauch, C., Diefenbacher, S. & Schnuerch, R. "A Field Study on Watching Eyes and Hand Hygiene Compliance in a Public Bathroom." *Journal of Applied Social Psychology* (2018): 10.1111/jasp.12501.

Plume, M. *Revealing Our Social World: A Brief Introduction to Sociology.* Cognella Academic Press, 2017.

Reynolds, J., & H. Xian. "Perceptions of Meritocracy in the Land of Opportunity." *Research in Social Stratification and Mobility* 36 (2014): 12–37. https://doi.org/10.1016/j.rssm.2014.03.001

US Department of Labor. *Table A-2. Employment Status of the Civilian Population by Race, Sex, and Age* 2015. https://www.bls.gov/news.release/empsit.t02.htm

Wolfensberger, W. *The Principle of Normalization in Human Services.* New York, NY: National Institute on Mental Retardation, 1972.

Wolfensberger, W. "Reflections on a Lifetime in Human Services and Mental Retardation." *Mental Retardation* 29, no. 1 (1991): 1–15.

Wolfensberger, W. *A Brief Introduction to Social Role Valorization: A High-Order Concept for Addressing the Plight of Societally Devalued People, and for Structuring Human Services.* 3rd ed. Syracuse, NY: Syracuse University Training Institute for Human Service Planning, Leadership & Change Agentry, 1998.

Wolfensberger, W. *The New Genocide of Handicapped and Afflicted People.* 3rd ed. Syracuse, NY: Syracuse University Training Institute for Human Service Planning, Leadership & Change Agentry, 2005.

CPSIA information can be obtained
at www.ICGtesting.com
Printed in the USA
FSHW020032171220
76886FS